Anonymous

British Rule in South Africa

A Collection of Official Documents and other Correspondence

Anonymous

British Rule in South Africa
A Collection of Official Documents and other Correspondence

ISBN/EAN: 9783744751865

Printed in Europe, USA, Canada, Australia, Japan

Cover: Foto ©Suzi / pixelio.de

More available books at **www.hansebooks.com**

BRITISH RULE IN SOUTH AFRICA.

A COLLECTION OF

Official Documents and other Correspondence,

SUGGESTING THE ADOPTION OF A POLICY WHICH SHALL
ENSURE THE PEACE AND PROGRESS OF

THE ORANGE FREE STATE AND TRANSVAAL REPUBLIC

AND

THE ABORIGINAL TRIBES,

IN THEIR RESPECTIVE RELATIONS WITH

THE CAPE OF GOOD HOPE AND NATAL.

PRINTED AND PUBLISHED BY
W. FOSTER, ST. GEORGE'S-STREET, CAPE TOWN
1868

PREFACE.

THE circumstances connected with the British occupation of the Cape of Good Hope are in some degree peculiar, and it has been perhaps unavoidable that the measures adopted by successive Governors have represented rather a series of shifts and compromises than any well-matured and definite policy on the part of Great Britain. It is, at any rate, very certain that, during the last thirty years, some most serious blunders have been committed, and that we are now suffering the evil effect of the vacillating and inconsistent policy which has been applied to the settlement of our domestic troubles, and of our difficulties with the Border Tribes. It is only very lately indeed that we have received the gracious assurance that the theories and traditions of the Colonial Office will no longer be adhered to in spite of remonstrances from those whose local knowledge, political experience, and unblemished reputation for loyal attachment to the Crown, may fairly be deemed titles to respect and consideration. This gratifying change in our relations with the Department, which is practically our only Court of Appeal, may not unfairly be attributed to the light thrown upon the real bearing of colonial questions by such writers as Mr. Merivale, Mr. Money, whose work upon Java is a valuable manual of government, and Mr. Arthur Helps, who has drawn most striking lessons for our future guidance from the history of the Spanish Colonies of South America.

The unexpectedly disastrous termination of those internal disputes which led to the original settlement of the Colony of Natal, and of the Orange Free State, as well as the prodigious loss of life and property entailed upon the

Empire by the Kafir wars, may surely be ascribed as much to a want of proper and reliable information by the Home authorities as to the influence or intrigues of interested parties within the Colony.

The recent embroilment of the Orange Free State with the Basutos, which led to the latter being received under British protection, has naturally excited a great deal of public attention; and, although there is every reason to rest assured that the political significance of the dispute has been fairly represented in Downing-street by Sir Philip Wodehouse, it has occurred to the compiler of these pages that the present time offers a favourable opportunity for supporting His Excellency's measures in so far as they have received Imperial sanction, and also for suggesting their extension on a larger scale than he has perhaps ventured to recommend.

The object of the present Publication is to place before our fellow-colonists, and others in the Mother Country connected with us by ties of association and interest, an intelligent expression of public feeling in the existing crisis. Many sources of information have been resorted to, and the opinions of different classes of society embodied, and much that has already appeared in the local press has been reprinted. The influence of newspapers, though powerful, is also ephemeral, and it may be fairly presumed that even careful readers are occasionally precluded from noticing some particular issue where points of fact have been adduced which have an important relation to the whole case. Thus, *e.g.*, the letters signed "Colonist" have been reproduced *in extenso* at the risk of incurring the imputation of tautology, because the writer has endeavoured logically to follow up every phase of the argument which has been developed by the progress of events, and to leave no occurrence of importance unnoticed. For the same reason, there has been annexed the memorial presented by some influential London merchants to His Grace the Duke of Buckingham, in anticipation of his reception of the Orange Free State Deputation, and which, in fact, may be regarded as a "counter-blast" to the representations of the delegates. It is a faithful record of the history of the abandonment of the Sovereignty, and the arguments with which it ably advocates the re-assertion of British authority beyond the Orange River cannot easily be refuted.

If matters rest where they are, a collision between the inhabitants of the Free State and the Basutos is imminent, and in the event of any outbreak, the latter would naturally apply for, and be entitled to, assistance from this Colony. The position of British subjects within the State (and it will be observed that the *quæstio vexata* of the legal independence of *all* its inhabitants is far from being decided) will again be fraught with trouble and difficulty. The exercise of force would, of course, quickly repress all resistance to the authority of Great Britain, but the employment of such means would on every account be deprecated, as tending to widen the breach which already exists between the Colonists and those whom real or imaginary grievances originally drove over the Orange River, and as offering a specious argument to those factious demagogues whose interest lies in fomenting disaffection to the British Crown.

There can be but little doubt that, if the suffrages of all intelligent residents in the Free State who have a substantial stake in the country were fairly collected, a decided majority would be in favour of British rule; and that, as the advantages of such an arrangement became apparent, the task of dealing with the Transvaal Republic would be simple and straightforward, rendering any appeal to coercive action entirely unnecessary.

The anarchy, lawlessness, and demoralization, the commercial stagnation, and utter insecurity of life and property which prevail in the Free State—suggestive rather of a mediæval community under the ban of a Papal interdict than any picture of modern times—are graphically described in the following pages, and call loudly for the interference of the British Government, while the pecuniary loss this state of things entails upon our mercantile community, though in one sense a secondary consideration, is one which is not likely to be forgotten.

The existence of slavery, with all its attendant horrors, in the Transvaal Republic, and the continued recurrence of those raids against tribes who are anxious to proffer fealty to England, which, if not actually authorized by those in power, are never discountenanced, are a disgrace to civilization; and, apart from missionary views of such questions, which it is not within the province of this Pamphlet to plead, all must feel keenly and strongly the extraordinary apathy which permits an obscure and semi-barbarous State to violate every principle of humanity in the perpetration of cruelties which Great Britain has attempted to suppress at the cost of precious blood and millions of treasure.

It is perhaps premature to speculate upon the consequences which might follow the discovery in any quantity of gold or precious stones beyond our boundary, but is it not highly probable that the reports of their abundance, which have already been circulated, may induce an immigration from various parts of the world of a horde of adventurers, whose presence in a country free from the restraints of law and order would be a new and powerful element of discord?

The chronic disturbances on the Western and Northwestern Frontier have now risen to a height which should convince us that the antagonism between the Boers and the Native Tribes is as deep-seated as it is fatal to the progress of the out-lying settlers.

The only substantial guarantee for the future prosperity of South Africa, for the development of its pastoral and mineral resources, and for the extension of Christianity and civilization to the Aborigines, would be a policy which should extend our frontier over the whole continent from Walwich Bay to the Zambesi River; which should give a Lieutenant-Governor and a nominated Legislative Council to the Orange Free State and the Transvaal Republic, subsidise the leading Native Chiefs, appoint men of character, energy, and experience as British Residents at the head-quarters of every important tribe, and ensure respect to our traders and explorers, as well as security to border farmers, by adding largely to the strength and efficiency of the Frontier Armed Mounted Police.

If this scheme should ever be favourably entertained, it will be found that its details present few of those difficulties which are believed to be inseparable from any policy having Annexation or Confederation for its basis; and there can be no doubt that its adoption, in one shape or another, would alone secure to us and our descendants permanent peace and prosperity.

It is also hoped that this publication will be considered to have appeared at an opportune moment, if it have the least effect in persuading the Orange Free State Government, now that their delegates have returned from England, to enter upon amicable negotiation with the Queen's representative at the Cape, "for a solution of its difficulty with the Basutos on the basis of mutual concessions, and a willingness also to come under British rule;" or if it be in any remote degree instrumental in inducing Her Majesty's Government to retrace the fatal step taken in 1854, and to resume British Sovereignty northward of the Orange River in South Africa.

Cape Town, *December*, 1868.

CONTENTS.

	PAGE
I. Extract from Speech of Sir Philip Wodehouse at the Prorogation of the Cape Parliament, September 2, 1868...	1
II. The Transvaal Convention between Her Majesty's Assistant Commissioners, Major W. Hogge and C. M. Owen, Esq., and a Deputation of Emigrant Farmers, headed by A. W. H. Pretorius, Commandant-General, January 17, 1852	2
III. Articles of Convention between Sir G. Russell Clerk, K.C.B., and J. P. Hoffman, President, and other Delegates, Feb. 23, 1854	3
IV. Protest of the Committee of the Delegates of the Sovereignty, February 17, 1854	6
V. Resolutions of a large Public Meeting, held at Bloemfontein, February 17, 1854	8
VI. Resolutions of a Public Meeting at Smithfield, March 2, 1854	9
VII. Cape Town Petition to the Imperial Parliament in February, 1854	10
VIII. Memorial from the Cape Merchants in London to His Grace the Duke of Buckingham, August, 1868	13
IX. Resolutions of the Natal Legislative Council, recommending to the favourable consideration of Her Majesty's Government the Annexation of the two Republics, the Orange Free State and Transvaal, August, 1868	19
X. Resolutions of the Natal Legislative Council respecting Slavery and the High Commissioner, August, 1868	20
XI. Cape Town Address to Sir Philip Wodehouse on his return from Aliwal North, May 13, 1868, and his Reply thereto	22
XII. Resolutions unanimously passed by a Public Meeting at Port Elizabeth, June 13, 1868, and the Governor's Reply	24

		PAGE
XIII.	Letter of Port Elizabeth Chamber of Commerce, March 23, 1868, to Sir Philip Wodehouse, and His Excellency's Reply	26
XIV.	Suggested Petition to the Queen, referred to by the Port Elizabeth Chamber of Commerce	28
XV.	Resolutions unanimously passed at a Special Meeting of the Port Elizabeth Chamber of Commerce, December 31, 1867	31
XVI.	Resolutions passed at an adjourned Monthly Meeting of the Cape Town Chamber of Commerce, February 10, 1868	32
XVII.	Letters to the Editor of the *Cape Standard*	33
XVIII.	Letters to the Editors of the *Cape Argus*	198
XIX.	Leading Articles of the *Friend of the Free State*	209
XX.	Orange Free State Statistics (compiled from the *Friend*)	215
XXI.	Speech of the Hon. John Robinson, Esq., in the Natal Legislative Council, August, 1868	217
XXII.	Federation Memorial presented to Sir Philip Wodehouse at Aliwal North, April, 1868	219

FREE STATE AND BASUTO QUESTION.

Official Documents, Resolutions of Public Meetings,

&c., &c.

EXTRACT FROM SPEECH OF SIR PHILIP WODEHOUSE AT THE PROROGATION OF THE CAPE PARLIAMENT, SEPTEMBER 2, 1868.

There remains still for final adjustment one question of importance in its effect on the native tribes,—that of the reception as British subjects of the tribe of the Basutos, which I sincerely hope may be so accomplished as not only to secure their welfare, but to pave the way for other beneficial changes in due season on the northern bank of the Orange River. Speaking entirely on my own responsibility, giving expression only to my own opinions, I may say that I regard the measures which severed from their allegiance the European communities in those regions to have been founded in error; and that it will be a blessing for all if, with their general and hearty concurrence, they can be restored in a general sense to their former position. I should not wish to be regarded as an advocate of the actual union of any of them with the Colony of the Cape. This Colony is already large enough—probably too large—for the population by which it is likely for many years to be inhabited; and the extension of it beyond the Orange River would, it is to be feared, cause a renewal of those demands for disunion, whether under the name of Separation or Federation, which have done so much mischief, and which I rejoice to see dying out. What is to be hoped for, in my opinion, is the creation, beyond the river, of a large and well-organized Government, bound to this Colony only by a common allegiance, by the ties of kinship, by congenial laws, by just covenants, and by a common desire to extend the blessings of Christianity, peace, and civilization to all within their reach.

THE TRANSVAAL CONVENTION BETWEEN HER MAJESTY'S ASSISTANT COMMISSIONERS, MAJOR W. HOGGE AND C. M. OWEN, ESQ., AND A DEPUTATION OF EMIGRANT FARMERS, HEADED BY A. W. H. PRETORIUS, COMMANDANT-GENERAL, JANUARY 17, 1852.

The Assistant Commissioners guarantee in the fullest manner, on the part of the British Government, to the emigrant farmers beyond the Vaal River, the right to manage their own affairs and to govern themselves according to their own laws, without any interference on the part of the British Government; and that no encroachment shall be made by the said Government on the territory beyond, to the north of the Vaal River: with the further assurance that the warmest wish of the British Government is, to promote peace, free trade, and friendly intercourse with the emigrant farmers now inhabiting, or who hereafter may inhabit, that country; it being understood that this system of non-interference is binding upon both parties.

Should any misunderstanding hereafter arise as to the true meaning of the words " The Vaal River," this question, in so far as regards the line from the source of that river over the Draakenberg, shall be settled and adjusted by commissioners chosen by both parties.

Her Majesty's Assistant Commissioners hereby disclaim all alliances whatever and with whomsoever of the coloured nations to the north of the Vaal River.

It is agreed that no slavery is or shall be permitted or practised in the country to the north of the Vaal River, by the emigrant farmers.

Mutual facilities and liberty shall be afforded to traders and travellers on both sides of the Vaal River; it being understood that every wagon containing ammunition and fire-arms, coming from the south side of the Vaal River, shall produce a certificate signed by a British Magistrate or other functionary duly authorized to grant such: and which shall state the quantities of such articles contained in said wagon, to the nearest Magistrate north of the Vaal River, who shall act in the case as the regulations of the emigrant farmers direct. It is agreed, that no objection shall be made by any British authority against the emigrant boers purchasing their supplies of ammunition in any of the British colonies and possessions of South Africa; it being mutually understood that all trade in ammunition with the native tribes is prohibited both by the British Government and the emigrant farmers, on both sides of the Vaal River.

It is agreed, that so far as possible, all criminals and other guilty parties who may fly from justice, either way across the Vaal River, shall be mutually delivered up, if such should be required, and that the British Courts, as well as those of the emigrant farmers, shall be mutually open to each other for all legitimate processes, and that summonses for witnesses sent either way across the Vaal River, shall be backed by the Magistrates on each side of the same respectively, to compel the attendance of such witnesses when required.

It is agreed, that certificates of marriage issued by the proper authorities of the emigrant farmers, shall be held valid and sufficient to entitle children of such marriages to receive portions accruing to them in any British colony or possession in South Africa.

It is agreed, that any and every person now in possession of land and residing in British Territory, shall have free right and power to sell his said property and remove unmolested across the Vaal River, and *vice versa;* it being distinctly understood that this arrangement does not comprehend criminals, or debtors, without providing for the payment of their just and lawful debts.

ARTICLES OF CONVENTION BETWEEN SIR G. RUSSEL CLERK, K.C.B., AND J. P. HOFFMAN, PRESIDENT, AND OTHER DELEGATES, FEBRUARY 23, 1854.

1. Her Majesty's Special Commissioner, in entering into a Convention for finally transferring the Government of the Orange River Territory to the representatives delegated by the inhabitants to receive it, guarantees on the part of Her Majesty's Government, the future independence of that country and its government; and that after the necessary preliminary arrangements for making over the same between Her Majesty's Special Commissioner and the said representatives shall have been completed, the inhabitants of the country shall then be free. And that this independence shall, without unnecessary delay, be confirmed and ratified by an instrument, promulgated in such form and substance as Her Majesty may approve, finally freeing them from their allegiance to the British Crown, and declaring them, to all intents and purposes, a free and independent people, and their Government to be treated and considered thenceforth a free and independent Government.

2. The British Government has no alliance whatever with any native chiefs or tribes to the northward of the Orange

River, with the exception of the Griqua chief, Captain Adam Kok; and Her Majesty's Government has no wish or intention to enter hereafter into any treaties which may be injurious or prejudicial to the interests of the Orange River Government.

3. With regard to the treaty existing between the British Government and the chief Captain Adam Kok, some modification of it is indispensable. Contrary to the provisions of that treaty, the sale of lands in the Inalienable Territory has been of frequent occurrence, and the principal object of the treaty thus disregarded. Her Majesty's Government therefore intends to remove all restrictions preventing Griquas from selling their lands; and measures are in progress for the purpose of affording every facility for such transactions,—the chief Adam Kok having, for himself, concurred in and sanctioned the same. And with regard to those further alterations, arising out of the proposed revision of relations with Captain Adam Kok, in consequence of the aforesaid sales of land having from time to time been effected in the Inalienable Territory, contrary to the stipulations of the Maitland Treaty, it is the intention of Her Majesty's Special Commissioner, personally, without any unnecessary loss of time, to establish the affairs in Griqualand on a footing suitable to the just expectations of all parties.

4. After the withdrawal of Her Majesty's Government from the Orange River Territory, the new Orange River Government shall not permit any vexatious proceedings towards those of Her Majesty's present subjects remaining within the Orange River Territory, who may heretofore have been acting under the authority of Her Majesty's Government, for or on account of any acts lawfully done by them, that is, under the law as it existed during the occupation of the Orange River Territory by the British Government. Such persons shall be considered to be guaranteed in the possession of their estates by the new Orange River Government.

Also with regard to those of Her Majesty's present subjects, who may prefer to return under the dominion and authority of Her Majesty, to remaining where they now are, as subjects of the Orange River Government, such persons shall enjoy full right and facility for the transfer of their properties, should they desire to leave the country under the Orange River Government, at any subsequent period within three years from the date of this convention.

5. Her Majesty's Government and the Orange River Government shall, within their respective territories, mutually use every exertion for the suppression of crime, and keeping the peace, by apprehending and delivering up all criminals who may have escaped or fled from justice either way across the Orange River; and the courts, as well the British as those of

the Orange River Government, shall be mutually open and available to the inhabitants of both territories for all lawful processes. And all summonses for witnesses, directed either way across the Orange River, shall be countersigned by the magistrates of both Governments respectively; to compel the attendance of such witnesses, when and where they may be required; thus affording to the community north of the Orange River every assistance from the British courts, and giving, on the other hand, assurance to such colonial merchants and traders as have naturally entered into credit transactions in the Orange River Territory, during its occupation by the British Government, and to whom, in many cases, debts may be owing, every facility for the recovery of just claims in the Courts of the Orange River Government. And Her Majesty's Special Commissioner will recommend the adoption of the like reciprocal privileges by the Government of Natal, in its relations with the Orange River Government.

6. Certificates issued by the proper authorities, as well in the colonies and possessions of Her Majesty as in the Orange River Territory, shall be held valid and sufficient to entitle heirs of lawful marriages, and legatees, to receive portions and legacies accruing to them respectively, either within the jurisdiction of the British or Orange River Government.

7. The Orange River Government shall, as hitherto, permit no slavery, or trade in slaves, in their territory north of the Orange River.

8. The Orange River Government shall have freedom to purchase their supplies of ammunition in any British colony or possession in South Africa, subject to the laws provided for the regulation of the sale and transit of ammunition in such colonies and possessions; and Her Majesty's Special Commissioner will recommend to the Colonial Government, that privileges of a liberal character, in connection of import duties generally, be granted to the Orange River Government, as measures in regard to which it is entitled to be treated with every indulgence, in consideration of its peculiar position and distance from the sea-ports.

9. In order to promote mutual facilities and liberty to traders and travellers, as well in the British possessions as in those of the Orange River Government, and it being the earnest wish of Her Majesty's Government that a friendly intercourse between these territories should at all times subsist, and be promoted by every possible arrangement, a consul or agent of the British Government, whose especial attention shall be directed to the promotion of these desirable objects, will be stationed within the colony, near to the frontier, to whom access at all times may readily be had by the inhabitants on both sides of the Orange River, for advice and information, as circumstances may require.

PROTEST OF THE COMMITTEE OF DELEGATES OF THE SOVEREIGNTY, FEBRUARY 17, 1854.

BLOEMFONTEIN, ORANGE RIVER SOVEREIGNTY,
17th February, 1854.

To His Grace the Duke of NEWCASTLE,
Her Majesty's Secretary of State for the Colonies,
&c., &c., &c.

THE SOLEMN PROTEST OF THE COMMITTEE APPOINTED BY THE ASSEMBLY OF DELEGATES OF THE ORANGE RIVER SOVEREIGNTY.

We declare the late acts of Her Majesty's Special Commissioner, Sir George Russel Clerk, to be illegal, unconstitutional, and in violation of the terms of Her Majesty's Commission, whereby he is enjoined to "enable the inhabitants to establish peaceable and orderly Government" in the Orange River Sovereignty; his proceedings on the contrary being certain to involve the country in irretrievable anarchy, confusion, and misrule; in confirmation of which assertion, we subjoin a statement of the transactions which have taken place since the arrival of Sir G. Clerk in this country, condemning and protesting against his acts in connection therewith.

On his arrival in the Sovereignty, an Assembly of Delegates, publicly elected throughout the several districts, was convened at Bloemfontein on the 5th September last by a Government notice dated 9th August, 1853, and published by his authority. That Assembly, at his recommendation, elected as a Committee of their number "for the purpose of considering a form of government for this territory, and for communicating with Her Majesty's Special Commissioner on all matters connected therewith;" the Committee being "specially enjoined not to receive this country from this British Government until the questions alluded to in Sir G. Clerk's reply of yesterday are satisfactorily settled, and full authority received from the Imperial Parliament ratifying all his acts."

The Assembly of Delegates further instructed their Committee "not to entertain any proposals for the formation of an independent government until certain questions should have been adjusted to their entire satisfaction;" it being left the Committee "to entertain any other question which might appear to them important to the interests of the country."

After the appointment of the Committee, the Assembly recorded their protest against the withdrawal of British protection, and then adjourned.

A copy of the resolutions passed by the Assembly of Delegates having been sent to Sir G. Clerk on the 9th September, he replied that some of the proposals were very reasonable, and that some he could not entertain, without, however, specifying any but the fourth, regarding a guarantee against interference from beyond the Vaal River.

On the 9th September a deputation of our number waited upon Sir G. Clerk, and expressed, in the name of the Committee, their desire to render him their assistance in any way in which it might be available. He replied, that he was not yet sufficiently advanced in his duties, or sufficiently acquainted with the different matters to be attended to by him, to be able at that moment to avail himself of their services; and stated that he would give the chairman due notice when he desired the Committee to re-assemble.

On the 10th November the Committee again met for the purpose of electing a Vice Chairman, when Sir G. Clerk was duly made acquainted with their sittings, but did not avail himself of their services.

A system of agitation was then commenced by certain persons, countenanced and encouraged by Sir G. Clerk, for the evident purpose of prejudicing their representatives in the eyes of the public. The leaders of this agitation held *private* meetings in different places, at which certain pseudo-representatives were chosen.

On the 10th January a Government Notice appeared, summoning "all persons who, on the part of the inhabitants, are now prepared to discuss with Her Majesty's Special Commissioner the terms upon which the independent government of this territory will be transferred to their hands," to assemble at Bloemfontein on the 15th February.

We, being the only persons legally and constitutionally authorized for the purpose, assembled on the appointed day, and informed Sir G. Clerk of our readiness to treat with him.

The pseudo-representatives above mentioned also assembled and held a meeting, from which the public were excluded by Government authority.

Sir G. Clerk entered into negotiations with these persons with the view of resigning the Government of this portion of Her Majesty's dominions into their hands, or to a Government about to be formed by them, and refused to acknowledge or treat with us the lawfully elected representatives of the people, without even deigning to give any public notice of his intention to ignore us, or recognize others as such.

In so doing and in guaranteeing to them, that their so-called new Government will be considered independent, he has unlawfully exceeded the powers invested in him by the Royal commission.

We are well aware that the bulk of the inhabitants whom we lawfully represent will never agree to succumb to the government thus attempted to be forced upon them; and we declare that Sir George Clerk, by consenting to its formation, after having been informed by our chairman of the probable consequences, has made himself answerable for the anarchy, and insecurity of life and property, which must inevitably ensue; and as the representatives of this people we hold the British Government responsible for all the consequences of the above-mentioned illegal and unconstitutional acts of him, their accredited agent.

On the part of the Committee of Delegates,

(Signed)   H. J. HALSE, Vice-Chairman.

GOD SAVE THE QUEEN!

RESOLUTIONS OF A LARGE PUBLIC MEETING, HELD AT BLOEMFONTEIN, FEBRUARY 17, 1854.

1. That the sentiments expressed in the following Resolution, passed this morning by the Committee of Delegates, be adopted by this meeting :—

"That the Committee having been informed by Her Majesty's Special Commissioner that he is now engaged in treating with persons who are not legally authorized for that purpose, protest against all his acts in connection with such persons in the strongest terms, and declare that the resignation of the Government of the country into their hands is in direct contravention to the terms of his Commission, and that we, or those we represent, never will submit to any Government so formed, and that the Special Commissioner be requested to forward a copy of our protest to Her Majesty's Secretary of State for the Colonies, to whom we will also forward a copy direct."

2. That this meeting denounces the proceedings of Her Majesty's Special Commissioner as illegal and unconstitutional. That it regards his attempt to thrust upon the inhabitants of the Sovereignty a Government composed of persons who have been elected at private meetings of only a section of the community, and not convened by public notice, with unmitigated disgust, and we hereby declare our determination not to acknowledge the authority of such Government or to obey its mandates, and we call upon our fellow countrymen to support us to the utmost of their power in this determination.

3. That as our allegiance has been always, and up to this moment is, entire and undivided, and as the Special Commissioner, Sir George Clerk, has acknowledged that he has been invested with no power whatever to absolve us therefrom, nor any more, of course, to annul, by his own single authority, the Act of Parliament of William IV., we declare that his proceedings have been unauthorized by his Commission, and contrary to Her Most Gracious Majesty's will and wish, as expressed in that document.

4. Resolved, that we declare all dealings of the Special Commissioner, Sir George Clerk, with any persons, not freely elected, whom he may, by either public or private, open or underhand, means, pretend to call representatives of the people of this Sovereignty, are, *ipso facto*, null and void, and shall not be recognized by us.

5. That should it become a certainty that the Special Commissioner will carry out the unjust measure of abandonment, and hand us over to the power of men in whose election we have had no voice, and in whom we have no confidence, whenever that measure be gazetted, that the Committee of Delegates, assisted by a permanent com mittee at Bloemfontein, shall proceed to organize a suitable and efficient Government for this country, which Government we pledge ourselves to support to the utmost extent of our power.

RESOLUTIONS OF A PUBLIC MEETING AT SMITHFIELD, MARCH 2, 1854.

That this meeting has this day learned by the *Bloemfontein Gazette* that Her Majesty's Special Commissioner has entered into a convention with, and handed over the Government of this country to men in whom we have no confidence, who were neither legally elected nor represent the majority of the people, while the delegates duly elected by the people were prepared to take over the Government on sound constitutional principles.

That this meeting has learned with feelings of indignation, that a body of men termed the New Government, countenanced by Her Majesty's Special Commissioner, Sir George Russell Clerk, has authorized the levy of four hundred Burghers, with pay of 4s. per diem each, guaranteed by Sir George Clerk, for purpose of forcing independent government upon us, and compelling us to submit to the rule of men in whom we have no confidence, and whom we will not recognize or obey. That as loyal British subjects we are resolved not to be deprived of the rights and privileges of Englishmen by Sir George R. Clerk, and that till our allegiance has been repudiated by an Act of Parliament, we will establish a Provisional Government acknowledging allegiance only to Her Most Gracious Majesty Queen Victoria.

Resolved, that we will not submit to any appointment of Landdrost, or other officers, made by Mr. Hoffman's Government, but should any such appointments be made, to be stationed at Smithfield, we will expel them forthwith.

Resolved, that this meeting, before separating for the day, do with heart and lungs nurtured and invigorated by the untainted air of freedom, and with right true loyal feelings, join devotedly, first, in our most beautiful and sacred National Anthem, and then sincerely and vigorously in three times three hearty cheers for our beloved Sovereign Lady Queen Victoria, and may her reign and that of her children be long and permanent, happy and glorious, over the Orange River Sovereignty.

CAPE TOWN PETITION TO THE IMPERIAL PARLIAMENT, IN FEBRUARY, 1854.

THE HUMBLE PETITION OF THE UNDERSIGNED INHABITANTS OF CAPE TOWN AND ITS NEIGHBOURHOOD.

HUMBLY SHOWETH,—

That the Orange River Sovereignty was taken formal possession of by Governor Lieutenant-General Sir Harry Smith, in February, 1848, while holding the office of Her Majesty's High Commissioner, for settling and adjusting the affairs of the countries bordering upon this country, by whose authority the lands were either sold or granted in perpetual quitrent, and whose proceedings were duly confirmed by Her Majesty's Ministers.

That these authoritative arrangements for the settlement of the country as a British possession, induced numbers of Her Majesty's subjects to settle therein, and to embark their capital in trade and agriculture, by which means it rapidly advanced; and in the course of the following five years had assumed the aspect of a thriving British Settlement, producing abundance of black cattle, extensive flocks of wool-bearing sheep, stock, and other articles of various descriptions, adapted to the purposes of trade and commerce, thus affording every prospect of being enabled, at no very distant period, under the fostering care of Her Majesty's Government, to defray the expense of such military force as might be required for its protection, while the loyal and respectable portion of the inhabitants are most anxious to remain under Her Majesty's rule and government.

That in the early part of 1853, Her Majesty was graciously pleased to issue Her Royal Commission to His Excellency Sir George Clerk, requiring and enjoining him "to take all such measures, and to do all such matters and things, as can and may lawfully and discreetly be done" by the said Sir George Clerk, by virtue of the said Royal Commission, "for settling the affairs of the Orange River Sovereignty, and for determining the disputes which exist between the natives and other inhabitants thereof, and for enabling the said inhabitants to establish peace and orderly government therein."

That on his arrival at Bloemfontein, Sir George Clerk invited the said inhabitants to select delegates for the purpose of communicating with him on the subject of his mission ; and accordingly each district sent one or two delegates to represent them at the conference with His Excellency.

When this meeting took place the delegates were confounded by Sir George Clerk's announcement that his mission was—not for arranging the affairs of the Sovereignty, and determining the disputes between the natives and other inhabitants, with a view to the establishment of peace and orderly government, but for the reverse of all these, viz., for the total abandonment of the settlement as a British possession, and the establishment of independent power throughout the Sovereignty, on the very border of our Colonial territory, and between that and a highly important portion of the native tribes.

Of course, when the delegates heard this announcement, it became impossible for them, when such appalling prospects opened to their view, to lend their countenance to a project of so alarming a character ; consequently, after some unavailable interview and correspondence, Sir George Clerk formally dissolved them as a representative body.

But the subject was one which too deeply involved the future peace and welfare of their adopted country to enable them to abandon it, while any hope remained of arresting its ultimate overthrow. They therefore determined upon dispatching their chairman, Dr. Fraser, and the Rev. Andrew Murray, the Minister of the Dutch Reformed Church at Bloemfontein, to represent their case to Her Majesty's Government, and who proceeded by the *Queen of the South* mail-steamer.

The departure of these gentlemen having been made known to Sir George Clerk, it was naturally hoped and expected that

His Excellency would not have pressed forward his measures till the result of the deputation to England should be known, but that he would have reported the anticipated result of the measures he had been instructed to adopt, and wait for further instructions.

But these hopes and expectations have been disappointed, and that too in a manner which has rendered the disappointment more appalling.

On the 23rd February last, Sir George Clerk executed a convention with twenty-five individuals at Bloemfontein, by which the Orange River Sovereignty was to be delivered over to them, and proclaimed a "Free State."

It must be supposed that Sir George Clerk could not have known, when he thus recognized these men as "the representatives of the people," that several of them are not British subjects—not residents in the country, whose interests they affect to represent—that many of them have been engaged in rebellion against Her Majesty's Government; that for the apprehension of the most prominent among them, Sir Harry Smith offered a reward of five hundred pounds, and that others had been fined after they had surrendered. Yet such is the fact, which the public records of the Colony establish; and these are the people to whom has been confided, under the authority of the Secretary of State, the lives and properties of Her Majesty's subjects in the Sovereignty, the future welfare of the native inhabitants, and the peace of South Africa.

A Foreign Republic upon the confines of the Colony is ill calculated to establish peace and maintain orderly government on either side the boundary. The disputes between the native and other inhabitants will probably be determined promptly enough by the annihilation of one or the other, and by deluging the land with the blood of both, and thus the affairs of the Sovereignty will be settled, but in a way that will ultimately compel Her Majesty's Ministers, they may rest assured, to resume possession of the abandoned territory at a vast expenditure of public money, amid the horrors of war, which will far exceed any which has yet been waged in South Africa.

For the sake then of the peace and prosperity of this productive settlement;

For the protection of Her Majesty's thriving possessions at Natal, the overland communication between which and the Colony is entirely cut off by the abandonment, and is thus rendered an easy prey to the Foreign Republic;

For the preservation of our border territory, and the maintenance of the peace which His Excellency Sir George Cathcart has so happily established with the Kafir tribes;

And especially for the sake of the native population, whose chance of civilization will thus be utterly obliterated, and whose reduction to slavery will become more than probable, notwithstanding the provision against the slave trade contained in the convention;

But above all, for the honour of the British nation, and for the sake of justice in behalf of those who have invested their capital and labour in the country, with implicit confidence in the good faith of Great Britain;

Your petitioners humbly pray, that the arrangements made by Sir Harry Smith, and confirmed by Her Majesty's Government, may not be abrogated, and that the convention which the Special Commissioner has entered into with persons who do not, as His Excellency has been led to think, represent the people of the Sovereignty, may be revoked, in order that the Orange River Sovereignty may remain a possession of the British Crown.

MEMORIAL FROM THE CAPE MERCHANTS IN LONDON TO HIS GRACE THE DUKE OF BUCKINGHAM, AUGUST, 1868.

To the Right Hon. the Duke of BUCKINGHAM *and* CHANDOS,
Her Majesty's Secretary of State for the Colonies, &c., &c.

MAY IT PLEASE YOUR GRACE—

We, the undersigned, all more or less connected with and interested in the Colony of the Cape of Good Hope, understanding that two Delegates from the adjoining territory, known as the Orange Free State, are at present in England, beg to submit the following brief particulars for your Grace's consideration :—

That in or about the year 1888 a large number of the Cape Colonists, being dissatisfied with British rule, for various reasons, but chiefly in consequence of the abolition of Slavery which had previously existed there, emigrated beyond the boundaries of the Colony, and established themselves on a tract of country since known as the Orange Free State, and inhabited partly by natives of various races, and from time to time their number was increased by emigrants from Europe and from the Colony.

The occupation of this territory led to the usual and inevitable results—cattle were stolen from the Farmers, and they in return made reprisals, and thus in frequent petty conflicts lives were sacrificed on both sides. This lawless state of things, too often marked by acts of tyranny and oppression on the part of the stronger race, led eventually to the interference of the

Colonial Government, on an appeal for protection being made by some of the Native Chiefs against the aggressions of Colonists, most of them British-born subjects.

Prior to the action of the Colonial Government the population of the Orange territory had been largely augmented by the influx of a number of Boers from the territory beyond the Vaal River, these people having fled there after having been in open rebellion against British authority in the adjoining district of Natal. An attempt on the part of the Colonial Government to establish Magisterial supervision over the Orange River territory was resisted, chiefly at the instigation of these people, who endeavoured to cast off their allegiance, and proclaimed the territory a Republic, independent of British rule.

This precipitate measure, and the revival of a species of domestic slavery among the emigrant farmers, led to armed interference on the part of the Home Government ; the territory was entered by a British force, and the rebellious farmers, having rashly attacked the troops on their march, were defeated, and the country was at once proclaimed as British territory, under the designation of the Orange River Sovereignty.

The assumption of authority by the Crown over this large and valuable country was hailed by the emigrants of Dutch and English descent, as well as by the native tribes who were scattered over the territory, as the advent of a better state of things. A British Resident was appointed, and the course of affairs was marked by unchecked peace and steady prosperity. A small garrison, at no time exceeding 400 men, was found adequate to support the Resident's authority. The malcontents went further Northward and Eastward, and established what is now known as the Vaal River Republic ; and a large number of colonists, both of English and Dutch descent, relying on the stability of British authority, went to reside in the Sovereignty, purchasing and receiving grants of land, and investing largely in other property.

During the continuance of the Kafir war of 1852, the British Resident in the Sovereignty unwisely and needlessly allowed himself to be forced into a conflict with the Basutos and other native tribes, in which he met with failure and disaster. This mismanagement produced serious complications, and the then Governor of the Cape Colony and High Commissioner, Sir Harry Smith, was superseded in his Government before he could apply a remedy.

Sir George Cathcart succeeded to the Government, and, with the avowed object of sustaining the prestige of the British name, he marched into Basutoland, and attacked the Basuto army.

The enormous cost of the Kafir war, and the charges on the Imperial revenue arising out of this expedition, naturally aroused the attention of the Home Government, and to prevent further expenditure a gentleman trained in the Civil Service of the East India Company was sent to ascertain whether it was practicable to make arrangements for the abandonment of the whole of the territory.

Proposing to be guided in his decisions and report by the opinions of those most interested, the residents themselves, meetings were called throughout the Sovereignty for the election of Delegates, through whom the public voice was to be expressed.

The expression of public opinion and feeling thus gained through those twenty-four Delegates was clear and unmistakeable ; it was that on every consideration of right, honour, and expediency, the British Government could not abandon the Sovereignty.

The views and opinions of the vast majority of the residents in the Sovereignty, both of European and Native descent, being at variance with what was evidently a foregone conclusion, was entirely disregarded by Her Majesty's Commissioner, who thought fit to recognise, instead of them, a small knot of persons elected by no competent authorities, possessing no representative character whatever, notoriously disaffected towards British authority, and devoid of that moral character which could alone give their opinions any weight.

But it was on the expression by this convenient clique of their readiness to undertake the formation of a new Government, that the small detachment of troops was withdrawn, and, by a proclamation, the Queen's authority over the territory was declared to have ceased.

This unlooked-for decision was loudly and earnestly protested against as a breach of good faith on the part of the Queen's Commissioner, who, professing to be guided by public opinion, had notoriously disregarded it.

The abandonment of the Sovereignty was effected in opposition to the declared opinions of all the English residents ; by far the largest and most influential residents of all other races ; it was earnestly remonstrated against by all classes of the Cape Colonists ; it was in despite of the urgent entreaties of the surrounding Native Chiefs, even those with whom we had been recently at war ; and in stern opposition to the opinion and advice of every missionary who resided in the country, or knew anything of its affairs.

When, in the year 1854, the fatal measure of withdrawing British rule was decided upon, and the territory was abandoned to the inhabitants, they were not formally absolved from their allegiance to the British Crown, and to this day, therefore, they are legally British subjects, a fact which has either been lost sight of by the Home and Colonial Governments, or otherwise disregarded for obvious reasons.

Many of the English abandoned the territory in disgust, and a Republic, under the name of the Orange Free State, with an elective President and Council, was at once formed, with results which all who knew what the disorganised state of society is in the Free State, fully anticipated.

The residents, unable to find among themselves the materials for forming a Government (after a period of comparative quiet, the effect of the arrangements of the previously existing Government) have drifted into a series of harassing and protracted wars between the Free State and the native tribes, involving great loss of property and the sacrifice of many lives. In the progress of events, the Free State Government adopted the idea that the Missionaries labouring among the native tribes were inimical to European interests, and they passed a law depriving the native inhabitants of the Mission Stations of their right in the soil.

This harsh and uncalled-for measure pressed with great severity on a number of French Protestant Missionaries, who had long laboured successfully amongst the Basutos, and who in consequence had to abandon the mission stations on which large sums of money had been expended, and where their principal native congregations were collected.

Moshesh, the Chief of the Basutos, with whom the Free State has been frequently at war, has, after repeated requests, been received with all his tribes as British subjects, and the Basuto country has been proclaimed British territory, a proceeding which has been resented by the Free State authorities as an interference between them and a hostile tribe, a large portion of whose territory they had taken by force of arms, and whom, at no distant period, they expected to reduce to abject and unconditional submission.

The Free State Government having refused to allow their President to treat with the Governor of the Cape Colony as to the fixing a proper line of boundary, and having determined to send home a deputation to appeal against the Governor's proceedings, with what instructions your Memorialists are not aware, it is incumbent on them to place before your Grace the views and opinions of by far the larger portion of the residents in the Free State—of all those commercially connected with it—of all the native tribes and races, and of a vast majority of the colonists of the Cape of Good Hope, whose interests are identical with those of the Orange Free State.

Your Memorialists do not hesitate to state that by all these classes re-annexation in one form or other as a British Dependency is most earnestly desired; and they would go further and say, that by all these classes strong, earnest, and often repeated remonstrances against the withdrawal of British authority were made, as being derogatory to the honour of the Crown, inimical to the best interests of the people, and alike fatal to the extension of law and order and the spread of Christianity and civilization.

It is impossible to convey in language to your Grace an idea of the state of demoralization to which a large proportion of the Free State inhabitants have been reduced by the protracted wars carried on against the native tribes; but it is sufficient to state, as of the most pressing and important interest to the Cape Colonists, that for the past three years, under the pretext that the State is at war, all the Courts of the Free State have been closed, and in consequence they have no legal means of recovering debts, which in the aggregate amount to not less than £300,000 (Three Hundred Thousand Pounds). That the wars with the natives are carried on by paper money, issued on the security of the public lands, and current at about the value of 11s. to 12s. in the pound—by levies in kind on the residents, and by a special tax of £40, on each occasion of war, on non-resident landowners. The paper issue is a legal tender in the Free State, and as there is no check on its issue beyond the will of the Volksraad, a further depreciation seems inevitable.

Among the more comprehensive questions involved, there are others which impress themselves very forcibly on your Memorialists, as rendering it highly desirable in the interests of humanity, for the honour of Great Britain, and the welfare of her Colonies in South Africa, and the due control of a large territory, the inhabitants of which are still British subjects, though not under her protection, or amenable to her jurisdiction, that means should be taken for re-asserting British authority over the region in question. These may be stated as follows :—

a The anomalous position of residents in the Free State, who as subjects of the Queen, and separated only by geographical lines from the Colonies of the Cape of Good Hope and Natal, are allowed to exercise independent authority, and are regarded and treated as Foreigners.

b The inevitable complications which must result from the altered position of the Basuto nation in relation to Great Britain and to the Orange Free State.

c The assumed position taken up by the Transvaal Republic, who by Proclamation have recently defined its boundaries, adding an immense extent of territory to the Republic, including the country over which a Chief named Matjen rules, and embracing a large portion of the land containing the recently-discovered Gold Fields, and extending to the great Lake N'gami. A very important addition has also been made on the eastern boundary, reaching to the River Umzuti (including the Pongola and Umzuti Rivers), to where it discharges into the ocean on the east coast, and including one mile of territory on each side of the river. This river is navigable for a considerable distance inland, and discharges itself into Delagoa Bay to the south of the Portuguese settlement there, thus securing a good and safe harbour, which may also eventually become available for the Orange Free State.

d The great changes which may be expected in the condition of the territories through the discovery of gold and diamonds, and the possibility of Foreign Governments extending their dominion over them.

e The furtherance of the interests of humanity in putting down that modified system of slavery which is known to prevail in the territories north of the Vaal River.

Taking these circumstances into consideration, and others which might be adduced, we believe that it would be of very great benefit and advantage to the natives if the British Government should assume the protectorate of such of the tribes as may desire the same; also that it would be a great advantage to the Free State people and the Cape and Natal Colonists, if British authority was resumed in the Free State, with the consent and concurrence of the people; and finally, that it is desirable that no unnecessary delay should occur in taking the necessary steps, inasmuch as there is good reason to believe that there will be a considerable migration of Europeans to the gold and diamond fields, which, as already mentioned, are in the territory of some of the chiefs who desire to enter into alliance with the British Government.

In expressing so decided an opinion as to the political, moral, and social advantages to be derived from an extension of British authority over the Orange Free State and adjacent territories, your memorialists have not lost sight of the fact that consideration of expense in maintaining British authority over the Sovereignty was the moving cause of that protection being withdrawn.

But your memorialists do not hesitate to say that these considerations were based on erroneous data and imperfect information, as well as on a thorough misconception of the actual state of things existing in the Sovereignty and the adjacent Basuto territory.

Speaking from a general knowledge of the various races inhabiting the territories to the north and north-east of the Colony, and from the experience gained in the neighbouring Colony of Natal, where large bodies of natives are in subjection to British authority, your memorialists are led to believe that the further extension of the authority of the Crown which they advocate, might be effected without imposing additional pecuniary burdens on the Colony or the Imperial revenue.

We have the honour to be
    Your Grace's obedient humble Servants.

RESOLUTIONS OF THE NATAL LEGISLATIVE COUNCIL, RECOMMENDING TO THE FAVOURABLE CONSIDERATION OF HER MAJESTY'S GOVERNMENT THE ANNEXATION OF THE TWO REPUBLICS, THE ORANGE FREE STATE AND TRANSVAAL, AUGUST, 1868.

1. That the interests of the two South African British Colonies, viz., the Cape Colony and Natal, are in many respects so closely united with the Republics situated on their several borders, that a union of these under British rule can scarcely fail to conduce to the material welfare of the whole, both as a means of promoting an interchange of friendly relations amongst them, as well as of providing, by judicious combination, for their adequate security and confidence in time of danger ; and establishing and regulating commercial intercourse on a permanent and satisfactory basis to all parties.

2. That the comparative dependence of these Republics on the Cape Colony and Natal, together with the similarity of the religion, laws, and customs of the white inhabitants to those of the same classes inhabiting the two latter colonies, favours the belief that sooner or later they will be desirous of coming under the dominion of the British Government.

3. That the Council is therefore of opinion, that with a view to furthering the objects above set forth, it would be highly desirable for Her Majesty's Government favourably to consider any proposal which the authorities of these Republics, being empowered thereto by the inhabitants, may put forward, affecting their annexation to either the Cape Colony or Natal, or embracing suggestions with respect to any other form of allied or separate administration deemed suitable by the majority of the white inhabitants of such states.

4. That a respectful address be presented to the Lieutenant-Governor, transmitting to His Excellency copy of the above resolutions, and requesting His Excellency to forward the same to the Right Hon. the Secretary of State for the Colonies, for the favourable consideration of Her Majesty's Government.

RESOLUTIONS OF THE NATAL LEGISLATIVE COUNCIL RESPECTING SLAVERY AND THE HIGH COMMISSIONER, AUGUST, 1868.

1. That in the opinion of this House, the office of High Commissioner, as exercised at present in relation to this Colony, is inimical to the maintenance of the prestige and influence of Her Majesty's Government amongst the Native Tribes of South East Africa, and the House is guided to this conclusion by the following considerations :—

a The High Commissioner, as Governor of the Cape Colony, resides at Cape Town, which is about 700 miles from the northern frontier of the Eastern Province, where alone independent native tribes are to be met with.

b That Natal is surrounded on three sides by territories chiefly occupied by large and powerful independent tribes, with whom the local authorities cannot deal, irrespective of the consent of the High Commissioner at Cape Town.

c That in times of disturbance amongst the surrounding communities, the Government of Natal is deprived of that power of timely and effectual action which it might otherwise exercise with great benefit to the interests of peace and civilization.

d That ever since the annexation of the Orange River Sovereignty (since abandoned) in 1848, the emigrant farmers who settled over the Vaal River, and formed a Government of their own, under the style of the South African Republic, have carried on a system of slavery, under the guise of child-apprenticeship—such children being the result of raids carried on against native tribes, whose men are slaughtered, but whose children and property are seized, the one being enslaved and sold as "apprentices," the other being appropriated.

e That in 1862 this system of slavery was brought to the notice of the High Commissioner and the Secretary of State by Lieutenant-Governor Scott, in the form of a statement made by a Bushman woman named Leya, who had been captured and enslaved by the boers of the Transvaal Republic, but no steps were taken to put an end to the practice in question.

f That on the 25th of April, 1865, Lieutenant-Governor Maclean forwarded to the High Commissioner a statement made by Mr. W. Martin, of Maritzburg, dated June 1st, 1865, in which clear and positive evidence, acquired during two visits to the country in 1852 and 1864, was given at length, and in which certain wrongs suffered by the writer, in direct contravention of the treaty entered into between Her Majesty's Special Commissioners, Hogge and Owen, in 1852, were set forth.

g That the existence of this system of slavery, attended as it is by indescribable atrocities and evils, is a notorious fact to all persons acquainted with the Transvaal Republic; that these so-called "destitute children" are bought and sold under the denomination of "black ivory;" that these evils were fully admitted by persons officially cognizant of them at a public meeting held at Potchefstroom, the chief town of the Republic, in April, 1868, and that the whole subject has been brought fully under the notice of the High Commissioner.

h That the following reply was sent to Lieutenant-Governor Maclean by the High Commissioner :—" I can assure you that I fully sympathize with you in your desire to put a stop to what is so strongly described by Mr. Martin, but I am really quite at a loss to discover in what manner I could interfere with any prospect of success. There can scarcely be a doubt that the President, if referred to, would strenuously deny the existence of such traffic. A *bonâ fide* inquiry would be almost impracticable, and, moreover, it would be beyond the power of the Transvaal Republic, admitting it to have the inclination, to put down a trade which the Boers must find to be very tempting and pro--fitable. Under all the circumstances, I trust that you will, on further consideration, be prepared to acquiesce in my desire to abstain from addressing Mr. Pretorius on the subject."

i That as a *bonâ fide* inquiry to be instituted by the Government of the Transvaal Republic would be, under the circumstances, " quite impracticable," it is highly important that Her Majesty's Government should take other steps to ascertain the truth and to put a stop to a trade which, however "tempting and profitable to the Boers," is a direct breach of the treaty entered into with Her Majesty's Commissioners; is an outrage on humanity and civilization, and is an aggravation of the traffic which Her Majesty's Government has so long sought to suppress upon the East Coast.

j That so long as this traffic in children is suffered to exist, there can be little hope for the progress of civilization amongst the native tribes living in the Transvaal Republic, while the prevalence of such practices in the immediate neighbourhood of independent and colonial tribes has a most pernicious and injurious effect, and tends to lower the position and influence of the white race.

k That it is impossible for the High Commissioner, living so far as he does from the scene of these atrocities, to judge clearly and fully their character and tendencies, but it would be in the power of the Government of Natal, had it the right to act, to interfere in the matter without entailing any troublesome or costly complications on the Home Government.

l The state of peace which the colony of Natal has enjoyed ever since its establishment, combined with the constant recognition here of all the just rights and claims of the natives, have secured for the local Government the confidence of the neighbouring independent tribes, and would enable the representatives of Her Majesty's authority here, were they freed from the control of the High Commissioner, to exercise a most salutary and beneficent influence over the native races of South-eastern Africa.

2. That a respectful address be presented to the Lieutenant-Governor, forwarding copy of above resolution, and praying His Excellency to transmit the same to the Right Honourable the Secretary of State for the Colonies, for his consideration, together with copies of all documents bearing upon the subject.

CAPE TOWN ADDRESS TO SIR PHILIP WODEHOUSE ON HIS RETURN FROM ALIWAL NORTH, MAY 13, 1868, AND HIS REPLY THERETO.

CAPE TOWN, May 13, 1868.

To His Excellency Sir P. E. WODEHOUSE, *K.C.B., Governor of the Cape of Good Hope, Her Majesty's High Commissioner, &c., &c.*

SIR,—We seize the opportunity of your Excellency's return to Cape Town from Basutoland to convey our grateful sense of the energy and ability with which you have endeavoured to carry out the instructions of Her Majesty's Government to restore peace in South Africa.

The British Basuto Protectorate is, in our opinion, wisely calculated to put an end to the wretched and protracted warfare between the Boers and the Basutos, which has been so manifestly disastrous to both, and was even fraught with danger to the happy continuance of the peaceful relations so long subsisting between this Colony and the Native tribes, both within and without its border.

It may reasonably be expected that the Basutos, as British subjects, will be more efficiently restrained from committing outrages on the life and property of their neighbours, than under the former control of the chiefs.

Taking a deep interest in the welfare and progress of our former fellow-colonists, relatives and friends, northward of the Orange River, we cannot help regretting that the Volksraad did not empower the President to meet your Excellency in amicable conference at Aliwal North, because we feel persuaded that you were prepared to give the fullest consideration to the just claims of the Orange Free State.

We do not, however, yet despair that the people of that State will see that it is to their real interest to urge upon their representatives, when they next meet in Council, the justice and expediency of at once entering into negotiation with your Excellency, as Her Majesty's High Commissioner, with a view to a settlement on satisfactory terms of the only material point at issue—the future boundary line of Basutoland, now British territory.

Your Excellency, we respectfully submit, cannot be ignorant that there is but one opinion throughout the Cape and Natal, that the abandonment of the Sovereignty in 1854 was a measure most prejudicial to the interests of both these British Colonies, to the country which the Convention of Sir George Clerk professed to make independent and free, and to the Aborigines of South Africa, who have so long claimed the protection of Great Britain.

Without desiring to dictate to our neighbours of the Trans-Orange Republic, we think that we may assume that the extension of British Rule to the Orange Free State would be attended with great advantage to all parties concerned; and we venture to express the earnest hope that, in the event of the subjects of the Queen of England in South Africa who have been abandoned petitioning Her Majesty, to whom they owe their natural allegiance, to be placed again under the protection of the British Flag, your Excellency may deem it right to exert your powerful influence with the Home Government on their behalf.

We are not unmindful of your Excellency's past services in the administration of the Government of this Colony, but we have no hesitation in recording our opinion that it would be an appropriate close to your useful and honourable career in South Africa to be instrumental in the annexation of the Orange Free State, as well as Basutoland, to the British Colonial Empire.

We have the honour to be, Sir,
Your most obedient and humble servants,
(Signed) J. B. EBDEN, J. J. LE SUEUR,
J. T. EUSTACE, H. DOUGLAS, &c., &c.*

---

* Addresses similar in purport, numerously and influentially signed, were presented to His Excellency from Port Elizabeth, Simon's Town, Swellendam, Bredasdorp, George, Colesberg, Albert, Victoria West, &c.

GENTLEMEN,—I beg that you will accept my best thanks for this flattering expression of your approval of the efforts I have recently made for giving effect to the instructions of Her Majesty's Government, with regard to the reception of the Basutos as subjects of the British Crown.

I believe that in dealing with these matters we are all actuated by the same desire to restore peace, to promote good government, and certainly to secure to the people of the Free State a substantial return for the exertions they have made, and the losses they have sustained, during this melancholy strife with the Basutos.

I am convinced that such a return is unattainable except through our intervention, and I look forward to the day, when I may yet have an opportunity, in negotiation, of satisfying the Government of the State of the sincerity of my feelings for them. I have no desire to question the soundness of the opinion you have expressed, that the severance of the Free State from this Colony was a misfortune for both communities. But their re-union now is beset with many difficulties; the question has never been discussed between Her Majesty's Government and myself, and I am without instructions respecting it. A proposal to that effect must manifestly emanate from the people of the Free State, and must take the form of an unmistakeable expression of the general will.

It is not for me to say what would in such case be the decision of Her Majesty's Government or of the Colonial Parliament, but I have no doubt that such a representation would receive a respectful and patient consideration at their hands.

I have again to thank you for the address you have been kind enough to present to me.

(Signed)   P. E. WODEHOUSE.

RESOLUTIONS UNANIMOUSLY PASSED BY A PUBLIC MEETING AT PORT ELIZABETH, JUNE 13, 1868, AND THE GOVERNOR'S REPLY.

1. That the inhabitants of Port Elizabeth, in public meeting assembled, embrace the present opportunity of expressing the satisfaction afforded to them by the admission of the Basutos as British subjects, and by the addition of their territory to the British dominions.

2. That the difficult task of carrying out the intentions of the Home Government, in respect to the Basutos, has, in the opinion of this meeting, been conducted by His Excellency Sir Philip Wodehouse with great energy and discretion; and that

throughout the negotiation His Excellency has endeavoured, by every means in his power, to secure the co-operation and friendly feelings of the Orange Free State Government.

3. That there is but one opinion throughout the colonies of Natal and the Cape, that the abandonment of the Sovereignty in 1854 most injuriously affected the interests of the British colonies, as well as those of the Orange Free State, and of the aboriginal tribes of Southern Africa; and that this meeting regards with satisfaction the admission of the Basutos as British subjects, principally because it is the fitting step to the much-desired reunion of the Orange Free State to this Colony, with which it is so intimately connected by family ties and commercial interests. This meeting is also of opinion that no effort should be spared to induce the British Government to confer upon the Orange Free State the same advantages and' privileges that it has extended to the Basutos.

4. That, in the opinion of this meeting, the motion of which notice has been given by Mr. Wollaston for Thursday next, in the House of Assembly, is of the utmost importance, and it is hoped that it will receive the cordial support of all the members of the Legislature.*

5. That the chairman be requested to forward copies of the foregoing resolutions to His Excellency the Governor and the members of the House of Assembly for Port Elizabeth.

COLONIAL OFFICE, June 23, 1868.

H. W. PEARSON, Esq., *Port Elizabeth*.

SIR,—I am directed by His Excellency the Governor, to acknowledge the receipt of your letter dated the 15th instant, accompanied by copies of resolutions adopted at a public meeting held at Port Elizabeth, in reference to the admission of the Basutos as British subjects, and the annexation of their territory to the British Dominions. His Excellency desires me to state for the information of the inhabitants of Port Elizabeth, that he has received with satisfaction this evidence of their approval of the efforts he has made to arrive at a

---

* The following is the notice of motion referred to :—" That a select committee be appointed, with power to take evidence and call for papers, to consider and report upon that portion of His Excellency the Governor's speech having reference to Basutoland and the Free State, the Despatch of the Right Honourable the Secretary of State for the Colonies, and correspondence on the same subject, to be laid upon the table of the House, and upon the question generally, as affecting the interests of this Colony in its relations with the Free State, and the progress of civilization in South Africa."

friendly understanding with the Orange Free State on the
affairs of Basutoland.
I have the honour to be, Sir,
Your obedient Servant,
(Signed) R. SOUTHEY, Colonial Secretary.

LETTER OF PORT ELIZABETH CHAMBER OF COMMERCE, MARCH 23, 1868, TO SIR PHILIP WODEHOUSE, AND HIS EXCELLENCY'S REPLY.

PORT ELIZABETH CHAMBER OF COMMERCE,
PORT ELIZABETH, March 23, 1868.

To His Excellency Sir P. E. WODEHOUSE, K.C.B.,
Governor and High Commissioner, &c., &c., Aliwal North.

SIR,—The Committee of the Chamber, taking advantage of your Excellency's important mission as Her Majesty's High Commissioner to Aliwal North, have instructed me as their chairman, respectfully to submit a few remarks for your consideration on the present position of affairs in the Orange Free State, with which the interests of this Colony are so intimately connected.

I have the honour, while adverting to the proclamation contained in the *Government Gazette* of the 18th instant, to express, on behalf of the mercantile community of this place, the extreme satisfaction afforded to them by the admission into the allegiance of Her Majesty of the Basutos as British subjects, and by the addition of their territory to the British dominions.

2. We are well aware of the anxious solicitude evinced by your Excellency towards the native races of South Africa, and attribute, in a great degree, to your Excellency's representations, as High Commissioner, the interposition of Her Majesty's Government with a view to a prompt solution of the Basuto difficulty.

3. Your Excellency is no doubt well acquainted with the history of the Orange Free State from the days of the Sovereignty, narrated with tolerable accuracy in the printed copy hereunto annexed of a Petition to the Queen, cut out of an Orange Free State newspaper, to which I beg to refer; and I need scarcely add, that it would be a source of immense relief to this Colony, if, in the course of the negotiations with Mr. President Brand, it should so happen that your Excellency were to see the way to bring the Orange Free State again under British rule, by annexation, federation, or otherwise.

4. The stake of British merchants in the Orange Free State is worth protecting (the claims of Port Elizabeth merchants alone being estimated at upwards of £300,000). The country itself offers a wide field for enterprize ; and, as a pastoral country, is certainly superior to the average lands of the Colony, requiring only a Government that would command public confidence to make it one of the most prosperous and flourishing of our South African provinces.

5. It already contributes in wool about one-fourth part of our exports from Algoa Bay, and consumes about a corresponding value of our imported goods. The country moreover is at present but partially occupied, and it is in this direction chiefly that the Colony has to look for an extension of its trade and commerce.

6. The financial position of the Orange Free State will be found, on proper investigation, by no means so alarming as might at first sight appear. There is undoubted security for the discharge of its present public debt, and the legal tender notes at present in circulation, amounting to £130,000, could easily be redeemed. The dread of a further issue of paper is the main cause of their present depreciation, and if allowed to take place will entail the most ruinous consequences.

7. The inhabitants of the Orange Free State are, it is believed, generally favourable to a British Federal Union, wishing, however, to enjoy the privilege of local self-government, but to be associated with the other provinces in matters of common interest.

8. For the last two or three years, the merchants in this Colony have suffered incalculable loss from the indiscriminate closing of the Law Courts throughout the Orange Free State, and I beg to call your Excellency's attention to the following extract from Article 5 of the Convention of 21st February, 1854 :—
"And the Courts, as well the British as those of the Orange River Government, shall be mutually open and available to the inhabitants of both territories for all lawful processes." By which it would appear that the Orange Free State Government have entirely departed from the conditions set forth, thus rendering the interference of our Government not only justifiable but absolutely necessary for the due protection of the rights of British subjects.

9. And the Committee feel confident that whatever course of action your Excellency may find it necessary to pursue, the large mercantile interests involved in the Orange Free State will not fail to claim full consideration at your Excellency's hands.

I have the honour to be, Sir,
Your obedient humble Servant,
By order of the Committee of the Port Elizabeth Chamber of Commerce,
(Signed) R. D. BUCHANAN, Chairman.

GOVERNMENT-HOUSE, CAPE TOWN, May 26, 1868.

To JOHN FRY, *Esq.*,

Secretary of the Port Elizabeth Chamber of Commerce.

MY DEAR FRY,—In reply to yours of the 22nd inst., I am desired by the Governor to inform you, for the information of the Chamber of Commerce, that His Excellency duly received the letter alluded to in yours dated the 23rd of March, as will be seen by the reference to it in the Speech ; and the reason for its not having been answered is, that it bore chiefly on the question of the annexation of the Free State to the Colony.

His Excellency was most anxious at that time, as indeed throughout, to avoid giving the Free State Government a pretext for asserting that he was plotting its overthrow, and therefore thought it better to leave the letter from Port Elizabeth unanswered.

His Excellency hopes that the Chamber will appreciate the motives which made him keep silence. I have only to add that you are at liberty to make any use of this letter you please.

Yours very truly,

G. ST. V. CRIPPS.

SUGGESTED PETITION TO THE QUEEN REFERRED TO BY PORT ELIZABETH CHAMBER OF COMMERCE.

" Federalist" writes to the *Friend* :—As I perceive from your leading articles that you are very decidedly in favour of the extension of British rule in some shape (not annexation to or incorporation with the Cape Colony or Natal, I believe), it has occurred to me that when Sir Philip Wodehouse comes to Bloemfontein, or meets the President, perhaps at Thaba Bosigo, it would be a good opportunity for " the abandoned subjects of Her Majesty" to commence a constitutional agitation, with the view of this State being converted into a portion of the British Colonial Empire. I have been *officious* enough to draft a petition to the Queen, which I forward to you herewith. The document will speak for itself, and if you approve and give insertion to it, can be altered by those more cognisant with the feelings of the people generally, so as to obtain signatures. The petition has been drafted in haste and rather in ignorance how the British-Basuto Protectorate will be received by the inhabitants. I confess I am one who think that if they know their own interests they would greatly prefer having their neighbours British subjects, instead of savages under no control but that of their chiefs.

To Her Most Gracious Majesty VICTORIA, *by the Grace of God Queen of Great Britain, Ireland, &c., &c.*

MADAM,—We, the undersigned inhabitants of the Orange River Free State, in South Africa, beg leave to approach your Majesty with the profoundest respect for your Crown and person.

Your Majesty will, we trust, forgive us for recalling to your memory that the country which we inhabit was formerly a portion of your Majesty's dominions, having been taken possession of as an integral part of the British Empire in the year 1848.

Relying on the security afforded by the British flag, many of us for the first time ventured to leave the Cape Colony, cross the Orange River and seek our fortunes in the land which had thus been taken under your Majesty's protection. In doing so, we felt that while we were changing the land of our habitation, we were not changing our nationality, but that we still retained the pride of being British subjects, and the safety of living under British laws and Government, or even deemed that we had rights which Englishmen never voluntarily forego, and which other nations seldom fail to respect.

In consequence, principally, of disturbances arising between your Majesty's troops and the neighbouring nation of Basutos, under their chief Moshesh, Sir George Clerk was sent as your Majesty's Commissioner, to this then Sovereignty of the Orange River, for the purpose of settling its affairs and abandoning, in your Majesty's name, the future possession and government of it.

The intelligence of this step, determined upon by your Majesty's advisers then in office, alarmed and dismayed all your loyal subjects who had taken up their residence, invested all their means, and cast their lots in this country, relying on the fact that it was British territory, and protected by the power of your Majesty's arms. They petitioned your Majesty to recall the sentence of abandonment, they besought your Majesty to extend the protection of the British Empire, in some shape or for some period, to this land; they sent deputations to England to attain this end, upon which their lives and fortunes depended, but in vain. It seemed good to your Majesty's advisers that the people of this country should henceforth protect themselves as they best could, and that they should submit to the pecuniary losses which their forced loss of nationality entailed upon them.

From that day until the present time, this State has struggled against the disadvantages of a weak Government; a national credit limited by the small resources of the land, and unsustained by the aid of a mother country; a colony whose colonists have been cut adrift from the parent State. It has been perpetually harassed and impeded in its progress by a warlike nation of savages on its border, who have kept its inhabitants in a state of perpetual alarm by robberies, forays, and deeds of violence.

In self-defence, and to save itself from utter ruin and destruction, it has again and again been obliged to take up arms against these people, and to waste, in long protracted wars, the energies which a peace would, under the blessing of Providence, have secured it wealth and prosperity. The treachery and faithlessness of this perpetual enemy has again compelled this State to resort to warfare, and it is now using its utmost powers to avenge the cruel wrongs which it has suffered in the spoliation of its lands, and the murder of its citizens by these ruthless barbarians on its frontier, but also in the hope that it may finally and effectually crush their perpetual aggressive spirit, and compel them to live in amity and peace with their neighbours.

In the midst of these efforts, in which we are sacrificing our time and our very means of existence, we have been surprised at hearing that your Majesty has been recommended to take under your gracious protection the enemy who has brought us so much suffering and bloodshed, and who was the original cause of the withdrawal from this land of the very boon now bestowed upon him.

We do not doubt the wisdom, and we feel assured of the good intentions indicated by your Majesty's determination to include the country of the Basutos under the flag of Great Britain, with the view of restoring and maintaining general peace in South Africa; but we do, with profound respect, urgently ask your Majesty whether you will refuse to us, who once enjoyed it, that which you now grant to others whose defiance and determined opposition to your Majesty's arms entailed the forfeiture of it upon us? And as we are told, that it is because the Chief Moshesh and his people have asked for the protection of the British Crown, have begged to be made British subjects, and have tendered their submission to your will, that your Majesty has granted their requests, so do all now, in the name of justice, and as men who were born or have lived under the British flag, as men who, on the faith of what we conceive our birthright, and relying upon the name of Great Britain, have become denizens of this land—so do all now ask your Majesty again to extend your protection to us, to let us once more call ourselves British subjects, and your Majesty our most gracious Queen. We cannot believe that your Majesty will turn a deaf ear to this our appeal; we make it in all earnestness and sincerity, and we look forward with confidence to a favourable response as an act of justice and peace to us, and an act eminently in accordance with the sentiments and deeds of one whom we have never ceased to venerate as a wise and good Sovereign, even while forbidden to claim Her as our own protector and ruler.

RESOLUTIONS UNANIMOUSLY PASSED AT A SPECIAL MEETING OF THE PORT ELIZABETH CHAMBER OF COMMERCE, DECEMBER 31, 1867.

1. That, attention having been called to the Anti-Blueback movement at Bloemfontein, and the resolutions passed at a public meeting there, held on the 18th December, 1867, this meeting cordially expresses its concurrence generally in the views therein embodied, and takes this opportunity of declaring its firm conviction that by judicious taxation alone can the Orange Free State Government extricate itself from its present pecuniary circumstances.

2. That, in the opinion of this meeting, the issue of paper money in 1865-6, by the Orange Free State Government, without any proper provision for its conversion into gold or silver at the will of the holder, was opposed to all sound principles of political economy, and could not fail injuriously to affect the agricultural and commercial interests of the country.

3. That the depreciated value of the paper money already issued, amounting to £180,000, negociable only at a discount of from 25 per cent. to 30 per cent., affords the best evidence of utter want of public confidence in the measure as a financial scheme, and that, in the face of such a depreciated currency, the very idea of Government entertaining for a moment the additional issue of legal tender notes is calculated to cause the utmost consternation amongst mercantile men having business relations with the Orange Free State, and, if carried out, would, in the opinion of this meeting, destroy entirely the credit of the State in the Colony, and be attended with the most calamitous consequences to all concerned.

4. That the prolonged and indiscriminate closing of the Courts of Judicature throughout the Orange Free State territory, in affording a convenient shelter to the dishonest portion of the community, is not only productive of severe loss and embarrassment, but is highly demoralizing in its tendency; and in the opinion of this meeting, common justice demands that special protection should be afforded only to those engaged in active service in the field.

5. That, in view of the intimate relations, alike social and commercial, between the Orange Free State and this Colony, it is highly desirable, for the welfare of both, that a closer and more binding union than can ever be expected under the present system should exist between the two countries, either by Federation or otherwise. That this meeting pledges itself heartily to support any measure having this union for its object, and moreover expresses its full belief that any feasible terms, for the future good government of the country, mutually agreed upon by the Orange Free State and the Cape Colony, would readily be confirmed and ratified by Her Majesty's Government.

RESOLUTIONS PASSED AT AN ADJOURNED MONTHLY MEETING OF THE CAPE TOWN CHAMBER OF COMMERCE, FEBRUARY 10, 1868.

1. That this Chamber expresses its sympathy with and approval of the Anti-Blueback movement at Bloemfontein and Port Elizabeth, and deems it unnecessary to dwell on the self-evident evils of an irredeemable currency, so ruinous to the country where it exists, and so dangerous to the interests of the neighbouring colonies who have commercial dealings with the Orange Free State.

2. That this Chamber is impressed with the conviction that any plan of forming a more close and binding union between the Orange Free State and this Colony would be attended with the best results, commercially and otherwise, to both communities.

3. That in the opinion of this Chamber the step about to be taken by Her Majesty's Government, in creating a British Protectorate over the Basuto nation, is calculated to put an end to the warfare between the Boers and the Basutos, so disastrous to both.

Letters to the Editor of the Cape Standard.

GOLD IN SOUTH AFRICA.

Sir,—Your sub-leader of this morning has doubtless excited the curiosity and active ambition of becoming rich of many of your readers, who will be "awaiting with interest further particulars about the Transvaal gold-fields."

To remove any "scepticism" which may exist "in respect to the alleged discovery of this mine of South African golden wealth," it has occurred to me to transfer to your columns an extract from a letter just received from Port Elizabeth from a gentleman who takes great interest in the colony, and who is rather noted for forming sound opinions on most matters:—

The discovery of gold in Moselekatse's country seems to be true. Mr. Mauch, a respectable German resident known to Mr. Jones (of the firm Dunell, Ebden, and Co.) writes confidently on the subject, and, if the gold fields he describes equal his expectations, then verily South Africa will be regenerated. The next accounts will be interesting. The gold country is said to be 400 miles from Potchefstroom, or about 1,000 miles from Port Elizabeth. This distance is nothing for an article worth say £50 per lb. weight. The specimens which have been received have been tested and pronounced to be the genuine metal.

The *Graham's Town Journal* evidently believes the information of Mr. Mauch, and very properly counsels immediate action on the part of our Government. The annexed passage from its leader will speak for itself:—

The colony will look to the Government to act promptly in this case. Should further intelligence be conclusive as to the alleged extent and richness of the fields, it would be the duty of the Government to proceed to take action in concert with the other European Governments in South Africa, in order to bring the territory under authority and law. As the paramount state in South Africa, the Cape should assert its claims to chief control. The district is, it seems, within the territory belonging to Moselekatse's tribe, and the earliest opportunity should be taken on the part of the united Governments of the Cape, Natal, Transvaal, and Free State to negotiate the terms on which the fields should be occupied. . . . Our own Government should at once obtain information, and on the receipt of intelligence confirmatory of that already before the public, should immediately take action so as to secure the interests of the Cape and of Natal.

*It is to be hoped that this matter will at once claim the consideration of Sir Philip Wodehouse; if gold really exists in the Transvaal territory, steps should be taken that the Cape colonists may share in the treasure; if it does not, the sooner the false hopes which are likely to be raised by the alleged discovery of gold within our reach are set at rest the better it will be for our contentment.

January 14.   AFRIKANDER.

The Withdrawal of the Troops.

Sir,—I take the earliest opportunity of congratulating your readers upon the glad tidings conveyed by the *Argus* of this morning, that Her Majesty's Government have "decided not to withdraw any of the troops this year, or to demand of the Colony any additional contribution for its defence."

While it may readily be admitted that this happy result is mainly to be ascribed to the "representations" of *both* Houses of the Colonial Legislature, "backed by the despatches of Sir Philip Wodehouse," it seems hardly fair under the circumstances to ignore the constitutional efforts of the 1,100 Cape Town petitioners, who set the example of petitioning to the Eastern Province.

But for their petition to the House of Lords, so well drawn by the classic pen of one, whose claims to judicial honours were so fully recognised by the press at both ends of the Colony on a recent occasion, when it was generally expected that he was about to be elevated to the Bench, Earl Grey would not, in his place in the British Senate, have propounded the statesmanlike views on behalf of all classes of Her Majesty's subjects in Southern Africa; nor would the Duke of Cambridge have declared his conviction that, on Imperial grounds alone, the Cape of Good Hope ought to be continued as a garrison for the Queen's soldiers.

To my mind the masterly arguments of the Governor's Prorogation Speech, which have stood the test of public criticism both here and in England, have been the means of inducing the Duke of Buckingham to reverse the determination of his predecessor at the Colonial Office; but, with all respect for His Excellency, I venture to repeat that there is some evidence to show that the Duke of Cambridge and Earl Grey have had something to do with "the change that came o'er the spirit of his dream" between the opening and the prorogation of the last Parliament.

At the risk of being deemed presumptuous, I must refer to an opinion expressed by me in your columns in August last:—

The speech of Earl Grey in the House of Lords demands the warmest praise and gratitude of the Colonists of the Cape of Good Hope, for it has already had the effect of drawing from the able pen of the Governor, in his prorogation of the Parliament, a most masterly exposition of the true bearing of the question of the presence of the British Troops upon "the peace and tranquillity of the distinct races," and the general welfare of the Colony.

If any one doubt the accuracy of this conclusion, which to me appears self-evident, let him carefully contrast, both in substance and in spirit, the arguments used by His Excellency in his Prorogation Speech, with those by which he endeavoured at the opening of the Parliament to reconcile the representatives of the people to submit to the hard terms of the despatch of the Earl of Carnarvon.

In justification of that opinion, let me quote the two annexed passages of the opening speech, which, when placed in juxtaposition with the lucid conclusion of the prorogation speech, will speak for themselves:—

In October last I repeated that representation, but have been unsuccessful; and perhaps it was unreasonable to expect that Her Majesty's Government, by making such an exception in our case, should expose themselves to just remonstrances from other Colonies, in whose case the principle had been fully enforced.

And again :—

But some alleviation of the heavy blow which has fallen upon you may be found in the fact, which must be obvious to any careful observer, that what may be termed the political organization of the native tribes for purposes of hostility is fast waning. I have carefully made it my business, during my administration of the Government, to guard against hostile combinations, to awaken in the natives a sense of the value of good government and security for life and property, and to give them confidence in the justice of those in authority over them. In our own interest, as well as in theirs, such ought ever to be their policy; and by such means we may hope, as years pass by, to render the safety of the Colony independent of the presence of military force.

So much for the insinuation of the *Argus* that the constitutional "representations" of the Cape Colonists "have had little to do with the decision of the Home Government."

But, after all, it is no disparagement of a colonial Governor to say that "he has pinned his faith to the sleeve of such a distinguished statesman" as Earl Grey, and I sincerely trust that the Colony will lose no time in gratefully acknowledging the valuable services of Sir Philip Wodehouse, particularly as at one time he incurred censure for his apparent lukewarmness in its behalf.

The *Argus* says :—" The Government do not, however, surrender either the policy or the scheme with regard to the defence of the Colonies which they have announced," and the question now arises, how ought the Cape to act to render the probability of the removal of the Queen's troops from South Africa remote ? In your leading article the other day, in reply to the observation of the President of the Chamber of Commerce with respect to the silence of the Cape Town press on Earl Grey's letters, you stated :—" If the press has said less than Mr. Ebden would have wished, it is because it sees that Parliament will ere long re-assemble, and that it will be more opportune to open discussion on this subject then than now." You have also well said :—" There is a close intimate connection, as every one ought to know, between the establishment Responsible or Party Government in this Colony and the withdrawal from it of the protection of British troops," and the frontier press generally adopts this view of the case. Why should there not be then some Parliamentary action to record the fact, which seems to have been taken for granted by the Governor, that " there is no strong desire on the part of the people of the Colony for the establishment of Responsible Government," but that on the contrary they prefer " the continuance of that very moderate amount of control which the British Government still retains, and of which the presence of the British troops is an accompaniment ?"

An Eastern, formerly an adherent of the Responsible Government party, thus writes :—

To keep the troops in the Colony I for one would readily relinquish for the present all claim to Responsible Government ; and I hope that a decided Parliamentary majority may adopt Earl Grey's views on this question. Our Port Elizabeth papers, you will observe, warmly support such a policy. The most important question, however, to my mind, just now, is the annexation of the Orange Free State, so largely affecting the future welfare and progress of South Africa.

Your interesting and well-argued leaders on the resumption of the sovereignty afford the best evidence that you concur in the opinion quoted regarding it, and best speak for themselves.

Many practical men on the Eastern frontier will agree with you that the unsettled relations between the Free Republic and the Basutos are calculated to disturb the peace and tranquillity which exist between this Colony and the native tribes both within and without its border, and will cordially endorse the opinion expressed by you in the following terse words :—

It is questionable whether a handful of English troops in the Free State, and the *prestige* of British power would not do more for the pacification of the border tribes than the addition of several regiments to our force on the Cape frontier. In fact, if the Orange River territory were once more a British sovereignty we believe that less instead of more troops would be needed in South Africa. And thus, as far as military expenditure is concerned, we think the objection to resume the rule of the Free State by Great Britain on that score is unfounded.

It cannot be disputed that you are right in arguing that the inhabitants of the Free State ought to take the initiative themselves in agitating for the extension of the benignant sway of the Queen of England to their territory, and there can be little doubt that the Englishmen and the Afrikanders to whom you allude would form a majority in favour of the proposed change.

The terms of annexation, whether by means of federation or otherwise, can always be arranged ; and it is thought that a portion of the Customs duties might with advantage be devoted to the improvement of the Government and credit of the Orange Free State, the anarchy and bad faith of which threaten to overwhelm with ruin the mercantile interests of Port Elizabeth.

January 16, 1868.   COLONIST.

THE "ADVERTISER AND MAIL," EARL GREY, AND RESPONSIBLE GOVERNMENT.

SIR,—Your well-argued leader of yesterday, which you conclude with the practical deduction that "The next Hustings' cry is likely to be, the Troops or Responsible Government," has not been long in rousing the *Advertiser and Mail* to throw its shield of protection over its political "pet panacea for all our ills."

Its leading article of this morning rather severely denounces "the controversy which is going on with respect to the withdrawal of the troops as amusing, and in some points absurd," while, at the same time, it does not seem quite fairly to represent the arguments of those who are still discussing this important and interesting question.

1. I, for one, readily agree with your contemporary so far as to award the "special honour" of the victory to the Governor, although we differ somewhat in the mode of reasoning by which we arrive at the same conclusion. It appears, however, to me, that the annexed extract from the *Advertiser and Mail*,

It is hardly just, however, of our contemporary yesterday to say Sir Philip Wodehouse moved in the matter at all only after he had been aroused to a sense of his duty by condemnatory leading articles, and mild, though honest correspondence in our contemporary's columns,

is not a quite accurate version of the *Standard's* view of the case.

What you did state was :—

We might even go further, and referring to the speeches of His Excellency the Governor on the opening and the proroguing of Parliament, contrast the former with the latter, and say that the comparative hopefulness of the Governor's last utterances were, in a great measure, due to the energetic movement inaugurated not in Parliament, but among the people themselves.

A reference to these speeches will, it is thought, bear you out, but at any rate it would answer no good purpose further to labour this point. Whatever may have been the moving cause of his action, Sir Philip Wodehouse most ably and earnestly advocated the cause of the Cape colonists in the despatch in which he supported the Parliamentary resolutions, and deserves their gratitude, which it is hoped that they will not be slow to express.

No one suspects the *Advertiser and Mail* "of playing either the panegyrist or the lackey" to the Governor, but it is "hardly just" to insinuate that others hesitate or are disinclined to do him "justice."

2. The *Advertiser and Mail* has *at last* noticed what it terms the "eccentric antipathy" of Earl Grey to Responsible Government, who, it is alleged, "numbers as his votaries in this

Colony, *only Mr. Ebden, sen., and Mr. Pote, and the Standard, and perhaps half-a-dozen others, including Mr. Reuben Ayliff, M.L.A. for Uitenhage.*" Is it not somewhat strange thus entirely to ignore public opinion in the Eastern Province, and to treat with the contempt of silence the approval bestowed on Earl Grey's letters by the *Graham's Town Journal*, the *Eastern Province Herald*, the *Fort Beaufort Advocate*, the *King William's Town Gazette*, and probably by other frontier newspapers?

The *Advertiser and Mail*, while it is bound to admit "the ability and independence of the noble Earl," is not complimentary "as to his influence among English statesmen." Notwithstanding the no very flattering epithets which have been applied to him, many both in this Colony and in England will differ from your contemporary in assigning to this eminent statesman so contemptible a position in the House of Lords; and I am tempted to make a quotation from some Essays on the English Constitution, in the *Fortnightly Review*, which may not, perhaps, be deemed very irrelevant:—

The criticism of the acts of late administrations by Lord Grey has been admirable. But such criticism, to have its full value, should be many-sided. Every man of great ability puts his own mark on his own criticism; it will be full of thought and feeling, but then it is of idiosyncratic thought and feeling. We want many critics of ability and knowledge in the Upper House—not equal to Lord Grey, for they would be hard to find—but like Lord Grey. They should resemble him in impartiality; they should resemble him in clearness; they should most of all resemble him in taking the supplemental view of a subject.

Be this as it may, the alleged want of influence in the British Senate of Earl Grey is no answer to the argument contained in his letter to Mr. Pote, "that the maintenance of British military force in the Cape Colony ought only to be allowed on the condition that the colonists, on their side, consent to the retention by the Crown of the authority necessary for enforcing a system of impartial government over the white and coloured races, by which the interests of both may be protected." But is it true, as the *Advertiser* says, that Earl Grey is the "only authority" against Responsible Government at the Cape of Good Hope? Is he singular in the opinion he has so well expressed? Does not Sir Philip Wodehouse, before whom perhaps, if not "before the noble Earl," the *Advertiser* might feel disposed "to bow down," adopt the self-same argument in the annexed admirable extract from the prorogation speech, to which reference has been so often made in the columns of the *Standard?*—

The question really seems to be, in whose hands is the chief Government of the country to be vested—in Great Britain or in the colony itself? *—for I think that so long as any British soldiers are left here, the ultimate responsibility will remain with the former: and I also feel very strongly that the best interests of this colony require that it should so remain, at any rate for some time to come.* We have here to deal with colonies inhabited by two races, whose habits and whose characters are totally different, who possess each of them the ability to do incalculable mischief, and in the hands of one of which is deposited the whole legislative and executive authority. I cannot doubt that, under these circumstances, the welfare of both, the preservation of peace and tranquillity so essential to both, will best be secured by the continuance of that very moderate amount of control which the British Government still retains, and of which the presence of the British troops is an accompaniment. A very slight observation of passing events, within the colony and without, will be sufficient to show how powerless any Government, standing alone, would be for checking an outburst of hasty resentment on the part of one class against another,—with what difficulty it would be able to regulate a prolonged struggle, when once hostilities had begun. I have on these grounds supported the resolutions of the two Houses, with the more confidence from perceiving the absence of any strong desire on the part of the people of the colony for the establishment of *Responsible Government*. *I consider that, under that form of Government, it would be most injudicious—it would be prejudicial to the mother country and to the colony—to leave the troops of the former for the support of the policy of the independent ministry of the latter.*

Let me also call in aid of the position taken up by His Excellency, that it is not reasonable to expect Great Britain to fight with her soldiers, and at her cost, the battles with the native tribes of our own creation, the opinions of the Earl of Carnarvon, the late Secretary of State for the Colonies, and of Earl De Grey, so long a member of the late Lord Palmerston's Cabinet.

In the debate in the House of Lords, last session, in the matter of New Zealand, the former stated, " At the same time the position of affairs was a very inconvenient one, because on the one hand, we are maintaining a large military force, and on the other, the colonists were really directing our policy as regards the natives, that is to say, *the conditions of war or peace rested with the colonists, but it was incumbent with us, if war ensued, to carry it on ;*" and the latter said, " He was not one of those who desired the disruption of the ties between the Mother Country and the Colonies, for he believed the connection was advantageous to both, *but if colonial authorities were allowed to employ our troops, and to spend our money in order to relieve them from the consequences of their own policy*, complications would certainly arise in our relations with them, which would certainly result in disruption."

As also bearing upon the point under discussion, I must be permitted to make the subjoined quotation from the despatch of the late Duke of Newcastle, which was written by him, as Secretary of State for the Colonies, at the time when he applied the new Imperial military policy with respect to the colonies of Australia:—

That form of Government (Responsible) being unequivocally established, it is, I imagine, admitted on all sides that the Imperial Government has no further responsibility for maintaining the internal tranquillity of the country. Its obligations, therefore, to contribute towards the defence of *colonies in full possession of internal self-government, and unaffected by any exceptional circumstances of situation or population,* is limited to the contingency of war, and the danger of war. But in the case of the Australian colonies, *free from the presence of formidable native tribes*, and free, also, as occupying a vast island, *from the perils to which a land frontier exposes other communities*, those obligations will always be in the main sufficiently discharged by Her Majesty's Navy, which must form, both in peace and war, the true Imperial contribution to the security and protection of Australia.

Enough then, it is thought, has been said to prove that, although England may find it to her advantage to keep a large military force at the Cape on the ground of Imperial interests, she is not likely to part with her control over the management of her native question, or, in the language of the Governor, " *to leave her troops for the support of the policy of the independent ministry of the colony.*" In other words, Responsible Government does seem inconsistent with the continuance of the present military force at the Cape.

8. While I cannot entirely coincide with the *Advertiser and Mail*, "that the Imperial policy of England, with respect to her troops, has nothing to do with the internal government" of the Cape of Good Hope, I incline to its opinion that the Queen's soldiers have been retained here " for Imperial purposes—for maintaining the prestige and securing the power and peace of the Empire."

The Duke of Cambridge, as well as Earl Grey, in the House of Lords, and General Peel, the late Secretary of War, in the House of Commons, have recently dwelt upon the great value to the British Empire of the Cape of Good Hope as a military station, both on account of its geographical position and its climate, and Dr. Hutchinson has opportunely brought to notice the fact that the late Marquis of Wellesley and the Duke of Wellington have recorded similar opinions.

The Cape, from its contiguity to " formidable native tribes," is entitled to exceptional consideration, and will not, it is submitted, bear comparison with the two cases cited of Mauritius and Ceylon, in both of which a comparatively small military garrison is required and kept. The case of Canada is also hardly parallel, for there " strong Imperial armaments are maintained with Responsible Government," not to fight with natives but to protect this valuable portion of the dominions of the British Crown against any attack of the United States of America.

The member for Uitenhage, who has incurred the displeasure of the *Advertiser and Mail*, may well be excused for having at his *first* political dinner not quite correctly stated the arguments of Earl Grey against Responsible Government, but it is rather amusing to see how greedily the zealous advocates of Government by Party seize hold of the mistake which he has committed, and attempt to make capital out of it.

Doubtless the Imperial military expenditure is important in a mercantile point of view, but the loss of it would be as nothing compared with the blow which would be inflicted on the future security of the Colony, and the peace and tranquillity of the Aboriginal tribes by the departure of the British soldier from the shores of Southern Africa.

Wednesday, 22nd January, 1868. COLONIST.

THE RESUMPTION OF THE SOVEREIGNTY, OR ANNEXATION OF THE FREE STATE.

Sir,—Although your readers have no doubt already been convinced by the able manner in which you have handled the subject, that some change of dynasty in the Orange Free State is absolutely required to put an end to the anarchy, confusion, and bad credit there prevailing, I venture to endeavour, by some further remarks, to provoke discussion in your columns upon a question of such general interest at the present moment. Many will agree with the opinion, so well expressed in the annexed extract from the *Great Eastern* in allusion to the Natal memorial on behalf of the ill-treated French missionaries in Basutoland, and the Lieutenant-Governor's reply thereto :—

> The documents are the most important which have for a long time appeared in print. There are mixed up with this, and other matters connected with the proceedings of the Free State, questions which affect the welfare of this Colony to a very much greater extent than is generally calculated upon. Nothing that is being done within the Colony itself at this moment involves such serious considerations as do the acts of those outside the Colony, who are disturbing the peace, muddling their own and our finances, and preventing an industrious tribe from growing bread for themselves and us.

Whatever difference of opinion there may exist as to the practicability or expediency of annexing the Free State to this Colony, few, it is thought, will not readily admit that the extension of British rule to the territory between the Orange and Vaal Rivers will not but be attended with beneficial results to the Colonists of the Cape of Good Hope, Natal, and the Sovereignty, and "last, though far from least," to the interests of the Aboriginal Tribes of South Africa.

There seems to be much in the idea propounded by your very interesting correspondent, "A Frontier Man," who, it is hoped, will continue to throw light on a matter he so well understands, that " but for the unfortunate battle of Berea the Sovereignty would never have become the Free State."

Doubtless Sir George Cathcart, who justly merits the encomium bestowed upon him "of being among the best and most conscientious Governors the Cape ever had," was frightened with the large Imperial military expenditure of the protracted Kafir war, which he brought to a close, and perhaps overestimated the force which would be necessary to keep in check the military prowess of the Basutos, and was thus instrumental in the British Supremacy being withdrawn from the country beyond the Orange River.

Since 1853, however, the aspect of things in South Africa has much changed. As a consequence probably of the wise frontier policy inaugurated by Sir George Cathcart, and extended and improved upon by Sir George Grey, it is now true, as Sir Philip Wodehouse has stated, "that what may be termed the political organization of the native tribes for purposes of hostility, is fast waning." Indeed upon this point you have drawn a sound practical conclusion in the subjoined passage from one of your leaders, which will well bear being quoted for a second time :—

> It is questionable whether a handful of British troops in the Free State, and the *prestige* of British power would not do more for the pacification of the border tribes, than the addition of several regiments to our force on the Cape frontier. In fact, if the Orange River territory were once more a British Sovereignty, we believe that less instead of more troops would be needed in South Africa. And thus, as far as military expenditure is concerned, we think the objection to resume the rule of the Free State by Great Britain, on that score, is unfounded.

For my own part, I cannot see the entire force of your objections to the annexation of the Free State to this Colony, and feel inclined to go with two able organs of public opinion in the Eastern Province in this matter. The *Great Eastern* concludes a late leader, in which it quotes largely from the *Standard*, with the following sensible and pertinent remarks :—

> We do not know from whence our esteemed contemporary ascertained that the Free State produces nearly one-third of the wool grown in the Colony. But we will take the assertion to be the real fact. If that be so, and it be true, too, that the wool passes through the natural ports—ports of this Colony—we ask why the Free State should not be annexed to this Colony? If our ports are its ports, and it exports and imports with us through the same outlets and inlets, it is surely entitled to be a part and parcel of us.
>
> To declare the Free State British territory is surely a very important way of dealing with the subject. How is the State to be governed? If it contributes to our revenue, as is indicated, it is surely entitled to a share in the administration of that revenue. It is but fair to the State that, while it is restrained from making war, it should have as much right of considering questions of taxation either as the Eastern or the Western Province.
>
> We prefer the annexation of the Free State to the declaration hinted at by our Cape Town contemporary.

The *Graham's Town Journal* also takes a sound and not impracticable view of this case in the annexed passage, written in its usual amusing style :—

> The President—no one better—must by this time know that the country, and every man in it, except rogues, would be at once lifted into comparative prosperity, were there three or four Civil Commissioners and Resident Magistrates in as many places, one of Her Majesty's Judges—say Mr. Brand himself—placed over a Court of Justice in Bloemfontein, a detachment of Currie's Police on the Border, and half-a-dozen trans-Orange

representatives in the Cape Parliament. An immediate measure of this sort is what is needed, and not a fanciful Utopia made up of remote possibilities and imaginable contingencies.

You say, " To tack on to us, who have nothing to boast of in our own financial position, a large insolvent community, would be dangerous, if not ruinous." To this I would reply, that the establishment of more amicable relations between the Boers and the Basutos, and the restoration of order and good credit to the Free State, would tend to promote its progress and powers of *consumption of goods*, and thus increase the customs duties of Port Elizabeth, which increase, together with the quit-rents properly collected, and some fresh legitimate taxation, would meet the expenses incurred in consequence of the annexation. This idea is only thrown out for the purpose of being discussed, as I do not profess to have gone into any details or calculations.

My main object in intruding on your columns is to attempt to get an agitation, *either* for the resumption of the Sovereignty, *or* the annexation of the Free State—I do not much care which of the two—*initiated* within the Orange Free State; for the desire to be replaced under the benign influence and sway of the British Crown must emanate from the people themselves of the Free Republic, in order to be effectual in commanding the favourable consideration of the Home Government.

The following extract from the letter of a correspondent of the *Eastern Province Herald*, beyond the Orange River—

I have been three weeks in the Free State, and as the veld is splendid—every part looking fresh and green—I should have enjoyed myself very much had I found my old friends and the inhabitants in general in better spirits. The "Blueback" question depresses the European part of the population sadly; but the Boers—thick-headed and stupid as they are—think it a splendid feat, making their own geld. I am afraid the report of the probability of the Home Government re-annexing the Free State is too good to be true. Such a piece of good fortune, should it occur, would make the English and German Free Staters wild with joy, but there would be strong opposition on the part of a majority of the Boers, who think themselves perfect at most things, but especially in warfare and governing !—

affords a reasonable expectation that fair discussion would soon enlist on the side of adhesion to the British rule *the majority of the people of the Orange Free State.*

The *Standard* and the *Graham's Town Journal* have so fully commented upon the interesting interview between the President and the deputation of the Anti-Blueback Association, as to leave little to be said on the subject. But I would go further, and claim the President as an authority in favour of the opinion that the Orange Free State ought soon to become part and parcel of Her Majesty's dominions.

When His Honour said, as reported, " that a very few years would see a federation of all the States and Colonies of South Africa," he could not for one moment have dreamt that either the Eastern or Western Province of the Cape of Good Hope, or Natal, would ever throw off their allegiance to Queen Victoria or her successor, and enrol themselves as federate States under the flag of any Free Republic.

Mr. Brand, with his reputation as a lawyer, would possess much more moral influence for good in the country of his adoption as a Judge, appointed by the Queen of England, than in the "humiliating position" which he now holds as President, without the power to check the foolish legislation of the Volksraad, which is bringing discredit and disgrace upon the country subject to their misrule, and threatening to ruin those who have any commercial dealings with its inhabitants.

Mr. Keate, in his favourable response to the memorial above referred to, "relative to the expulsion by the authorities of the Orange Free State of the French Missionaries from Basutoland," says: "His Excellency will also take the earliest opportunity of communicating with Her Majesty's High Commissioner upon the subject, within whose competence it rests to deal with matters affecting the relations of the Crown with nations lying outside British territory in South Africa." This suggests to me the repetition of an idea, before expressed, that, while the terms of Annexation or Federation are being arranged, Her Majesty's Government should appoint a British Resident or Consul at Bloemfontein, for the purpose of protecting the interests of British subjects in the Colony, as well as the rights of the Aborigines.

The salary of this officer might be paid by the Colony, and he should correspond with the High Commissioner, and might perhaps exercise some beneficial influence on the policy of the Volksraad.

I cannot conclude without expressing a hope that the Cape Town Chamber of Commerce will, *at their next monthly meeting*, take some action to show their sympathy with the Anti-Blueback movement of Bloemfontein and Port Elizabeth, as well as with the proposed Resumption of the Sovereignty or Annexation of the Free State.

Saturday, January 25th, 1868.   COLONIST.

THE TRANSVAAL GOLD MINES.

SIR,—I called the attention of your readers the other day to the fact that the evidence with respect to the discovery of some gold-fields in Moselikatze's country appeared to be authentic.

The remarks, which were quoted from the *Graham's Town Journal*, have excited some ridicule in the columns of the press, and it is not much matter of wonder that "the news should be considered too good to be true."

The *Eastern Province Herald* observes :—

It must be recollected that the discovery of gold was just as generally disbelieved in Australia, when it was first made, until the arrival of nuggets confirmed the fact beyond a doubt. Sir Roderick Murchison is said to have predicted the discovery of gold-fields just about the spot where Herr Mauch says that they do actually exist. He undoubtedly formed his opinion from geological facts brought under his observation, and it is said from the land being in the line of the gold belt, which is that latitude known to encircle the globe, cropping up at times to the surface. We see nothing as yet to justify the sending home of large orders of any kind, *but we see much to justify intense anxiety, and a very critical examination of all facts " cropping up" from the gold region.*

Natal would be more benefited by the discovery of gold where it is alleged to be than the Cape, and the communications of Mr. Mauch appear to have created some enthusiasm with our go-ahead neighbours. In the *Natal Mercury* of the 28th of last month, there is an interesting and particular report of the "analysis of the auriferous quartz" received from the Transvaal, from which I make the following extract :—

And lastly, the intense clearness, freshness, and purity of the whole specimen, free from any sign of wear or exposure, proved beyond a doubt that it had very recently been broken from its native reef or rock. The impression left upon the minds of the cautious inspectors was that the specimen was undoubtedly a genuine one, and that it was found by Mr. Mauch under the circumstances described by him.

Surely, a sufficient *primâ facie* case is made out to justify some action on the part of the Cape Government, even if it be merely to prove the truth or falsehood of the alleged existence of gold in South Africa, which must greatly affect the prospects of this Colony. The Cape Parliament, with all their love for retrenchment, would not grudge a few pounds to obtain authentic information, or to be the first in the field to make favourable terms with Moselikatze.

It has occurred to me to suggest that the services of a gentleman, long connected with the Australian gold-fields as a commissioner, who is now on leave at the Cape, might be secured to explore the Transvaal gold-fields, and perhaps confer a lasting benefit on his native country.

27th January, 1868.   AFRIKANDER.

THE FREE STATE.

Sir,—The terse and closely-reasoned leading article of the *Standard* of this morning, the burden of which may be said to be that " it is unwise to allow any independent states or communities of any sort to take root in South Africa," will, in the opinion of many, bear a favourable contrast with that of the *Advertiser and Mail* of yesterday.

Your readers will deem it no " waste of printer's ink," or

exhaustion of their "patience," if you continue, in the manner you have commenced, to adduce good arguments in support of the important question of extending British rule to one at least of the South African Republics—the Orange Free State.

A subject which has already afforded such scope for fair discussion in the editorial columns of the press, both East and West, cannot be barren of general interest; and although an opinion was once entertained by one of your contemporaries to the contrary, the Cape colonists need not *now* despair of their representations, if reasonable and just, claiming the favourable consideration of the Mother Country.

It was, as you have pointed out, a remarkably curious coincidence that, on the same day in which the *Advertiser and Mail* had *ex cathedrâ* pronounced the opinion that, "the whole drift and tendency of Imperial policy is to restrict and curtail, not to extend and advance the area of Imperial dominion," the *Argus* should have received that rather startling, though gratifying telegram, that Queen Victoria had granted the prayer of Moshesh to be admitted her loyal subject, and that Basutoland was likely to be annexed either to this Colony or to Natal.

The fact that the Basutos can now claim the protection of the British flag will, it is suggested, facilitate rather than retard the happy consummation of the Trans-Orange Republic being converted into a portion of Her Majesty's Colonial Empire.

In the present aspect of this question, it would answer no good purpose to attempt to argue in favour of "the absorption of the Free State into the Cape Colony," further than just to make mention of an idea which is entertained by some practical men, that President Brand's territory might very well be divided between the Cape and Natal.

At any rate, it may be gathered from the article of the *Friend*, quoted by the *Advertiser and Mail*, that there exists beyond the Orange River a strong feeling in favour of a "reunion with Great Britain" in some shape; and it is submitted that no time ought to be lost to test the public opinion of the *majority* of the people of the Free State on this point. It is true that the *Friend* throws out some difficulty about *initiating* the agitation, "and canvassing for votes among the rural population," in favour of the substitution of the British Government, "without some hope, or reasonable guarantee be held out, that the request, when made, would be granted;" but, if the petition of Moshesh has obtained a favourable reply, why should not that of the European population of the Free State, including "many sons of England, who have never desired to renounce their inheritance," but have been *unwillingly* compelled to live under a Republican form of Government, be also successful?

In an article "communicated" to the *Great Eastern*, which

you have transferred to your columns, attention is directed to the fact that the late Duke of Newcastle considered that an Imperial Act of Parliament would be required " to release the abandoned subjects of Her Majesty from their allegiance," and that no such Act has been passed. This consideration might perhaps weigh with Her Majesty's Government in now " reversing the wretched, short-sighted policy of expediency" which transferred the Sovereignty to the rule of a Free Republic at the great sacrifice of the interests of British subjects, and which, as the result has shown, has proved inimical to the rights of some of the Aboriginal Tribes.

The *Advertiser and Mail* says :—

The Sovereignty was abandoned in 1852, because war with the Basutos was found to be a troublesome and costly sort of thing; and it is the height of absurdity to suppose that Her Majesty's Government would re-accept that Sovereignty on the avowed plea that the Free State authorities find war with that wily potentate to be still no less troublesome and costly. It is quite possible, if not probable, that many years hence the Free State, and the Transvaal too, may be annexed in federal union with the Cape and Natal; *but that will be after those States have learned to fight their own battles, assert their own valour, and vindicate their own position against all native foes.*

But is not the telegram of yesterday evidence that the conclusion of your contemporary with respect to the Imperial policy is not altogether correct? Are you not right in saying " that a more generous and statesmanlike policy prevails now respecting colonies than has done for years past in the Imperial Councils, and that an adjustment of this South African difficulty will be a worthy termination to the administration of Sir Philip Wodehouse" ? At the instigation of His Excellency, Her Majesty's Government have already adopted Earl Grey's arguments, and, *for the present at least,* wisely considered the Cape of Good Hope as an *exception* to the *general* rule with respect to the military defence of the colonies, and *now,* probably under the same influence, they step in as mediators between the Boers and Basutos, instead of allowing them " *to fight their own battles out.*"

Great Britain only preserves her consistency by throwing her shield of protection over the Basutos, as well as the other aborigines of Southern Africa ; but, at the same time, she will not " triumph over" or treat with any injustice " our Free State neighbours," whom we soon hope to welcome as fellow-subjects under her far-spreading flag.

The *Friend* says, " Our freedom was thrust upon us by Sir George Clerk, as the duly-authorised agent of the British Government," and " why should not then the overtures come from that Government whose fault and folly it is that we are free ?"

This can hardly be expected ; but, at the same time, it behoves those friends of the Free State, who in this Colony have entered upon the question of restoring the supremacy of the Queen to her abandoned subjects, to continue their exertions with the view of showing their approval of, and sympathy with, the movement about to be made in the same direction within the State itself.

An idea has been thrown out in the columns of the *Great Eastern*, that the Cape colonists have been "luke-warm" in assisting their brethren beyond the Orange River in their struggles for "re-union with Great Britain," and that "they now only seem to awaken from the lethargy into which they sunk on the abandonment being actually perpetrated, when they find the debts due to them in the Free State likely to be totally extinguished."

This would indeed be a *selfish* motive for action, and it is therefore to be hoped that the Cape Town Chamber of Commerce, at their meeting on Monday next, will follow the example set at Port Elizabeth, and record an opinion in favour of the extension of British rule to the Orange Free State, as well as against the danger to be apprehended from the obnoxious bluebacks. As every suggestion bearing upon the points of Federation or Annexation, with respect to what was once the Sovereignty, may be interesting to your readers at this moment, I venture to give you the opinion of a gentleman in the Eastern Province of some experience.

The Orange Free State must be brought under British rule again, and we must endeavour to get the inhabitants of Bloemfontein to make a move in that direction. Federation is the scheme. It could not be tacked on to the Colony, even if they desired it—our Parliament would, I fancy, object. It is not judicious to provoke the Hollanders; ignore their existence if you will, but try and conciliate all parties. I wish a petition to the Queen and British Parliament could be set on foot, as well as an address to Earl Grey. While thanking him for past services, we might improve the opportunity to enlist his philanthropic tendencies in behalf of the African races, who have been deserted by England ever since she recognized any power, other than British power, on the South African continent.

The idea of the supremacy of British rule may perhaps remind some of your readers of the not irrelevant allusion the other day of your able correspondent, "A Frontier Man," to the Act of Parliament of William the Fourth, which gives jurisdiction to Colonial Courts over crimes committed by British subjects in South African territory, up to the 23rd degree of south latitude.

The spirit of this enactment of the Imperial Legislature was doubtless to protect the native races; and may it not be argued that it is somewhat inconsistent with the *formal recognition of any independent South African Republic?* An earnest conviction that the more this important subject is discussed, the more likely is good to come out of it, must be my apology for trespassing at such length on your columns.

COLONIST.

Thursday, January 30.

THE BRITISH PROTECTORATE OF THE BASUTOS.

SIR,—I ventured on Thursday last to institute a comparison in your favour with the *Advertiser and Mail*, but a sense of justice now compels me to give a decided preference to the leading article of the *Argus* over that of the *Standard* of this morning.

You and your readers must forgive me for presuming to submit in your own columns, not in a " captious" but friendly " spirit," some criticisms rather condemnatory of the remarks with which you have ushered in the recent intelligence that the Queen of England has determined upon extending the protection of her flag over the Basutos.

1. It seems to me that your leader, which concludes with the annexed paragraph, " At present we are content to understand that Great Britain is about to enlarge her boundaries, and to increase her military force on this continent, and we trust that the conduct of the business in hand will bring no discredit *on the more generous policy, and larger views, which the Mother Country now avows to her dependencies*," is somewhat inconsistent with itself.

Surely, if the starting point of your argument had been that Great Britain meant well towards the Cape of Good Hope, you would hardly, as a good Conservative, have been instrumental in creating a popular prejudice against the representative of Her Majesty, to whom is to be "entrusted the diplomacy" of carrying out the proposed important change.

In your anxious desire narrowly to watch colonial interests, and to prevent us from "becoming involved in liabilities to meet expenses which may accrue at no distant day," you may have written, as you have done, without any intention unjustly to assail the Governor, but, I fear, the expressions used and insinuations conveyed are calculated to wound the feelings of a. gentleman who, whatever his faults may be, is most conscientious in the discharge of his high duties, and has the reputation of being an honest politician.

If British Kaffraria, which was foremost in the grand anti-annexation battle, has made its peace with Sir Philip Wodehouse, what good purpose can it answer to attempt to resuscitate the irritated feelings of the past?

The application of the " distinctive name" of " Annexation Wodehouse" to His Excellency may perhaps make him unpopular, but it is suggested that many thinking men will be of opinion that the Cape of Good Hope is not likely to suffer from the extension of her territory, if, by such extension, the cause of the Aborigines be advanced, at the same time that the continuance of old England's military succour, so essential for the protection of Her Majesty's subjects of all classes in the Colony, be secured.

2. It may be true that "the step to be taken," of throwing the shield of British rule over Moshesh and his followers, "was not suggested by the Legislature, the press, or the people of this Colony."

Your apparent opposition to it, however, seems to be not very consistent with your many able leading articles in favour of restoring to what was once the Sovereignty the sway of the British Crown ; nor does it entirely harmonise with your idea, which I quoted in my last letter, that " an adjustment of the South African difficulty would be a worthy termination of the administration of Sir Philip Wodehouse."

Has not the long-pending hostile attitude between the Boers and the Basutos been the great difficulty in establishing, on a permanent and satisfactory basis, the future peace and tranquillity of the European population as well as the Aboriginal tribes of Southern Africa ?

I am glad to observe that the *Argus* concurs in the opinion I formed on first impressions, caused by the news from England, that the British protectorate of the Basutos would facilitate instead of retard the conversion of the Orange Free State into a portion of Her Majesty's Colonial Empire, and I must ask permission to transfer to your columns the subjoined pertinent comments of your able contemporary on this part of the case, with which, I believe, many of your readers in the country will cordially sympathize.

Then, again, we cannot keep out of sight the probability that the step which has now been taken will ultimately lead to the re-establishment of the British Sovereignty over the *quasi*-European settlements beyond the Orange River. We do not mean to say that this idea had anything to do with the annexation of Basutoland, or that such a momentous change is imminent. British statesmen are not moved by ideas so much as by the practical requirements and exigencies of the hour, and it is quite certain that they will never interfere with the rights of an independent State which respects British rights and interests. The Free State is as safe from British invasion as the most powerful kingdom. Any annexation movement having reference to the Free State or Transvaal must come from those countries, or it will not be heeded by the British Government. Still the fact cannot be concealed that these petty attempts at independent government north of the Orange River have proved signal failures. They have brought neither peace nor commercial prosperity to those who compose them. The Free State is well-nigh ruined by Basuto wars and blue-backs, and the last number of the *Transvaal Argus* gives the most gloomy view of the condition and government of that country. We should not be surprised at any time to hear that the population of both these States, weary with the insecurity of life and property, and the peculation of officials, had imitated the example of Moshesh. We believe that there is yet a great work for British enterprise and power north of the Orange River, and we anticipate the day when the petty provincial conflicts which now consume so much of the political energy of the country shall be hushed under the rule of a confederation which shall gradually extend its power northward to the well-watered plains of Central Africa.

3. Naturally enough, as a true John Bull, you do not appear much to relish the idea that the " Emperor Napoleon should have been permitted to dictate the policy of Britain."

But it hardly amounts to this, although I confess I incline to the opinion that the *Argus* is not very far wrong when it says, " Then, again, we have reason to believe that a French Protectorate was imminent, if the British Government had turned a deaf ear to the prayer of Moshesh."

It is quite clear from the reply of the Emperor of the French to the address of the Evangelical Alliance, that he takes an interest in the missionary labours in Basutoland "of his ecclesiastical friends and good subjects," Professor Cassalis and his brethren, who, it is generally admitted, have not been " well treated by the Free State authorities."

An argument in the mouth of Louis Napoleon, somewhat to the following tenor and effect—England professes to be a great power and to be deeply interested in the cause of the Aborigines and the encouragement of Christian missions ; she is, and hopes to continue, in amicable alliance with France, and yet she permits an insignificant South African Republic, an offshoot from her own Colony, whose independence she has formally recognized, to insult and treat with injustice French missionaries, as well as to carry on a long disastrous warfare with the Basutos. If England do not interpose, France must in behalf of the Basutos, who have been so long under the civilizing influence of her missionaries—might perhaps have had some effect with Earl Derby's Conservative Ministry, "in precipitating the decisive step which has now been taken."

You seem also to be apprehensive that when Mr. Disraeli gives place to Mr. Gladstone the present policy may be reversed to the detriment of this Colony. But it is no longer a secret that, as the *Argus* says, " for some time past, Sir Philip has urged upon the Government the desirability of annexing Basutoland (or rather of England protecting it) as the only way of bringing to an end a harassing war, threatening the peace of the colonial frontier," and it is believed that, if Mr. Cardwell had remained at the Colonial Office, he would, long ere this, have "favourably responded to His Excellency's appeals." So much for the dread that a change of Ministry in England may affect this question.

4. No Cape Colonist can quarrel with you for the prudence and caution you evince in guarding against any accession of territory without some Imperial guarantee being given that the Colony is not alone to bear the brunt of the increased liabilities; but your alarm on this point seems a little inconsistent with "the more generous policy and larger views," for which you have on more than one occasion lately given the Mother Country credit.

For my own part, I am disposed to think that the *Argus* takes a sound practical view of the case in the following passage :—

> It will be no easy task to keep Basutos and burghers within their respective boundary lines, even though British power be invoked to assist. With these little affairs in hand it is the more satisfactory to find that the troops are not to be withdrawn. Indeed, we cannot doubt that the annexation of Basutoland had something to do with the recent decision of the Home Government.

Let me also quote on this point the annexed extract from a leader of the *Fort Beaufort Advocate*, which refers in congratulatory terms to the decision of the Home Government *not* to withdraw the troops from this Colony :—

> Who knows but that the whole question of South African politics may yet occupy the serious attention of the Imperial Government? It is not impossible, nor even improbable, that the late rumours respecting the re-annexation of the Free State, may have emanated from some indication of a desire on behalf of Her Majesty's advisers to take a closer view of the relations subsisting between British possessions in South Africa and adjacent states, and that the withdrawal of the military has been suspended, pending the decision which may ultimately be arrived at by Ministers.

5. You seem to be sceptical about what you term the impracticable idea of "annexing the new territory to Natal," but, perhaps, it may turn out that Mr. Shepstone, who thoroughly understands the native question in all its bearings, may have considered the point already, and be enabled to influence the Natal Legislature in its favour.

The Cape Parliament may possibly be again consulted upon the subject of annexation, and who knows but that there may yet be a fight between the rival colonies for the prize of Basutoland ? According to the telegram of the *Argus*, "there is great satisfaction in the Eastern Province at the proposed annexation of Basutoland," which the knowing ones say, both on account of its geographical position and the facilities of trade, ought to form part of this Colony instead of Natal.

After all, however, perhaps the mountain may be turned into a mole-hill, and the *Advertiser and Mail* proved to be right, "that the most probable issue of the affair will be simply the creation of a protectorate under a British resident ; while in any case the Basutos will have to raise by taxation whatever moneys may be required to maintain the establishment or establishments which this protectorate must entail."

6. There is one way of viewing this matter in which few will differ from you, and that is, "that the Orange Free State has many claims on our friendly consideration," and that its mortification or defeat is neither to be desired for our interests, nor would accord with our sense of justice."

But is there any good ground for expecting that the Governor, or rather the High Commissioner, will pursue his course of action in a "triumphant spirit," or exalt the Basutos over the Boers? Doubtless he will put an end to the war, already too long protracted, which both desire, but as the accredited agent of Great Britain he will act discreetly and justly.

I confess that the serious complications you anticipate as likely to arise out of British interference, by the signal warlike "successes" either of President Brand or Moshesh, do not seem to me very probable; and there can be little doubt that *both* would best consult the interests committed to their keeping by wisely welcoming Sir Philip Wodehouse as a mediator in the unseemly conflict between them.

Sir Philip has a difficult task before him, and it behoves the press of the colony to watch and criticise, but not in a hostile spirit, his proceedings; and I cannot help thinking that the organs of public opinion would further strengthen the hands of His Excellency by improving the opportunity of his presence in the Orange Free State, by encouraging the people in the State as well as in the Colony, to petition the Queen and the Imperial and local Parliaments, that they would permit the British flag to wave not only over Basutoland, but also over what was once the Sovereignty.

If confederation were not more the order of the day than annexation, a glance at the map might suggest that the Free State and Basutoland could be divided between the colonies of the Cape and Natal.

7. Having, I hope, touched upon all the points of your argument, I must be allowed to express an opinion that the reasons given by the editor of the *Argus* in justification " of the interference of the British Government in some shape," appear most conclusive. As he well puts it, " the Colony would have had the pleasure of keeping the Basuto nation, while the Free State enjoyed the fat of their land," *or*, " on the other hand, if the Basutos had overrun the Free State, the result would have been equally inimical to colonial interests."

I have thus, I fear, at tedious length, put my view of the contemplated British protectorate before your readers, and my apology for trespassing on your space and their patience must be an earnest impression that your observations and arguments, which I have attempted to answer, were, although well meant, calculated to raise some prejudice against the High Commissioner and the cause he has in hand, so important to the progress and civilisation of Southern Africa.

COLONIST.

Saturday, 1st February, 1868.

THE BRITISH PROTECTORATE OF THE BASUTOS.

SIR,—If my long letter has been in the most remote degree instrumental in drawing from your editorial pen the able justification of your political opinions, which formed the subject of my attempts at criticism, many of your readers will feel inclined to forgive me for having drawn so largely on their patience.

In the first place, let me cordially join you in "hoping that the intervention" of Her Majesty's present advisers on behalf of Moshesh "will resolve itself into the establishment of a Residency in Basutoland, leaving to the Free State the option, at its own free will, of proposing to the British Government and this colony an alliance which shall lead hereafter to a Federative reconstruction of the whole of the South African States and Dependencies."

We concur in the wish that the day may not be far distant when the British Ensign may be hoisted at Bloemfontein as well as at Thaba Bosigo, but we seem to differ on the point that the granting at the present moment by the Queen of England of the oft-repeated prayer of Moshesh, to be admitted her loyal subject, is calculated to facilitate this desirable result.

Great praise is, no doubt, due to you for your caution and anxiety that it should be clearly understood and recorded "that the cost and responsibility of bringing into more intimate union with, and more subject to the influences of civilization the Aboriginal race of the Basutos, should attach to the Imperial authorities," but you must excuse the expression of an opinion that you appear to take a rather exaggerated and despondent view of the "perils" which beset the mission of peace of Sir Philip Wodehouse to the Orange Free State.

In your summary of this morning of the Heads of News for dispatch per steamer *United Service*, you correctly state, "There has been a growing feeling in favour of an alliance with the Free State," but you add, "*it is apprehended that the Boers will resent the prior adoption of the Basutos as British subjects, and that complications may arise.*"

Of course, in this instance the "wish is not father to the thought," and no organ of public opinion in the Colony would more regret any interruption in the amicable relations between our neighbours of the Free State and ourselves than the *Standard*.

Is it not then almost a pity that the idea, of what the "Vicar of Bray," a correspondent to the *Friend*, calls the temerity of the Volksraad to "snub Her Majesty's representative," should have been even hinted at in your Conservative columns?

It is but just to you to add that the idea of the High Commissioner not meeting with a hearty welcome at Bloemfontein, is not entirely your own, but that it may be gathered from the annexed extract from the *Advertiser and Mail*:—

> It is said that Governor Wodehouse has requested Mr. Brand to stay hostilities until matters can be arranged by a visit of His Excellency to the scene of war. Whether the President will assent to this or not remains to be seen.

Some think and give out "that the peremptory forbidding the further prosecution of hostilities will be a bitter pill for the gallant burghers in the field to swallow ;" but it is hoped that President Brand will have sufficient weight and authority with the Volksraad to induce them gladly to accept the interposition of Great Britain, with a view of bringing to a peaceful settlement the matters in dispute between the belligerent Boers and Basutos.

Let us hope that the Queen's High Commissioner has received a favourable reply to his despatch *both* from the President and Moshesh, and that the din of war is already hushed, not to be re-heard, and that, when His Excellency meets the contending parties, he may be enabled to conclude the terms of a lasting peace to their mutual satisfaction.

In your liberal desire to promote " free discussion," you have transferred to your columns of this morning the opinions of the frontier press on the rumoured annexation of Basutoland, which may, I think, fairly be said to be more in conflict with the opinions expressed by the *Standard* than with those of the *Argus*, which have lately claimed my sympathy and feeble support.

These extracts best speak for themselves, but the moral I would draw from them is, that the British protectorate is likely to lead to the extension of British rule to the Orange Free State, an event of the utmost importance to all parties concerned.

I cannot resist quoting from the *Burghersdorp Gazette* and the *Graham's Town Journal* two short passages in corroboration of my view of the matter. The former says :—

> The annexation of Basutoland is the insertion of the thin end of the wedge, and the annexation of the Free State will soon follow as a necessity. In a few words, the verification of Mr. Brand's words to the deputation, that the day is not far distant when the whole of this part of South Africa, from the Transvaal downwards, will become one colony, appears about to be realized, and we cannot help thinking that Mr. Brand must have been doing something more than guessing when he made the remark.

And the latter states :—

> The information before us leads to the conclusion that the annexation of Basutoland is to be followed by negotiations which may result in the return of the Free State to its former allegiance. Whether this inference will be confirmed by facts, time will show. We need not say that such a consummation would be joyfully hailed by us. The extension of British South Africa to the remotest limits of existing European settlements, is one of the objects by which we guide our endeavours as journalists. The abandon-

ment of the Free State we have never ceased to condemn. The annexation of Basutoland, as well as of the Transkeian territory, is a measure we have long advocated, and which we have recently and repeatedly stated to be urgently and immediately required.

The *Great Eastern* says, " Why the annexation of Basutoland? Why not rather the annexation of the Orange Free State?" The answer to these questions is simply this : Moshesh has petitioned the Queen of England to extend her protection to him and his followers ; the Sovereignty, which has been declared an *independent* Free Republic, has not made known its desire to be reinstated under the regal sway of Her Majesty.

Let the people of the Orange Free State *only* make an appeal to the proper authorities for a change of dynasty, and the conversion of the Trans-Orange Republic into a British Colony " must follow as a matter of course." It is very gratifying to observe that the *Friend* takes over your able leading articles on the resumption of the Sovereignty, with a view of giving them a wider circulation in the Free State, and it seems to me that your telling arguments cannot fail, now that Moshesh has been successful in his petition to England's Queen, to rouse the people beyond the Orange River to commence an agitation with a view of becoming once more Her Majesty's loyal subjects, in the hope of being relieved from the difficulties and want of order and good government, which have so long checked their prosperity and progress. So much with respect to the general question of the British Protectorate of the Basutos.

I must now be permitted to add a word or two in reply to your comments on my letter. You say, " With respect to the general arguments of this letter, our readers must judge whether the criticism is accurate, or the imputations of inconsistency and *unfairness* are just." While I have no desire to depart from any of my arguments, I had no intention of charging you with arguing unfairly, and what I have written will not, I hope, bear that interpretation.

I am quite content that your readers should "judge" between us, but before they deliver their verdict, you must not be offended if I add another count to the indictment for inconsistency, which I have preferred against you.

The *Standard* is against what is called Responsible Government, and prides itself with justice upon having been instrumental in preventing the enthusiastic friends of Government by Party in Cape Town from gaining the day. It has correctly put forward that " henceforth the alternative will be Responsible Government or the retention of the troops," and has declared its decided preference for the latter alternative. The argument that the Cape ought not to have Responsible Government, because under the circumstances of this Colony the entire management of the native races ought not to be entrusted to it, was first clearly put forward by Earl Grey. The memorable words of the prorogation speech, which will bear constant repetition—

The question really seems to be in whose hands is the chief Government of the country to be vested—in Great Britain or the Colony itself? for I think that so long as any British soldiers are left here, the ultimate responsibility will remain with the former; and I also feel very strongly that the best interests of this Colony require that it should so remain, at any rate for some time to come. We have here to deal with colonies inhabited by two races, whose habits and whose characters are totally different, who possess each of them the ability to do incalculable mischief, and in the hands of one of which is deposited the whole legislative and executive authority. I cannot doubt that, under these circumstances, the welfare of both, the preservation of peace and tranquillity so essential to both, will best be secured by the continuance of that very moderate amount of control which the British Government still retains, and of which the British troops is an accompaniment—

have convinced His Grace the Duke of Buckingham, the successor at the Colonial Office of the Earl of Carnarvon, that Earl Grey was right.

The British Crown, in its anxiety to promote the cause of the Aborigines in South Africa, is about to take a step calculated to ameliorate the condition of the Basutos. Surely, it cannot be of much importance to discuss and decide whether that step has been prompted by Louis Napoleon, by Exeter Hall, or by Sir Philip Wodehouse, or by the Lieutenant-Governor of Natal, under the influence of Mr. Shepstone.

The point of my present argument is that the opposition, if any, to the Native policy of Her Majesty's Ministers, should, in the natural course of things, come rather from the Responsibles than the Anti-Responsibles. The fact that *one* at least of the consistent organs of the Responsible Government party in Cape Town, so far from opposing, warmly supports the proposed British Protectorate of the Basutos, is to my mind a strong argument in its favour. Would it not be a splendid opportunity for the sincere opponents of " an Irresponsible Executive" to endeavour to make capital out of the contemplated intervention of Her Majesty's Ministers, in a a matter so deeply affecting the interests of this Colony, if it were wrong?

After your explanation of your " bearing towards and expressions respecting His Excellency the Governor," I must, to be consistent with myself in the wish of avoiding " the rubbing an old sore," be as brief as possible.

I never for a moment dreamt of insinuating that you had ever breathed a word against " the *private* character of Her Majesty's Representative," but the feelings of a gentleman may be wounded by severe attacks, not founded on sufficient evidence, against his " *public* character."

No one ought to quarrel with your independent spirit in not being afraid to " hit hard" a public man when he is wrong, but I am not singular in the impression that you have been rather unmerciful towards the Governor. I at least cannot be accused of "subserviency" or "effeminate amiability" towards Sir Philip Wodehouse, for I have not the honour of his personal acquaintance. It may have been presumption in me to have said a word in his behalf, but I was not prompted by any private personal motive, but by an earnest desire to see the important matter now committed to him by Her Majesty brought to a favourable issue.

Tuesday, February 4, 1868.

COLONIST.

The Chamber of Commerce, the "Advertiser and Mail," and the "Argus."

Sir,—The *Advertiser and Mail* inaccurately, but perhaps unintentionally, states that the Chamber of Commerce has been called upon to "record their solemn vote for the Annexation of the Orange Free State," and thereupon peremptorily proceeds, in a short sentence, to pronounce its dictum, that it will amount to "a solemn farce," if the Chamber, on Monday next, dare to discuss the "series of resolutions on Free State affairs," which has now been before the public for some days.

The *Argus*, in a *long* leading article, in which it professes to "entertain the highest esteem for the President of the Cape Town Chamber of Commerce," alludes in its usual bantering style to the "receipt of an autograph letter from the private secretary of His Royal Highness the Duke of Cambridge," having emboldened the old and experienced colonist to travel out of his mercantile sphere, and concludes with a bit of chaff for the purpose of overwhelming with ridicule the poor President, as well as the course of action which he has, in the exercise of his discretion, submitted for the adoption or rejection of the members of the Chamber.

But these much-esteemed gentlemen, from their respective editorial chairs in the Heerengracht and St. George's-street, kindly grant permission to the Cape Town merchants to discuss and decide the self-evident proposition that an irredeemable paper currency is a bad thing, but forbid them even to argue the question whether the extension of British rule to the Free State, as well as to Basutoland, is or is not intimately connected with the social and commercial interests of this Colony.

They appear also to be horrified at the idea that the Chamber of Commerce, who were the first, notwithstanding their opposition at the time, to request the Governor to support the petition of the Cape people to the Queen and her faithful Lords and Commons against the then contemplated withdrawal of the troops, should now record, and convey in grateful terms to His Excellency, their just appreciation of the value of his services, in having been mainly instrumental, by his able support of the Parliamentary remonstrance, in attaining the favourable issue, for the present, at least, to the important question of the military defence of South Africa.

The resolutions of the President speak for themselves, and may require some alteration and amendment to meet the views of the majority of the members present "at the special meeting convened for Monday next."

I crave leave, however, through the medium of your impartial columns, to submit to the Vice-President, and those members who are likely to follow him, some reasons why the advice of the *Argus* should not be listened to, that "all the resolutions, except the first perhaps, should be quietly withdrawn."

1. I cannot see the force of the objection taken by the *Argus* in the annexed passage :—

It may be and is a very proper thing for mercantile bodies to declare their sentiments with reference to mercantile questions, but when a number of gentlemen, many or few, seek to gain additional weight for their opinions by putting them forward as emanating from a recognized organization, we conceive they transgress the rules of propriety.

What is the use of the organized association of a Chamber of Commerce but to give to the resolutions of that Chamber, upon questions affecting the mercantile interests of the Colony, when they have been formally recorded after ample discussion, *more* weight and influence than the individual opinions of any number of merchants?

In their private counting-houses merchants may very properly confine themselves to the actual operations of business, and to the pleasing calculations that the profits on baftas and other articles of British manufacture will more than balance the losses on wool; but, in their monthly meetings, within the walls of the Chamber of Commerce, they should give a wider scope to their thoughts, and take a more enlarged view of the general prospects of trade in the Colony.

I hope I may venture, without incurring the risk of offending the merchants of Cape Town and Port Elizabeth, to express an opinion that there is not much danger of political controversies diverting their due attention from the ordinary occupations of business.

It may be said we agree with the *Argus* that the tariff of import duties and the regulations of the Custom-house are subjects proper to be discussed by the Chamber of Commerce, but we differ from the President that the extension of British rule to the Orange Free State and Basutoland has any bearing on the commercial interests of the Cape.

Surely the restoration of peace, order, and credit to a large tract of country, the inhabitants of which are our customers for goods to supply their wants, and both import and export through our sea-ports, may be considered to be somewhat a "mercantile question."

The bankrupt state of the finances of the Orange Free State, caused by the ruinous and long-protracted war between the Boers and the Basutos, has led to the very liberal issue of bluebacks, which cannot fail to be attended with prejudice to the interests of the creditors of the State; and it does not require much reflection or argument to arrive at the conclusion, that the obnoxious paper currency, not convertible into gold or silver at the will of the holder, would not be patronized by any Government under the auspices and control of the Queen of England and her Parliament.

2. It may suit the purpose of the Editors of the *Advertiser and Mail* and the *Argus* to insinuate, without narrowly scanning the resolutions, that they are intended to convey the approval of the Chamber of Commerce " of the annexation of Basutoland and the incorporation of the Free State to the Colony," but the *second* resolution, which declares in favour of the " restoration of British rule to the territory which was once the Sovereignty," *expressly* declines to " enter into the question of the practicability or expediency of annexation," out of deference to the prevailing feeling against the extension of the limits of this Colony, the danger of which is, to my mind at least, much exaggerated.

The *fifth* resolution, which was added after the receipt of the memorable and satisfactory telegram of the *Argus*, is confined to the recording of the approbation of the Chamber of the proposed British protectorate over Moshesh and his tribes, and to the expression of an opinion that it was likely to lead to the other desideratum—the hoisting of the British flag at Bloemfontein.

3. The adjournment of the meeting until Monday next will enable many of the members of the Chamber of Commerce, who were not present on Monday last, to come prepared with their speeches and votes in favour of the resolutions, so obnoxious to that portion of the Cape Town press, which seems desirous of monopolizing the privilege of free discussion of political subjects, or with amendments more appropriately conveying their opinions; but it is hoped that few of the Cape Town merchants will be terrified into silence by the dread of the displeasure of either of your able contemporaries.

4. The *Argus* says:—

As far as regards the issue of any additional bluebacks in the Orange Free State, holding the views we have so repeatedly expressed, we were pleased to find that the President of the Cape Town Chamber had given notice of his intention to propose a resolution of sympathy with the Port Elizabeth Chamber, but, when it became apparent that the reference to the bluebacks was merely intended as a peg upon which to hang an expression of opinion upon subjects totally foreign to the functions of such an institution, we were not surprised that the majority of the members present at the meeting hesitated to commit themselves to his leading.

What is the correct version of this matter ? The President, being desirous that the Cape Town Chamber should, at their *ordinary* monthly meeting, express and report sympathy with the kindred institution at Port Elizabeth, posted up, in order to avoid the trouble and delay of a *special* meeting, the following notice :—

At the next meeting of the Chamber, to be held on Monday next, the 3rd of February, certain resolutions will be submitted by Mr. Ebden, expressive of the sympathy of the Chamber *with the proceedings of the Port Elizabeth Chamber of Commerce* on the subject of the proposed additional issue of bluebacks by the Free State Government.

Upon the minutes of the proceedings of the Port Elizabeth Chamber's meeting will be found, amongst other resolutions in favour of the financial difficulties of the Free State being remedied by "judicious taxation," and against the issue of inconvertible paper money and the closing of the courts of law, the subjoined resolution, upon which the *second* and *third* resolutions of the President are founded :—.

That in view of the intimate relations, alike social and commercial, between the Orange Free State and this Colony, it is highly desirable, for the welfare of both, that a close and more binding union than can ever be expected under the present system should exist between the two countries, either by federation or otherwise. That this meeting pledges itself heartily to support any measure having this union for its object, and moreover expresses its full belief that any feasible terms for the future good government of the country, mutually agreed upon by the Orange Free State and the Cape Colony, would readily be confirmed and ratified by Her Majesty's Government.

It is submitted then, that these resolutions might very well have been discussed at the *last* meeting, and that the objection which was raised, that the members would be taken by surprise by such discussion, was more technical than real ; although, of course, it must be admitted that there was no formal notice about the minor points relating to the approbation of the British protectorate of the Basutos, the appointment of a British resident at Bloemfontein, and the vote of thanks to the Governor.

5. While the *Argus* professes *not* to criticize the resolutions, it really does so, for "it merely suggests that it is a little inconsistent in a single breath to protest against the policy of a friendly State and to recommend the annihilation of its Government." I cannot see the justice of this criticism. As it strikes me, the gist of the argument of the Port Elizabeth resolutions, which in *spirit* were copied by the President of the Cape Town Chamber of Commerce, is, that there ought to be "a close and more binding union between the Orange Free State and this Colony, either by federation or otherwise," because the evils which are in existence beyond the Orange River, such as financial difficulties leading to the creation of paper money, continued hostilities between neighbouring native tribes, and the denial of justice by closing the courts of law, &c., &c., all of which seriously affect the welfare of this Colony,

may fairly be ascribed to the " present system of Government" *now* prevailing in the *small*, though *independent*, South African Republic of the Free State.

6. While it may be conceded to the *Argus* that it would be rather inconsistent with the duties of the Chamber of Commerce to take up the cause of the Bishop of Natal, or of the recusant minister of the Dutch Reformed Church, it is diffidently suggested that, if a competent discussion within the precincts of the Chamber would end in an abundant supply of Cape coal to the steamers visiting Table Bay, or in the establishment of *profitable* manufactories of sugar from beetroot, few would think that the members of the Chamber, who had been instrumental in attaining these happy results, were worthy of censure for having absurdly meddled with matters of public interest.

To put rather an analogous case—the Port Elizabeth Chamber of Commerce, of whose active sympathy with the Anti-Blueback Association of Bloemfontein even the *Argus* expresses approval, have in their annual report, about to be published, alluded to Mr. Mauch's alleged discovery of the Transvaal goldfields. Suppose the Chamber of Commerce to be in possession of authentic information on this subject, would it be a waste of time on their part, or beyond their sphere of usefulness, to discuss the expediency of organizing an exploring party to the gold regions of Moselikatze, so as to prevent him giving any undue preference to Natal or the Transvaal Republic?

7. Although Mr. Watson is reported to have cited the non-interference of the Liverpool Chamber of Commerce with the greenbacks at the time of the American war as a precedent to be followed by the Cape Town Chamber, I think I may conclude from what occurred at the meeting, that the *first* resolution will be carried as *a matter of course*.

The Cape Town merchants will, however, excuse me for suggesting that, if this resolution stand *alone* on the minutes of the proceedings of the Cape Town Chamber of Commerce, after the Port Elizabeth Chamber has expressed an opinion of the social and political aspect of the question, it may give rise to the repetition of an idea, borrowed from the *Great Eastern*, before referred to in your columns, of the *selfish* motive—viz., the payment of the debts of the colonists, alone actuating them in the expressions of sympathy with their brethren across the Orange River—" the abandoned subjects of Her Majesty."

These remarks have been submitted *more* with the hope of persuading the Chamber of Commerce *freely and fairly to discuss all the resolutions*, than by any well-grounded dread that the President of that Chamber will fall in the estimation of public opinion by the censure which has been bestowed upon him by the *Argus*.

COLONIST.

Thursday, 6th February, 1868.

The Governor and the Free State.

Sir,—Referring to "the despatch of Sir Philip Wodehouse to the President of the Free State," which appears in your columns of this morning, you say that you "will not pretend to judge how this *very remarkable* document will be received by the people of the Free State."

I am bold enough, however, to venture an opinion that this clear and conciliatory expression of the intentions of Her Majesty's Government in accepting "those overtures which the Chief Moshesh has so repeatedly made for becoming, with his tribe, subject to Her Majesty the Queen," is justly entitled to a cordial welcome, not only from the President and Volksraad, and those under their rule, but also from the Cape Colonists, who have the real interests of their neighbours beyond the Orange River at heart.

To me it seems that this statesmanlike paper, which "is courteous in its language," and not, I think, fairly open to the objection of being wanting in proper diplomacy, has not met with so good a reception from the *Standard*, the *Argus*, or the *Advertiser and Mail* as it deserved; although, perhaps, in suggesting that you and your contemporaries have indulged rather too freely in hyper-criticism upon the Governor's despatch, I may lay myself open to the same imputation from you all with respect to my presumptuous comments on your leading articles.

The reason which His Excellency puts prominently forward for the interposition of the Queen of England on behalf of Moshesh, is the termination of "the prolonged hostilities between the Orange Free State and the Basutos," which have been so fruitful of evil to all parties concerned—the Cape of Good Hope, Basutoland, and the Orange Free State.

To put the ideas of Sir Philip Wodehouse in another, though doubtless less telling shape—this Colony has been overrun by Basutos, and has felt the danger of its "relations" with the Aboriginal tribes being "embarrassed" by the war—the tribe of Moshesh, as well as their "deserving missionaries, who have so long laboured amongst them," have severely suffered—and the Free State has been driven into debt and difficulty so detrimental to its future progress.

The *Argus* condemns the part of the despatch which refers to "the internal condition of the Free State," and says it ought to have been omitted, and thus appears to agree with you that Her Majesty's High Commissioner was deficient in what you call "*diplomatic tact*," in "letting the Free State feel that it was a weak power" in comparison with Great Britain.

It is an aphorism, that the truth ought not always to be told, but, it is submitted with some confidence, that many who approach the consideration of the important step about to be taken by Her Majesty, for the amelioration of the Basutos, without being guided by a too "captious spirit" of criticism, will be of opinion that the Governor acted wisely and discreetly in using as an argument with the President, in support of the object Great Britain has in view—"the restoration and maintenance of general peace" in Southern Africa, the *expediency* of the Boers no longer pursuing the profitless avocations of war in the present bankrupt state of their country's public finances.

Sir Philip Wodehouse also, with a terseness of expression for which you fairly give him credit, goes on to recommend the Government of the Free State at once to "suspend hostilities," on the *reasonable* grounds that the British "Power, which is actuated by the most friendly sentiments towards the Free State," will "give the fullest consideration to the just claims of that State, and endeavour to restrain for the future the Basutos from making aggressions on the border of their neighbours."

Doubtless there is something in the point you appear to take with reference to the telegram *vià* Aliwal North, which announces the "Great Free State Victory," that serious "complications" may arise *before* the terms of peace can be finally concluded between the belligerent Boers and Basutos.

If I rightly understand your line of argument, you anticipate that such signal success will attend the military operations of the *new* commandoes, the leaders of which are so eager to gain laurels for bravery *before* the din of war is for ever hushed in the Trans-Orange regions, that by "right" of conquest, "under the law of nations," the *whole* of Basutoland, except perhaps the mountain country unfit for cultivation, will belong to the Orange Free State, and that England will not be able to afford the promised protection to her *new* subjects without expatriating them from the land of their birth, and distributing them over the colonies of the Cape and Natal, or selecting some other tract of country, in which they may peacefully and successfully follow their agricultural habits.

In reply to this, I would suggest that Great Britain is not likely to infringe the law of nations, and, if it be true that the land which, as the *Argus* has said, "was wrested by a handful of Burghers last war from the Basutos," is essential to their support, the probable and equitable result will be, *provided* the title of conquest is fairly established, that if, in justice to Moshesh and his tribe, the British Government be compelled to take the land, they will grant fair compensation to the Free State. So, after all, it is not perhaps a very extravagant presumption that the irredeemable paper bluebacks may be made convertible into gold and silver out of the military chest, which arrangement, to use a vulgarism, might "suit the book" of the Volksraad.

The *Advertiser and Mail* says:—

From the *Tyd*, which may be considered the organ of the *more purely Dutch element* in the population of the Free State, we observe that this movement of His Excellency—just at the time when the Free State had aroused itself to a final effort, and when decisive victory seemed to be within its easy grasp—is considered as unwarrantable and "shameful" intervention; and, if it hereafter appears from the correspondence that His Excellency gave the State no reason to expect any intervention as possible or probable, we do think that the authorities there have good reason to consider themselves most unjustifiably aggrieved.

With all respect to the worthy editor, who so thoroughly ridicules, in common with the *Argus*, the notion of the Chamber of Commerce discussing any political subject, although it may bear upon the mercantile interests of the Colony, it is suggested that it would have been more prudent at this critical moment, if not more just towards His Excellency, to have waited for the production of the correspondence before he appeared to justify the insinuation that the "intervention" of Her Majesty's Government "was unwarrantable and shameful."

I am not behind the scenes, but if there be any truth in the exordium of Sir Philip's despatch—

I feel sure that the Government of the Orange Free State must long since have become aware, from the communications which I have from time to time had the honour of addressing to you, of the great concern with which Her Majesty's Government and myself have contemplated the prolonged hostilities that have prevailed between that State and the Basutos,

there cannot be good foundation for the charge that the Free State "authorities" are "most unjustifiably aggrieved" by the intervention of England's Queen in behalf of the sable enemies of that State coming upon them by surprise.

The *Friend* having taken over into its columns, for the purpose of circulation within the Orange Free State, your able leading articles in favour of the resumption of the Sovereignty, I think it may fairly be assumed from the heading of its Extra, which proclaimed the despatch from the Governor to the President—"The thin end of the wedge—Annexation of Basutoland to the Empire on which the sun never sets"—that this organ of the "abandoned British subjects" of Her Majesty beyond the Orange River hails with intense feelings of joy and satisfaction the early prospect of the territory which was once the Sovereignty again forming part and parcel of the widespreading Colonial Empire of Queen Victoria.

You must forgive me for remarking that it seems a little inconsistent in you that, at the same time that you express a mean opinion of Sir Philip Wodehouse as a diplomatist, and would almost lead people to believe that, in the language of

F

the *Argus*, " he would blurt out his meaning with the bluntness of a soldier," you seem to insinuate that in the mysterious " pigeon-hole" of Government House there will be found a despatch " sanctioning the annexation of the Free State, if it should make the request, and if this Colony will assent thereto."

While I will not depart from the opinion previously expressed on more occasions than one, that the extension of British rule to Basutoland will " facilitate rather than retard" the decay of the Republican dynasty of the Orange Free State, or, as it has been better expressed, that " the annexation of Basutoland is but the first step towards the restoration of British rule north of the Orange River," I certainly think that the *Argus* is quite right when it says " we do not believe that the British Government were moved by any such idea. They simply intended to stop a war fruitful of mischief to the combatants and the colony."

If this be so, the objection you take to the despatch, that " it is written either too much in the style of my Lord Paramount, or it conceals a meaning which is not expressed upon the face of it," appears entirely to fall to the ground.

Upon the whole, then, it cannot be fairly denied that this " despatch breathes a spirit of good-will towards the Free State and its Government," and it is submitted that it will not *justly* bear any other interpretation, if you take it as an axiom, that the interests of the Free State are identical with those of this Colony in promoting peace and civilization amongst the aboriginal tribes of Southern Africa.

It was cursorily thrown out the other day by me, that perhaps, after all, there might be a contest between the Cape and Natal Parliaments who should gain the prize of Basutoland.

The *Graham's Town Journal*, well informed and practical in its deductions on most subjects, certainly makes it appear that there is a great deal to be said in favour of the territory inhabited by Moshesh and his tribe being annexed to this Colony instead of to Natal ; and I have even heard a report, although I will not vouch for its accuracy, that some of the Responsible Government party in Cape Town are " disgusted" that the Home Government should have given the first choice to Natal ; but may not this alleged undue preference be ascribed to the very strong Parliamentary protest of the Cape Legislature against the annexation of British Kaffraria ?

I shall indeed feel much disappointed if the Governor's despatch, which truly merits more than my feeble praise, does not meet with the warm approbation of the Eastern Province press ; and many of the earnest well-wishers of the Free State hope that the favourable response by the President to this despatch will soon relieve their anxiety as to any bad counsel prevailing with the Volksraad to prevent the overtures of the

British Government at the hands of Sir Philip Wodehouse being received in a good spirit.

Sincerely joining with you in "hoping that nothing untoward will mar the consummation so ardently desired, of peace on our borders, and equitable arrangements to secure the maintenance thereof," and enjoying the sanguine anticipation that the "interference" by Her Majesty will be attended with the most beneficial results, not only to both the combatants in this long-protracted war, but also to the Cape colonists and the aborigines of South Africa, if *only* the motives which have prompted it, and have been well described in this able despatch, be not misunderstood or misinterpreted.

February 8.   COLONIST.

THE CHAMBER OF COMMERCE AND THE "ARGUS."

SIR,—I must not forego the opportunity of thanking you for your timely and apt quotation of the opinions of Lord Stanley, Mr. Gladstone, and the *Economist* in aid of the arguments with which I endeavoured to prove, in the face of the grave objections taken by *both* your contemporaries, that the Cape Town Chamber of Commerce was perfectly competent to discuss all the questions which had been submitted to them. As in your editorial capacity you have made no further reference to the subject, I will beg permission to make, in your column set apart for correspondents, some comments on the proceedings of yesterday at the Commercial Exchange. Although the resolutions which have been passed will, it is thought, contrast unfavourably with those of the Port Elizabeth Chamber of Commerce, the President has every reason to be satisfied with them, inasmuch as they clearly convey "an authoritative exposition of commercial opinion" in Cape Town in favour of the extension of British rule, in some shape or other, to what was once the Sovereignty, as well as an approval of the contemplated British Protectorate of the Basutos, which *two* points, doubtless, he regards as the most material. The *minor* points rejected are of comparatively little importance, except perhaps that the not even " putting the question" of a vote of thanks to the Governor may suggest the idea that at the Cape of Good Hope censure of those in authority is ever more congenial than praise; although perhaps it may be also susceptible of more favourable construction, that the gentlemen assembled thought that *now* that the Queen's troops had been allowed to remain in the colony, and that the war between the Boers and the Basutos was likely to come to a satisfactory end, Sir Philip Wodehouse would soon lose his unpopularity in Cape Town without their giving him a helping hand.

With all respect for Messrs. Stein and Watson, it is submitted that the objection of "being entirely in the dark," or "of not having the whole case before them," in which they so resolutely persisted, was in legal phraseology rather frivolous, for, *after* the despatch of the Governor to President Brand, which every person present at the meeting may be presumed to have read, it certainly seems difficult to imagine what further information was required with respect to the British Protectorate of Moshesh and his tribe, to enable the Chamber of Commerce to give an opinion as to the merits of this proposal of Her Majesty's Government. It seems to me that Mr. Searle, in his short but sensible speech, with every word of which many will, I think, concur, hit the right nail on the head when he remarked, "They ought in this matter to support the views of the Governor, for he had a very difficult task to perform, and he required the sympathy of the whole colony."

Surely when the *Advertiser and Mail* quotes, with apparent sympathy and approbation, the conclusion of the *Tyd*, that the contemplated "intervention" by Her Majesty on behalf of the Basutos is "shameful," it is high time that her loyal subjects in Cape Town, particularly those of influence amongst the mercantile body, who are of a contrary opinion, should be permitted publicly to avow their disapproval of the sentiment "of the organ of the more purely Dutch element" of the Free State, and to assist, at least with the expression of their good wishes, the execution of the purpose committed to her High Commissioner. However much many may feel constrained to differ from some of the *dicta* of the *Argus*, it must be admitted that it appears firm and consistent in its extreme anxiety to monopolize for the press the expression of opinions on public questions which even have some bearing on the commercial interests of the country.

If the Rev. Mr. Fuller had yesterday, as a member of the Chamber of Commerce, brought to the consideration of the "policy of extending the British sovereignty to the Basutos," which he has already so ably supported, his ability and superior information on political subjects, he would have conferred a great benefit on his country, but when he quitted the scene of his useful editorial labours, with the evident intention of stifling free discussion at the Commercial Exchange, it looked very much like as if he feared that his long leader, which I have ventured to criticise, would not, without his *vivâ voce* interference in the deliberations of the Cape Town merchants, have been successful in enforcing his much desired silence on politics within the walls of the Chamber. The editor of the *Argus* is remarkably fond of good-humoured chaff, and most adroit in using it to overcome with ridicule the "voluminous" and "blundering," although at the same time perhaps unanswerable arguments of those who unfortunately disagree with him, and he probably afforded much amusement by taking some of his favourite commodity with him to the Chamber of Commerce;

but I take the liberty of suggesting that he ought not to have misrepresented the intentions or line of conduct of some of the actors in "the little drama" in which he himself played so prominent a part.

He is reported to have said at the meeting :—

The Government was just now entering into negotiations with the Free State as an independent State, *and it seemed to him very strange that a formal resolution should go up from the Cape Town Chamber of Commerce asking for the annexation of the Free State.*

Will Mr. Fuller be good enough to place his finger on any one of the President's resolutions which will fairly bear this forced construction?

The *second* resolution, *purposely* with the fixed design of avoiding a difficult point, upon which there was likely to be considerable disagreement, *expressly* declined to enter upon the question of annexation, and *merely* " made known an opinion that the restoration of British rule to the territory which was once the Sovereignty, was likely to be attended with beneficial results to the interests of the Cape, Natal, and the aboriginal tribes of South Africa."

The *third* resolution was only intended to convey the idea that a " more close and binding union" (words borrowed from Port Elizabeth) " *either by Federation or otherwise, which emanated from the Free State*," &c., would probably be assented to by Her Majesty's Government.

If the reporters have done the speeches of the editor of the *Argus* justice, there appears to be a good deal in the observation of the Chairman, " that it seemed to him that Mr. Fuller was more in favour of the *original* resolutions," although the idea at the time was received with laughter; for there is no doubt that the objection as to the want of " definite phraseology," which has since been taken in the columns of the *Argus*, applies with greater force to the resolutions of more attenuated form, which have been substituted for the *original* resolutions. The great talk at the meeting about *not* declaring a " truism" may perhaps also account for the omission of the allegation that " the British Protectorate of Moshesh and his tribe was a step likely to facilitate rather than to retard the resumption of British rule over the Orange Free State."

So much for the proceedings of the Cape Town Chamber of Commerce, which upon the whole, may be deemed satisfactory, considering the decided efforts of two able organs of the press to thwart them. The learned Professor of the Heerengracht was not admitted a member of the Chamber of Commerce in time to vote against the resolutions; but a laboured leading article appeared in the *Volksblad* of last week, throwing as much contempt and ridicule as possible on the course of action proposed by the President of that Chamber.

I cannot conclude without congratulating your readers on their having been favoured with the perusal of the able article from the *Friend*, which appeared in your issue of this morning. You may excuse me for suggesting that the extract would have more appropriately commenced with the annexed passage, no doubt inadvertently omitted by you:—

> Our conjectures of last week proved in part, though not altogether, unfounded. We then suggested that either mediation or the annexation of *both* the Free State and Basutoland to the British Empire would probably be the subject-matter of Sir Philip's letter; *but to our disappointment, and we had almost added disgust, the annexation of the Basutos and Basutoland is alone contemplated.*

That I was pretty accurate in interpreting the heading of the Extra which proclaimed the despatch of Sir Philip Wodehouse, may be gathered from the following paragraph:—

> And, seeing our prosperity, who knows but what John Bull might ultimately be induced once more to take us over, and include us also "in the Empire on which the sun never sets?"

The *Friend* very fairly places "the manifest advantage to be gained in the Free State by the contemplated arrangement" in juxta-position with "the supposed disadvantages," and who can, after a calm and unprejudiced consideration of the case, doubt that the former far out-weigh the latter? This influential organ of public opinion in the Orange Free State also places full reliance on the sense of justice of Sir Philip Wodehouse, and puts this pertinent question, "Why should the Governor, for mere mischief sake, feel any pleasure in annoying and tantalizing this State without cause?"

The *Graham's Town Journal*, referring to the great victory of the Smithfield commando over the Basutos at Tantje's Berg, takes some trouble of entering into details with the *good* intention of proving that there had not been sufficient time either for President Brand or Moshesh to communicate with their respective armies in the field to stay hostilities in accordance with the wish expressed in His Excellency's despatch. Many real friends of the State will hope that this version of the matter will turn out to be correct, and that it is not true, as the *Advertiser and Mail* throws out, "that the Free Staters are determined to exert themselves to the utmost in the short time allowed them *before* Moshesh is brought under the protectorate of Great Britain." I may be wrong, but I cannot see what additional advantage the Orange Free State can hope to gain by not "suspending hostilities" after the receipt of Sir Philip's overtures. But perhaps the more prudent course will be to stop further speculation on this subject until the correspondence, which has recently taken place between the Governor and the President, be published.

COLONIST.

Tuesday, February 11.

The Governor and the Free State.

To the Free State we recommend moderation—to the High Commissioner promptitude. The Colonists who are so deeply interested in his success, appreciate the difficulty of his task, and will not ungenerously judge his conduct.—*Cape Standard*.

Sir,—The conclusion of your leading article of this morning is so full of meaning, and appropriate at the present moment, that you must permit me to make it my theme of discussion in your next issue. Although some of the opinions which you have expressed may not meet with general concurrence, it will, I think, be admitted that you are urged by "an anxious feeling," as to the result, to represent in a proper spirit the difficulties which appear to you to beset the establishment of the British Basuto Protectorate. As I earnestly believe that free discussion will end in the removal of some at least of those difficulties, I will endeavour, as fairly as I can, to argue those points which seem to me most material, and calculated to bring the question to a satisfactory issue.

1. Surely, if the task which has been confided to Her Majesty's High Commissioner be difficult, it is the duty of all those who wish well to our neighbours of the Free State, whose real interests are not inimical to the cause of the Aboriginal Tribes, to strengthen his hands by the expression of their sympathies with the grand object he has in view—" the restoration and maintenance of general peace" in South Africa, so essential to its prosperity and progress. While the Eastern Province Press, as well as the organ of the British abandoned subjects *within* the Free State, have already declared strongly in favour of the proposed step, and only regret that it does not go further and extend the protection of the flag of England to the Orange Free State, there is too much reason to fear that some of the leaders of public opinion in the West are disposed to thwart, rather than to assist, the carrying out of this humane policy of Her Majesty's Government.

The *Advertiser and Mail*, after attempting to excite ridicule by paraphrasing the terse and well-intentioned despatch of Sir Philip Wodehouse, and approving of the "Free Staters" having turned a deaf ear to "the sudden dictum of the High Commissioner to stop hostilities," and advising them to continue fighting with "the utmost energy," in the same breath that it professes to be against "a prolongation of the war," concludes by saying :—" Of course the President's reply must be, in many respects, embarrassing to His Excellency." At the risk of being deemed uncharitable I cannot resist asking the question—Does not the writer of this article lay himself open to the imputation that in this instance "the wish is father to the thought ?"

The *Zuid-Afrikaan*, in a leader which commences by expressing the laudable desire of seeing " Her Majesty's possessions in South Africa, so as to command the respect and perhaps the confidence of the world," throws as much contemptuous abuse as possible on Her Representative in this Colony, and contrasts the insignificant and "mercenary" office held by Sir Philip Wodehouse as " the Governor and Commander-in-Chief of the Queen of England's Settlement of the Cape of Good Hope in South Africa, with its territories and dependencies," with the much more honourable and important position of Mr. Brand, as the President of the Independent Republic of the Orange Free State. This journal, which is widely circulated amongst the respectable agriculturists of Dutch descent at this end of the Colony, and probably reaches the Trans-Orange regions, also very unfairly endeavours to create a prejudice against the British Government by misrepresenting the motives which have induced their " *rude, rough, and insolent intervention*" to put an end to the war between the Boers and the Basutos. When, on the *one* side, sentiments like these are freely published, the *Argus*, whose sympathies are certainly with the *other* side, must forgive me for dissenting from its opinion, that " the Chamber of Commerce have complicated the situation by their officious resolutions," *not " on the annexation of the Free State*," but *only* in favour of the hoisting of the British ensign at the fort of Bloemfontein, as well as on the mountain of Thaba Bosigo.

2. You say, " beyond all question the Free State will continue the struggle, and endeavour to improve its recent successes ;" and the *Argus* " does not blame Mr. Brand for the perfectly natural course he is pursuing, now that the occupation of Basutoland by a foreign power is imminent," of endeavouring to " secure a substantial slice of territory before it is handed over."

With all respect for both your opinions, I cannot see how the principle " of possession being nine-tenths of the law" can well be applied to this case, and how the Free State can be said to improve its position, when the time arrives to settle the boundaries of Basutoland by any *new* conquests of territory it now makes. If I am not mistaken, the principal cause of the present war is the continuance of occupation by the Basutos of the territory which is *alleged* to have " been conquered and ceded by Moshesh himself in the treaty of 1866." It is submitted that, if the Free State can succeed in establishing a legal or equitable title to this land, " under the law of nations," the British Government, if compelled, in justice to the original owners, to restore the land, will grant an equivalent in value to the claimants. At any rate, it is difficult to see why anything that can happen after notice, that Basutoland is to become a portion of the Imperial Colonial Empire, can give to the Orange Free State a better title to the ceded territory, which was acquired by force of arms during the last war. I cannot agree with you, that "vigorous action on the part of the Free State may materially alter the situation of affairs, and that the views of the English Ministry, and more particularly the Parliament, will entertain of this business may possibly be much modified." Whatever success may now attend the warlike operations of "Mr. Brand and his Burghers," it does not seem probable that the British Parliament will sanction the expulsion of the Basutos from their native land, unless the Cape and Natal are prepared to welcome them as fugitives, or some other congenial soil, suited to their agricultural pursuits, can be allotted to them. The annexed extract from the *Great Eastern* will not be thought irrelevant to the point I am now arguing :—

It is possible that the commando had not received the despatch of Sir Philip, or instructions from the President on it; but it is to be regretted, for the sake of the Free State, that these operations, successful in themselves, should have occurred at this critical time. It would have been better for the belligerents to have laid down their arms until the visit of Sir Philip, under every circumstance. Had the boers administered one crushing blow in spite of the despatch, there would have been at any rate the determination in it of showing Sir Philip that they could whip the Basutos singlehanded; but this so called victory will not have much effect. It is in reality the capturing of a certain number of oxen, sheep, and horses. Tieme still defies them, Thaba Bosigo still lays claim to the merit of being impregnable, and whilst that is the case, the war between the Free State and the Basuto—putting on one side the interference of the Home Government—is as far off as when the commandos went to the front some months ago.

3. Many practical men will concur with the position so forcibly taken by the *Argus* in its able leader of this morning, "that Mr. Brand would have done wisely in abstaining from pressing for the boundary line as fixed by the last treaty."

The Basutos, when they become British subjects, will be under control and prevented making aggressions on their neighbours, and thus the reason assigned by the Free State for establishing a character for firmness of purpose and insisting on the new boundary line, will cease to have force. It cannot be reasonably expected that, as the *Argus* well puts it, "the British Government" will do less than "insist, however unpleasant it may be, that the Basutos have room left to live and till their land;" but, as Sir Philip Wodehouse has assured President Brand that he is prepared to "give the fullest consideration to the just claims of the State," it by no means follows that the South African Republic will not be able to make out a good case for compensation out of the military chest.

Let me, as usual, make a quotation from my old friend, the *Graham's Town Journal*, to assist my argument on this head :—

Should the Free State obtain any marked successes before the annexation of Basutoland is proclaimed, the position of affairs will be somewhat curious. We have already said that one of the puzzling questions arising out of the Imperial decision will be, how much of Basutoland is to be dealt with? Should the commandos gain any more advantages, take one or two mountains, and drive the Basutos beyond the limits of the country already proclaimed by the Bloemfontein Government as conquered and annexed to the

State, what consideration to such facts will be given by the representative of Her Majesty's Government?—what value will be set upon them by the Free State? There is one answer to the question. Whatever the British— not the Cape—Government insist upon, must be conceded by both Basutos and Burghers.

4. There may be some weight in the objection you take that the proclamation of Basutoland as British territory, or perhaps more correctly, of the Basutos as British subjects, should have been simultaneous with the ratification of the terms upon which the Boers and the Basutos had been concluded, but perhaps the explanation of the delay in the High Commissioner's proceeding to the scene of action may prove satisfactory. At any rate, it does not seem very probable that, as you suggest, the "state of circumstances in March or April" will be so altered as to make any "change in the policy of the British Government desirable or practicable." All who have the interests of this Colony and the Orange Free State at heart, will cordially join you in deprecating anything approaching to a hostile attitude between the two countries; but, as you appear to throw out, the fact that the supply of ammunition can be so easily stopped, ought to prevent the Volksraad from relying too much on the *independence* of the Free Republic, or, from listening to bad counsel, to treat the overtures of peace with contempt.

5. I regret that I cannot fully sympathize with your comments on the leading article of the *Friend*, which meets with my unqualified approbation. While you appear perfectly to understand that Her Majesty's abandoned subjects of the Free State are sadly disappointed at the undue preference which has been given to Moshesh and his tribe, by bestowing British protection *only* on Basutoland, you anticipate difficulty in the immediate re-union of what was once the Sovereignty with Great Britain, and talk of some "supplemental treaty of alliance" between the Free State and this Colony. Although there may be some objection to the annexation of the Orange Free State, either to the Cape or Natal, which seems to frighten the Cape colonists as well as the Free Staters, I cannot see any valid reason why the territory, which only a few years ago was under the regal sway of England's Queen, should not again form part and parcel of the Colonial dominions of Her Majesty, and it would be easy to devise some form of Government suited to it under the auspices of the flag of Great Britain.

6. "You wish well to the Basutos," and very properly think that "the question of righteous dealing with the Aborigines" will be advanced by the new policy towards Moshesh and his tribe.

After the able letter of your correspondent, "A Frontier Man," so fresh in the memory of your readers, it would be tedious to dwell upon this large subject; but I cannot conclude without expressing my entire concurrence with his opinion that the contemplated British Protectorate of the Basutos has something to do with the decision of the Home Government in retaining the Queen's troops in South Africa.

Thursday, 13th February, 1868. COLONIST.

His Excellency the Governor and the Free State.

Sir,—Whatever may be the opinion of the people of the Orange Free State with respect to the contemplated British Basuto Protectorate, there is no longer any doubt that the able despatch of Her Majesty's High Commissioner has not met with a very favourable reception from the authorities of that State. The reply of President Brand, which he concludes by "regretting that he cannot coincide with His Excellency that the course proposed will lead to the future general peace of South Africa," speaks for itself, and has already called forth from one of the organs of public opinion in Cape Town unqualified approval, together with the opinion that Sir Philip Wodehouse has "got himself into a most decidedly unpleasant fix," and "that it is hard to imagine what answer he can give to it." There are many, it is thought, who will not join in warm admiration of the "simplicity" and "firmness" of its language, or of the strength of its arguments, but will rather consider that it displays a want of proper confidence in the sense of justice and good intentions of the British Government, and feel inclined to agree with the *Argus* of this morning, that it amounts to very little more than "a *resumé* of the history of the war," somewhat *ex parte*, and perhaps not quite fairly setting forth *both* sides of the question. Those also who are sanguine as to the success about to be taken by Her Majesty's Ministers for the laudable purpose of putting an end "to the present internecine struggle between the Free State and the Basuto tribes, so dangerous to the peace of this Colony," will entertain the hope that your last-named contemporary is not very far wrong when it says :—

We very much doubt whether Mr. Brand's letter at all represents the general feeling in the State. We shall know more about it when the Raad meets, but, if the *Friend* at all represents the feeling of the people, Mr. Brand's forebodings will not be echoed by the more enlightened of the burghers.

In my last I ventured to direct the notice of your readers to the ludicrous paraphrase of the Governor's despatch by the *Advertiser and Mail*, and I now beg leave to annex an extract from the *Port Elizabeth Telegraph*, which seems to me much more fair and comprehensive in its explanation of this most important document, and which gives good reasons why it merited a more cordial reception at the hands of the worthy President of the Orange Free State :—

In that communication Her Majesty's High Commissioner intimates, through the proper channel, to the people of the adjoining Republic, that Her Majesty having been most graciously pleased to accede to the repeated prayer of Moshesh, he had received Her Majesty's commands to take steps for consummating the wishes of his sable Majesty. In order to prepare the way for an early and amicable settlement of the various questions presently pending between the government of the former country and the latter nation or tribe, His Excellency very properly suggested to both the propriety of an immediate cessation of hostilities, giving as his reason for tendering such advice, that as one of the belligerents was then, in all probability, about to become the subjects of a Power actuated by the most friendly sentiments towards the other, it would be his endeavour, in carrying out the measure resolved upon by the Queen, to give the fullest consideration to the just claims of the latter, that is, of the Orange Free State. Considering the nature of the recommendation thus made, the source from whence it emanated, the near prospect it afforded of a possible speedy termination of a war that has brought honour and renown to neither of the combatants, and of a lasting peace between the contending peoples, we had not unreasonably hoped both would have cheerfully consented to an armistice. The Paramount Chief of the Basutos, to his praise be it said, was no sooner informed of the fact that his most ardent desire was about to be accomplished, and of the wish of his future Sovereign's representative in South Africa that a truce might be proclaimed simultaneously throughout the Orange Free State and Basutoland, than he at once despatched a messenger to the enemy's camp, expressing his readiness to give immediate effect to the latter. Instead, however, of meeting the friendly overtures of Moshesh in a becoming spirit, the President, after consultation with his Executive, intimated, in reply to the message sent by the former, that the war would be continued as heretofore, till the ceded territory had been evacuated by the Basutos, and certain Basuto murderers given up.

Nothing contained in the reply of President Brand has, it is submitted, shaken the argument before advanced, that the Free State cannot, by prolonging hostilities, even if the most signal success attend their arms, improve their position when the time arrives in April or March for entering into negotiations with the Queen of England's Representative with respect to the boundaries of Basutoland. The question appears to me simply to resolve itself into this : Will the *mere* fact of the belligerent Burghers acquiring for a *second* time by force of conquest the " territory annexed by proclamation of Commandant-General Fick to the Orange Free State," the limits of which are particularly defined in the President's despatch, give the Free State, when it comes to settle the point *amicably* with Great Britain, a better title to this land than the formal cession of it by Moshesh when " he was compelled to sue for peace" at the termination of the last war ? The object of the war being, as Mr. Brand says, the evacuation by the Basutos of the territory above mentioned, the annexation of which to the Orange Free State was ratified by the Volksraad on the 7th February, 1867, if a *third* party intervene and stop the pending hostilities, surely the fair basis of negotiation is the state of things in existence at the commencement of this war.

If, under all the circumstances, the Free State can establish an *equitable right* "under the law of nations" to the land in question, she will be allowed by Great Britain to retain it ; or, if justice towards the Basutos requires its being restored to the native possessors of the soil, she will obtain compensation for its loss. But no brilliant victories by the Burghers, nor needless slaughter of their sable enemies, nor wanton demolition of their crops, will prevent Great Britain from acting with even-handed justice towards those of the tribe of Moshesh who have escaped from the deadly ravages of war ; for henceforth they are to be British subjects.

The President says :—" I hope and trust that the Basutos will now be brought to pay regard to the treaties entered into by them, and to respect the lives and property of our people ;" but he seems to be unmindful of the fact that England's Queen, in throwing her shield of protection over the Basutos, becomes responsible for the good conduct of her *new* subjects towards a neighbouring *independent* Republic with whom she is in terms of friendly alliance. The tone and tenor of President Brand's reply certainly convey an impression that nothing short of absolute possession of the recently annexed territory will satisfy the Volksraad, and if so, serious difficulties may, after all, as you anticipated, arise, when it becomes necessary to decide how much of the land of its birth the tribe of Moshesh is to be allowed to retain, to prevent it from starving or becoming a nuisance to the neighbouring colonies of the Cape or Natal.

The subjoined remarks of the *King William's Town Gazette* on this point are not irrelevant :—

Yet President Brand does not appear inclined to submit without a murmur to what he cannot possibly avoid. He demands the removal of the Basutos from the territory ceded at the termination of the last campaign, and further requires the surrender of a number of Kafirs who are, in his estimation, guilty of the murder of certain of his subjects. To this last proposition we can see no objection, and it remains to be seen whether Moshesh will demur at it. But the first part of the condition involves a very serious question, and one which must be left in the hands of the Government. When Sir Philip Wodehouse, at the request of the President, prescribed the boundary of the Free State, he did so upon the condition that his opinion was to be respected. Since then the Staters, in their thirst for territory they cannot occupy, have driven the Basutos back, and forthwith claim an extension. At a time of extremity Moshesh acceded to their wishes ; but afterwards, conceiving that a promise extorted by compulsion was not binding, he re-occupied, and consequently induced another war. As this war is still in progress, and as neither side has yet laid claim to victory, the matter may be considered as *sub judice*. In this position of affairs the annexation of Basutoland is suggested, and Sir Philip Wodehouse will most probably take his own boundary for the country.

The President also expresses surprise at the proposition that Moshesh and his tribe were to become subjects of the British Crown, and seems to think it inconsistent with the Articles of Convention of the 23rd of February, 1854, which precluded

"Her Majesty's Government from entering into any treaty to the north of the Orange River *which might be injurious or prejudicial to the Orange River Government;*" but, in reply to this, it may be urged that Her Majesty, so far from having "*any wish or intention*" to injure or prejudice the Orange River Government, *positively* declares, by the mouth of her accredited representative, "that she is actuated by the most friendly sentiments towards the Free State, and that her endeavour will be, in carrying out this measure, to give the fullest consideration to the just claims of that State, and to take every precaution against the renewal of those disorders on the border, which have led to such repeated complaints, and have ultimately caused the present war."

For my own part, I do not despair that better counsels will yet prevail with the Volksraad at their extraordinary session, and that they will be brought by calm discussion to see " that a good thing is being done for the Free State" in making the Basutos British subjects, and that they will regard it as the first step towards the extension of British rule to the territory now governed by a free republic. The happy day when "the Union Jack will once more float in Bloemfontein" is not far distant, if there be any truth in the following remarks of the *Natal Mercury* :—

> This news, so important in its bearing upon the political relationships of Natal, the Cape Colony, and, indeed, of all south-east Africa, is contained in a despatch which we publish elsewhere, written by Sir Philip Wodehouse, Her Majesty's High Commissioner, to President Brand. Sir Philip announces the intention of the Queen's Government without any reservation, and states his intention to visit Basutoland for the purpose of completing the arrangement and defining boundary lines in March next. Our neighbours in the Free State have received the intelligence with mixed feelings. Their best men are only too anxious that Great Britain should cast the *ægis* of her power over the whole of Southern Africa, but they don't like to let the Basutos alone just when they appear on the point of submission. Nor do they approve of the annexation of Basutoland only. They want the Free State to share in the arrangement. They are tired of Republicanism, and sigh for the repose and security under British rule. They ask why the Basutos, who have given no little trouble to the British Government in times past, who have spilt the blood of British troops, and foiled the genius of British generalship on more than one occasion, should be taken into the Imperial fold, while the Free State people, who were British subjects formerly, until summarily cast off by the Government of that day, are left to shift for themselves in the wilderness, are left, as they aptly describe it, "out in the cold."

If the British abandoned subjects of Her Majesty, whose feelings are so well portrayed in the foregoing extract from the *Natal Mercury*, which only echoes the sentiments of the *Friend of the Free State*, will but give a hearty welcome to Sir Philip Wodehouse when he comes amongst them on his mission of peace, and request him to lay at the foot of the throne their petition, that Her Majesty will be pleased to restore them to her favour, and place them on the same footing at least with

Moshesh and his tribe, it will not be long before "the more close and binding union" between this Colony and the Orange Free State, in favour of which the Chambers of Commerce of Port Elizabeth and Cape Town have been so terribly "officious" as to express a decided opinion, will be an accomplished fact.

Before concluding, your readers must forgive me for quoting the opinion of the *Great Eastern* in support of my late arguments on behalf of the course pursued by the Cape Town Chamber of Commerce, which has been so strongly condemned :—

It is quite competent for the Chamber of Commerce to discuss the subject of annexation. The Chambers are not only competent, but it is a duty they owe to the commerce they represent to bring their influence to bear upon such measures. The re-establishment of British rule in the Free State, and the want of order in the Border States, bear more upon the commerce of this colony than any matter now before the public.

Saturday, 15th February.   COLONIST.

THE GOVERNOR AND THE FREE STATE.

SIR,—Whatever may be regarded the sound opinion as to the spirit and substance of the reply of President Brand to Sir Philip Wodehouse's despatch, it would be useless to endeavour to disguise the fact that the apparent independence it displays meets with much sympathy and support within this colony. It does not appear very difficult to account for this. As between Great Britain and the Orange Free State, the natural desire in the human breast to protect the weak against the strong is brought into play for the purpose of jealously watching against any infringement of "the law of nations by a neutral power," while the antagonism of feeling between the "two distinct races" prevents the wise resolve of Earl Derby's Cabinet to " restore and maintain the general peace of South Africa," by putting an end, *without further delay*, to "the internecine struggle between the Boers and the Basutos" being favoured by so hearty a response from the Cape Colonists, as it certainly deserves. Now that the tide of success in warlike operations seems evidently to have turned in favour of the Free State, the opportunity of humbling the pride of Moshesh and his tribe, and checking for ever "the thieving propensities" of these " irreclaimable savages," is too good to be lost, and the belligerent burghers are therefore counselled and encouraged bravely to fight on, and continue the work of slaughter, and conquer as much territory as possible, with a view of improving the position of the South African Republic, when Her Majesty's High Commissioner begins to arbitrate between the combatants, and to fix the future boundaries of Basutoland. There appears to be, in some quarters, a perfect horror even at the idea of Queen Victoria increasing the number of her sable subjects in South Africa, while the reasonable fear that the remnant of the tribe of Moshesh will not have land enough left wherein to live, and thus be compelled to annoy their neighbours of the Cape, Natal, and perhaps even the Free State, seems to be treated with indifference, or at least is not looked upon as the main question in dispute, which, after all, it is, whether the hostilities be at once suspended, or the wretched warfare be prolonged until March or April next.

While at Cape Town, in a leader which concludes apparently in expressing concurrence with the laudable wish of the *Friend* that British rule shall be extended to the Free State as well as to Basutoland, the *Zuid-Afrikaan* complains that the *læsa majestas* of the President has not been sufficiently resented, and throws out that "the bold and decided policy of the independent Republic" shall be the giving a preference to "the stern arbitrament of arms" over "accepting" from Her Majesty her peaceful "intervention at the eleventh hour of the day;" at Port Elizabeth, in the columns of the *Eastern Province Herald*, Sir Philip Wodehouse is unceremoniously dubbed "a confirmed negrophilist," in whose good intentions, where the interests of colonists and of natives are in antagonism, so little faith is placed," that even his gifts must cause distrust. Surely, this is hardly fair towards the Governor of the Cape of Good Hope, when it is recollected that the British Basuto Protectorate is not his *sole* act, but the solemn decision of Her Majesty's Ministers in Downing-street, about the time they were called upon to consider the bearing of the question of the then proposed withdrawal of the Queen's troops upon the cause of the aborigines and the general peace of South Africa as affecting the interests of this Colony; and perhaps also *after* the Emperor Napoleon had made some representation in behalf of "the deserving French missionaries who have so long laboured among the Basutos."

It is indeed gratifying to me to turn from these organs of public opinion in the West and East to the practical, sensible, and well-argued leading article of the *Argus* of this morning, from which, according to my usual bad habit, I must crave permission to transfer to your columns the annexed quotation :—

In two despatches addressed to Moshesh and Mr. Brand, Sir Philip communicated the decision of the British Government, and proposed an immediate cessation of hostilities, promising at the same time to come up as quickly as possible and arrange the boundary. Moshesh, as a matter of course, welcomed the intelligence, and sent a flag of truce to his enemies. Mr. Brand, however, did not at all relish the announcement, and naturally resolved to press his advantage, so that he might arrange the boundary on his own terms. He, moreover, expressed the opinion, in his reply to Sir Philip, that the proposed protectorate of Great Britain would not be of advantage to the Free State. This opinion it is hard to understand, unless upon the supposition that Mr. Brand fears the annexation of Basutoland will be followed by the surrender of the Free State, or that it will put a stop to the gradual encroachment of the Burghers upon the territory of their troublesome neighbours. We believe, however, that Mr. Brand is greatly mistaken. The Free State needs nothing just now so much as rest. The administration of justice and the adjustment of financial difficulties must be attended to, or the State will fall to pieces from sheer internal weakness. The British protectorate will train the Basutos to more orderly habits and teach them to respect the rights of their neighbours, while the Basutos will be safe from any aggressive spirit which may exist on the other side. Quietly folded in the mane of the British Lion, they will have leisure to cultivate one of the richest soils in South Africa. Before the war they supplied the Free State with its grain, and there is no reason why, if peace can be permanently established, a mutually beneficial trade should not spring up between the two countries.

Although I will not depart from the opinion, before expressed, that it behoves all those who are opposed to the so-called Responsible Government, not to thwart or to embarrass the execution of the policy of the Home Government, with whom rests the responsibility of the management of the native question, there cannot be any objection against suggestions being made in the columns of the press *in aid* of that policy being satisfactorily carried out by Her Majesty's Representative on the spot. Many will *now* think that there is a great deal in what you said the other day: "When a thing of this sort has to be done, it should be done at once," and that His Excellency would not go far wrong in taking your hint, and being "prompt in action" in this important matter. Unfortunately, the delay which has taken place in proclaiming, in a formal manner, the Basutos to be British subjects, has enabled the independent Free Republic rather to treat with scorn than otherwise the overtures of peace, which come *direct* from England, and this difficulty, which has been thrown in the way of Her Majesty's wish, that the din of war in South Africa should be at once hushed, appears, for the reasons above attempted to be explained, to meet with sympathy from some of Her Majesty's subjects within the Cape Colony, although at Natal the feeling of the people appears to be altogether on the side of the proposed British Basuto Protectorate, if the press there be a fair index of public opinion. I am also glad to observe that your special Graham's Town correspondent announces the pleasing fact that "the news about the annexation of the territory of Moshesh has given unqualified satisfaction there," and that, while he foresees that difficulties are likely to arise in the negotiations between Sir Philip Wodehouse, President Brand, and Moshesh, he hopes that the Parliament of the Cape will cordially co-operate with the views of the Imperial Government.

It would appear, from the annexed extract of the *Port Elizabeth Telegraph*, that it does not anticipate many "serious complications" in settling this question, but it is again most earnestly submitted that the idea of placing this Colony in any position approximate to one of hostility with our neighbours of the Free State ought to be most anxiously avoided:—

What the High Commissioner will most likely do is, to express in language that it will be impossible for his Honour to misconstrue, much less misunderstand, his regret that the latter should have rejected the counsel tendered by himself and the friendly advances of the Basuto Chieftain, and then hasten his departure for the North-east, and proceed with as little delay as possible straight to Thaba Bosigo, there to receive, on Her Majesty's behalf, her new subjects, and after having done that to demand of the belligerent burghers, in the Queen's name, an immediate cessation of hostilities, with the alternative, on refusal, of incurring Her Majesty's dire displeasure. The action taken by President Brand on the Basuto Chief's last request is calculated to retard rather than hasten a friendly solution of the questions now pending between their respective peoples; and unless the forthcoming meeting of the Volksraad takes a more enlightened view of the situation than the Executive appears to have done, we fear it will be necessary for Her Majesty's High Commissioner to add physical to moral suasion, in order to enforce compliance with His Excellency's wishes in reference to the cessation of hostilities over the Orange River.

Tuesday, 18th February, 1868.　　　　　　　　　　　　COLONIST.

PRESIDENT BRAND'S REPLY TO THE QUEEN'S REPRESENTATIVE.

SIR,—Not fully sympathising with those who, after the satisfactory evidence to the contrary, still doubt the good intentions of the Home Government towards the Cape of Good Hope, and are so ungrateful as to look upon the peaceful "intervention of His Excellency in the Queen's name as ungenerous and unjust in the extreme," I have declined to join the *Zuid-Afrikaan* and the *Advertiser and Mail* in their warm encomiums of the "independent" reply of the President of the Republic of the Orange Free State, and I now desire, through the medium of your columns, to show that my ideas on this subject, if not sound, are, at least, not singular.

The *Great Eastern* concludes a practically sensible leading article, the purport of which may be said to be the well-meant endeavour, before it is too late, of urging upon the Cape Colony to prevent not only Basutoland, but also the Free State, being annexed to Natal, whereby it would lose the advantage of the Imperial expenditure consequent on the Basutos becoming British subjects, as well as the trade of the two countries converted into British territory, with the subjoined clear opinion, clothed in the editor's characteristic language:—

Mr. President Brand's letter to the Governor is full of bounce and bluster. His Honour's history of the war exhibits the colour of the President's mind. He turns fiction into fact, and thinks that "tall talk" will frighten Sir Philip and the Queen's Government. It is no doubt painful to him and to his friends to feel that they are not to be allowed to disturb the peace and tranquillity of the country any longer, and that they are not to defy their colonist creditors by keeping their law courts closed. But the best, the most intelligent, and honest men of the Free State have long asked to have the Royal Standard of England planted over that of the Republic. The day upon which the Free State is re-annexed to the British nation, whether it be a part of this Colony or Natal, will be a day of great rejoicing at Bloemfontein, and wherever in the State good and true men are to be found.

I have also ventured to express regret that the President did not comply with the reasonable request of Sir Philip Wodehouse, and at once suspend hostilities, on the ground that if the origin of the war were just, the Free State could not hope to improve its position, when the time arrived for entering into negotiations with Great Britain's representative, by continuing the fight and conquering anew the territory which had been ceded by Moshesh at the termination of the last war.

It seems to me that the line of argument I have adopted is not inconsistent with that of the *Graham's Town Journal*, conveyed by the annexed extract from its temperate and closely reasoned leader on " Mr. Brand's reply" :—

The greater part of it is taken up with a narrative of the rise and progress of the war, and may be dismissed with brief comment. The course of the narrative shows that the war, as far as the State is concerned, is a just war, that it was undertaken to enforce the treaty of April, 1866, which Moshesh had violated, and avenge the murder of two subjects of the State, and that it is now being carried on with vigour and a prospect of success. The object of this statement is to prove that the proposed interference of the British Government is not justified by anything the State has done in going to war, or by anything it has failed to do in commanding the probabilities of peace. Against the first position we have nothing to say. In our judgment the war was not to be avoided by the Free State. As to the probabilities of peace, we are in great doubt. Of late the commandoes have done something; the affair at Tanjesberg is a notable achievement. But what evidence is there that the Basutos are being thoroughly subdued? If by peace is meant another treaty with Moshesh, no doubt that sort of thing could have been secured long ago. But that has been proved to be but a mockery and a sham. The only question worth asking is, whether the Free State can command an enduring peace. And we confess that we see no likelihood of its doing so in the next dozen or twenty years. Putting British interference out of sight, the probabilities are that a peace between the Burghers and the Basutos this year would stumble into a war the next, and that this see-saw of truce-making and truce-breaking would go on just long enough to exhaust the Free State of its wealth, and force it into habits of turbulence and national immorality. It is because we think so,.that we support the annexation of Basutoland, believing it to be the best chance— excepting its own annexation—the Free State has of a return to quiet and industry.

The *Friend of the Free State*, which, as being on the spot, ought to be a good authority, does not appear to differ much from the *Graham's Town Journal* as to the prospect of a lasting peace between the Boers and the Basutos, if left to themselves to fight it out, and apparently contradicts the sanguine anticipation of President Brand, " that the object of the war is nearly accomplished, and that the arms of the Free State will, under God's blessing, be everywhere successful," when it writes as follows :—

It is true that rather cheering progress has of late been made with the war. But the commandoes now once more appear to be at a stand-still. The Upper, or Joubert's, division has done little or nothing since the taking of Marakabi's stronghold on the 21st and 22nd ult.; beyond sending out a fruitless patrol of 600 men, who looked at the Caledon, found it full, shot one stray Basuto, and returned to the camp. The combined Smithfield division did a splendid day's work on the 28th ult., when it captured the

Taujesberg, one of the strongest natural fortresses in Basutoland; but unless it move on quickly, and take Kieme, the little advantage we have gained will soon be thrown away. Could we but believe that the Basutos would be entirely subdued in three months—as some of our friends pretend to do—we should deprecate the interference of Sir P. Wodehouse as much as they; but we cannot forget the vexatious delays and disappointments of the past three years. We could, undoubtedly, in course of time, take all the strongholds of the Basutos, but even then we should not have destroyed the people; and when our commandoos returned to within the old boundaries of the State, the Basutos would follow them, take up their old places of residence, and again prey upon our flocks and herds.

While the *Zuid-Afrikaan* regrets that the President of the Orange Free State should have erred in not more decidedly vindicating his *læsa majestas*, it will strike very many that the *Graham's Town Journal* takes a much more practical and common sense view of the matter in the annexed passage:—

Now, independence and self-respect are excellent qualities, and a President of a State as insignificant as is the one Mr. Brand represents, is entitled to possess them and also to exhibit them, even when in diplomatic communication with the representative of Her Britannic Majesty. But it is not independence and self-respect which we see in this part of Mr. Brand's reply. We do not like to say that we see in it the vulgar quality of impudence. But we may freely say that the common courtesy of diplomatic intercourse is conspicuous by its absence. Mr. Brand does not even regret that he cannot consider His Excellency's suggestions. Probably his Honour thinks that the elected chief of a republic should studiously avoid the good manners which may be all very well for the representatives of monarchies and monarchs. Mr. Brand ought to be a good judge of his position, and he may see it to be his policy to press the war; but policy is many-sided, and he should have paid some regard to the impression the language and temper of his despatch would be likely to have on his correspondent, who is not only Sir Philip Wodehouse, but, in this case, the representative of no small Power, whose suggestions may have something behind them, and are at all events worth notice.

This able journal also seems to me most triumphantly to answer the insinuation of Mr. Brand, that the present interference of Her Majesty's Government is inconsistent with the Convention of 1854 and "His Excellency's letter of the 20th of January, 1866;" but I shall spoil the argument if I attempt to paraphrase it, so I will give your readers the whole of its conclusion on this point:—

From this it would seem as if Mr. Brand considers that it is unalterably due to the Free State that its relations to tribes over the Orange should not, according to Article 2, be meddled with in any way by the British Government; and it looks also as if he thought that in 1866 Sir Philip took that view of the subject. Whereas the facts are that in 1866 the High Commissioner exercised his judgment as to whether that was a proper time to interpose, and decided that it was not; but now, in 1867, exercising his judgment again, and being expressly instructed to do so by the Home authorities, he decides that it is the proper time, and is perfectly consistent with himself in doing so. In 1866 His Excellency did not foresee another war in 1867—another war, "injurious and prejudicial" to the Free State, and to all South Africa. This he sees only too clearly in 1868, and as this alternation of war and peace threatens to become chronic, he steps in, or rather the Imperial Government steps in, and acts in accordance with, and not contrary to the Convention in 1854, or the spirit of the letter of 1866

So much for the reply of the worthy President, to which, in my opinion, the able and amusing editor of Graham's Town, far less conversant with diplomatic correspondence than Sir Philip Wodehouse, has given a satisfactory rejoinder; so the difficulty suggested by the *Advertiser and Mail* with respect to the embarrassing situation of His Excellency has already vanished into thin air. That I was not very wrong in attempting to account for the sympathy, on the part of the Cape Colonists, with the prolongation of the war, by the antagonism of feeling between the two races, may be gathered from a special correspondent of the *Great Eastern*, who writes thus :—

It is the opinion of many that the treaty of peace will have to be baptised in bloo l, before it is accepted by the Free State. Every person from the Free State agrees in saying that the burghers are now so distributed that they are careless as regards the future of the country or themselves, provided they obtain bitter and minute punishment of the marauders of Basutoland. A very fair index to the feelings of these people may be gathered from the savage act perpetrated at Klokonani, where the whites not only slew the Kafirs, but went to the extra trouble of hurling them over the rocks, for which act I invoke the deepest utterance of contempt that the human heart is capable of expressing on the base-hearted scoundrels who soiled their dirty hands with an act calculated to lower the *prestige* of our race in South Africa. Why, for pity's sake, does not the *Friend* suppress such revolting details, which are enough to stamp with infamy the whole nation !

The *Fort Beaufort Advocate*, from which I usually quote with pleasure, appears to me for once to be on the wrong side, when it says :—

We repeat, we entirely sympathise with the weaker power in this instance; and unless the British Government is prepared to carry out its new policy to a much greater extent than is indicated in His Excellency's despatch, and extend the protection equally over the State from whose hands it intends to strike the sword, it will act most unjustly, inflict a blow on the peace of South Africa which will ultimately redound to its dishonour, and to the ruin of the whole country. The reply of President Brand to the Governor's despatch is temperate and respectful, but firm. The President puts his case argumentatively, and like a lawyer " shows cause" why he should not, under the circumstances, abrogate the trust reposed in him by the people at the most critical moment of his administration, and give his unqualified adhesion to the course urged upon him by the Governor.

The fallacy of this reasoning, which is shared in by the *Eastern Province Herald* and some other Frontier newspapers, seems founded on the assumption that the Queen of England's protection of Moshesh and his tribe does not impose upon Her Majesty, which it clearly does, the responsibility of preventing her *new* subjects from annoying their neighbours, an *independent* nation, in terms of friendly alliance with Great Britain.

The *Great Eastern* properly remarks :—" It is very annoying to hear such questions raised as, shall we have to pay for protecting the Basuto border, and if so, what will it cost?" The idea that perhaps the expense of any new arrangements may be " shuffled off from the British Government on to the Colonists" makes the proposed British Basuto Protectorate less popular than it ought to be, but surely this fear is groundless now that Her Majesty has resolved to retain her troops in South Africa, and the Governor would do well in the present juncture to publish, for the benefit of those so deeply interested in the question, the despatch of the Duke of Buckingham, in reply to the Parliamentary resolutions which he so strenuously supported. Although it is said that the "Hollanders" resident in the Orange Free State are "very angry at the interference of the British," it is probable that the majority of the people of that State will see the advantage of having for their neighbours British subjects instead of savages, over whom their chiefs can exercise no sufficient control, and it is earnestly to be hoped that the President and Volksraad may yet, after calm deliberation, see fit to restrain for a while the fierce bloodhounds of war, and, in common with Moshesh, welcome the arrival of the Queen's High Commissioner, when he comes to enter into amicable negotiations for the purpose " of restoring and maintaining general peace" in South Africa, at the same time that he is prepared to give the fullest consideration to the just claims of the Free State, without of course infringing the rights of Her Majesty's new subjects, the Basutos.

February 22.   COLONIST.

HER MAJESTY'S HIGH COMMISSIONER AND THE FREE STATE.

"Sic volo, sic jubeo, stet pro ratione voluntas."

SIR,—It is vain to attempt to deny the fact that the laudable desire of the Queen's Government to restore peace to South Africa is not duly appreciated by all Her Majesty's subjects at the Cape of Good Hope, and that there unfortunately exists an opinion, both within this Colony and the Orange Free State, that "the British interference in the Basuto question" is ill-timed, as likely to prevent the belligerent Burghers from inflicting on their savage foes condign punishment. If there be any reasonable prospect that, by April next, when the Queen's representative is formally to declare Basutoland British territory, all the strongholds of Moshesh will have yielded to the conquering arms of President Brand, and the Basuto tribe materially reduced in numbers, I can understand the argument of the Free Staters, who naturally enough wish to retaliate on those from whose aggressions on their property they have so seriously suffered, and who have no great faith in the power of the Colonial Government to restrain "its own native tribes from stealing," or in the probability that it will "succeed better with the Basutos."

I confess, however, that I incline to the opinion of the *Friend of the Free State*, that a lasting peace is not so close at hand as is anticipated, if the Boers and Basutos are left to fight it out by themselves, and that it would be better for the Free State in future, in the case of stolen property, to have to look "for redress to the British Government" rather than "to the different Basuto chieftains." Many also, who reflect upon the subject, will "indulge in the hope that the annexation of Basutoland may be the thin end of the wedge, and lead to the incorporation of the whole country" with the British Colonial Empire. No doubt it may be argued that the addition of Basutoland to Natal or the Cape is "clearly a reversal of the former policy of Great Britain, and shows a complete change in those who direct the councils of the State," but in a colonial point of view, is it the worse for that? It is true that the able editor of the *Advertiser and Mail*, who, it is to be regretted, has not espoused the cause of the British Basuto Protectorate, in a leading article written for transmission to England by the last mail steamer, condemns the step about to be taken with respect to Basutoland, as inconsistent "with the policy for years past of Her Majesty's Government, to check the extension of British dominions in this country, as well as in all parts of the world," and very properly gives, as instances, the "abandonment of the Orange River Sovereignty," and, to use the words of a Frontier newspaper, "the giving up of the Transkeian territory to hordes of barbarians, whilst it was refused to Colonial farmers." But, instead of quarrelling with the want of consistency in the Home Government, does not the *Natal Mercury* more ably and earnestly advocate the interests of both the Colonies of the Cape of Good Hope and Natal, as well as the cause of the aboriginal tribes of South Africa when it writes as follows?—

The time is nigh when Great Britain must awake to the full sense of her mission on these shores. During the long reign of Palmerstonian principles, no proposal involving any enlargement of territory had the slightest chance of a hearing. Non-intervention and non-annexation were inflexible rules of policy. But the present Ministry appear to take a broader view of national responsibilities, and to understand more fully the great practical truth that national prestige is necessary to sustain commercial greatness. Non-annexation may be the means of necessitating active intervention. England has constituted herself the ruling power in South Africa, and she cannot afford to shirk any of the obligations thus assumed. She acquired the Cape by conquest. She established herself in the Eastern Province by military occupation. She took possession of Natal for Imperial purposes, and for the protection of the native tribes, and the Queen's subjects then resident there. She became the mistress of what was then the Sovereignty with the same ends in view. The abandonment of that country was, equally with its acquisition, an act of the Imperial choice, and was done in the teeth of the engagements entered into with, and the strong wishes of, the inhabitants. Since the Sovereignty was transformed into the Free State, constant strife, trouble, and disorder have prevailed there, and its relations with the Basutos have been a source of endless perplexity to the High Commissioner. The sooner that false step is retraced the better it will be for England. If the Home Government wishes to avoid future complications, it will act wisely to help South-Africa, as it has helped Canada. There, through the intervention and good offices of the Ministerial representatives, a group of independent States have been compacted into one grand and strong dominion. There the mother land has done her best to build up an empire, whose strength lies in its coherence and its unity. Before the Queen's possessions on this continent are placed in a position where they may be truly independent of Imperial aid, and cease to be any drain upon the Imperial exchequer, a similar binding process will have to be gone through. Governed by the same people, and under one common Sovereign, and according to the same general principles, the different States and Provinces of South Africa would be strong enough to put down all internal danger, and to resist all probable external aggression. Governed by different peoples, and owning no uniformity of plan, policy, or rule, the same territories will be a continued thorn in the Imperial side. Believing, as we do, that the Basuto will prove as manageable under British rule as our natives are, perhaps more so, we shall be glad—most glad—to hear the flying rumour confirmed ("that the English Government intend to yield to the wishes of the Basuto people, and accept them as subjects of the Crown").

I cannot conclude without expressing a hope that there is no truth in what the *Eastern Province Herald* has termed "a marked expression of sympathy with the Basutos," viz., "that the Governor has prohibited the transmission of all munitions of war from this Colony to the Free State." Although it is much to be regretted that the President and Volksraad have not lent a willing ear to the good advice of Her Majesty's High Commissioner, to stay the ruthless hand of war until the terms of a lasting peace can be satisfactorily arranged, very many in the Colony, who warmly approve of the British Basuto Protectorate, will be disposed to agree with the *Eastern Province Herald* that "the step (of ' serving out the Free State') is calculated to still further complicate the difficulty of arranging border affairs with the Free State Government." Even if it can be shown that the express terms of the Convention with Sir George Clerk, which have escaped my memory, are not infringed by the stoppage of the supply of gunpowder, &c., this decisive act on the part of Sir Philip Wodehouse would increase the number of sympathizers in this Colony with their brethren across the Orange River. No doubt it may be fairly argued, on the side of His Excellency, that the anxiously expressed wish of our Sovereign, that deadly war should cease in South Africa, cannot be allowed to be treated as a dead letter; but a little diplomacy may yet produce the desired effect, without incurring the risk of needlessly exciting the antagonism of feeling between the two distinct races in the Colony.

The Volksraad may not perhaps be easily convinced by reason, now that their feelings appear to have been excited, but I venture to throw out an idea that the immediate application of the rule,

"Sic volo, sic jubeo, stet pro ratione voluntas,"

will not facilitate the satisfactory carrying out of the wise resolution of Her Majesty's Government with respect to the "restoration and maintenance of the general peace" of South Africa.

February 25, 1868. COLONIST.

HER MAJESTY'S HIGH COMMISSIONER AND THE FREE STATE.

SIR,—You must allow me to take the earliest opportunity of referring to an error, unintentionally committed by your printer, in prefixing to my last letter the line from Virgil quoted at its conclusion. In that position it is inconsistent with the spirit and general tenor of my remarks. I never for one instant dreamt that the will of the Queen of Great Britain and Ireland, that bloody war should cease to rage in South Africa, should not be implicitly obeyed by the Cape Colonists. Without stopping to argue the point, all I intended was to convey a gentle hint, with the best motives, in the hope that it might reach high places, where a little reasoning with the President and Volksraad on the spot might be more efficacious in satisfactorily carrying out the peaceful policy of Her Majesty's Government, than the exercise of stern authority at a distance.

The *Graham's Town Journal* just received so completely expresses my views on this question, that I must beg permission to borrow its language :—

The Resident Magistrate at Port Elizabeth has received instructions to refuse permits for the despatch of arms and ammunition to the Free State. We do not greatly admire this. Its effect will be to exasperate the Boers, and incline them to use vigorously the powder and shot they have. Moreover, this sort of thing increases the sympathy of the colonists with the Free Staters. It would be far wiser for the Governor to declare at once that Basutoland is now part of the British dominions, and commence negotiations with the States' Government. His Excellency i- staying too long at Cape Town, while events at the scene of action are doing anything but waiting upon his will.

Although doubtless there is a great deal in the argument of the *Advertiser and Mail*, that, until His Excellency has proclaimed the Basutos British subjects, the laws of neutrality with respect to the Free State, at least, ought to prevail, it is diffidently submitted that the force of such argument is weakened by the rather strong language used in the following paragraph :—

This, however, we take leave to consider as a mere sham ; and whether the transmission of supplies is actually stopped or not, the intervention by His Excellency in the affair, even to the extent he has intervened, is alike mischievous and unjustifiable.

It may be "mischievous" for the reasons so clearly set forth by the *Graham's Town Journal*, but it can hardly be fairly termed altogether "unjustifiable" after the formal rejection by the Free Republic of the friendly advice of the representative of Her Majesty's Government, that hostilities should be suspended. Suppose, but only for the sake of the argument, that President Brand, under an earnest conviction that the blessing of Providence attended his successful arms, and that nothing short of the total annihilation of Moshesh and his tribe would satiate the vengeance of the belligerent burghers, now flushed by the great victory of Tanjesberg and the death of Bushuli, should give an unlimited order for ammunition and fire-arms with the view of protracting the war to a distant period, is Her Majesty's High Commissioner, after having written " Great Chief,—It gives me much pleasure to be enabled to inform you that Her Majesty the Queen has been graciously pleased to accede to your request, so frequently made by you, that you and your tribe should be received subjects of the British Throne," quietly to permit the deadly weapons of war free transmission from Port Elizabeth to the territory north of the Orange River, and destroy for ever in the minds of the aboriginal tribes of South Africa the *prestige* of Great Britain ?

If it be true, in the words of the *Graham's Town Journal*, " that the despatch from Moshesh, which His Excellency by this time has received, contains the formal cession of Basutoland to Great Britain, and places the responsibilities of possession and rule in the hands of Her Majesty's Representative, and that it is indeed likely that the British flag now waves over Moshesh's mountain," all real friends of this Colony and the Free State will anxiously hope that the peaceful overtures of Sir Philip Wodehouse will yet receive a favourable response from the Volksraad, after calm deliberation upon all the advantages likely to accrue to the Orange River Free State from the British Basuto Protectorate.

In thanking the editor of the *Zuid-Afrikaan* for his fair notice of my letters, I rejoice to find that " he verily believes that a large section of the Orange Free State would hail the day that they were again incorporated with the British Empire." He must, however, forgive me for remarking that it is hardly just towards me to insinuate that I wish the extension of British rule, to what was once the Sovereignty, to be effected "*vi et armis*." I have always maintained that the union with the British Empire, so far from being " compulsory," must be voluntary, and that the request for such union ought to originate within the Free State, and that the abandoned subjects of Her Majesty have no chance to be placed in the same position with Moshesh, unless they follow his example and implore Her Majesty to grant them the protection of the British flag.

While, on the one side, it is distressing to learn that a petition to the Volksraad is being numerously signed, praying for the repudiation of debts, the further issue of bluebacks, and the denial of justice by the Colony of the Courts of Law, it is, on the other side, most gratifying to be informed that an appeal is to be made to Her Majesty's High Commissioner, by very many of the inhabitants of the Orange River Free State, to use his influence with the Home Government to bring about, if not annexation to this Colony or Natal, at least the establishment of British rule, by federation or otherwise, in the territory now governed by a Free Republic.

February 28th. COLONIST.

THE BASUTO QUESTION.

NEW VERSION.

The '*Tizer* quoted Wicqueful,
And Puffendorf and Grotius,
  And proved from Vattel,
  Exceedingly well,
Such a deed would be atrocious.

'Twould move a Free Stater's bowels
To read the doubts he scribbled,
  But Sir Philip did
  As he was bid,
And squashed *them* while *he* scribbled.
—The *Cape Argus*.

SIR,—Without for a moment disputing the principle enunciated by the *Advertiser and Mail*, that, according to the law of nations, "honour and justice demand that, feeble though the Free State may be, its rights should be regarded not less sacredly than if it were the great American Republic, or the French Empire itself," I venture to think that, after your legal comments on the express words of the Articles of Convention of Sir George Clerk, which you quote, many will incline to the opinion that your able contemporary, doubtless with the best intentions, has painted in too vivid colours the grievous wrong about to be committed by the Governor's vigilance with respect to the permits of the transmission of "the supplies of ammunition" from Port Elizabeth to the northward of the Orange River. The spirit of the course of legislation for several years past in this Colony has been to make, subject to the restraint of the Executive power, the free trade and traffic in gunpowder and fire-arms, for, as you clearly have pointed out, the discretion vested in the Resident Magistrate or Justice of the Peace is not likely to be exercised in opposition to the positive directions of the Governor: and a moment's reflection seems to lead to the conclusion that, in a case of emergency, it is quite right that it should be so. For the sake of illustration, suppose the Governor, who has the best means of information, to be aware that there exists a conspiracy among the Tambookies, and that they are intent upon hoarding gunpowder with an evil design, would he not be justified in issuing a circular to the magistrates that no gunpowder should be sold to one of that peaceful tribe? Again put the extravagant hypothesis of certain European traders continuing abundantly to supply the Kafirs in the Transkeian territory with arms and ammunition, when there was evidence that the intentions of Kreli towards the Colony were hostile, would not the intervention of His Excellency to prevent such persons persisting in the dangerous traffic be just and commendable ?

A thoughtful and able correspondent of the *Great Eastern*, writing from Aliwal North, concludes a letter, which in strong terms denounces the alleged "contemptible trickery of advocating repudiation and the onslaught of the Kafirs in order to render the Free State subject to colonial laws," with the following passage :—

There is no doubt that we cannot allow the Boers to exterminate the Basutos, nor allow the latter to overcome the Boers; and the only safe method to avoid all future wars between them is to take away their power to kill each other. The Boers, according to information received, are carrying on the destruction of crops with the most assiduous perseverance, and with a determination to impoverish the country as much as possible.

Her Britannic Majesty's High Commissioner has informed President Brand that the "Power" he represents is "actuated by the most friendly feelings towards the Free State," and has assured him that "Her Majesty's Government have contemplated with great concern the prolonged hostilities that have prevailed between the State and the Basutos," and "without the slightest view to the political aggrandisement of the colonies, or to any other result from their interference than the restoration and maintenance of general peace" in South Africa. Moshesh has laid down his arms—waves the white flag, and cries for peace ; and, after all, is not the checking the supply of the deadly weapons of war beyond the Orange River one practical mode of staying further bloodshed ?

There seems to be a great deal in the argument tersely conveyed by the concluding sentences of your leading article of this morning :—

The legislation on the subject (the trade in gunpowder, &c.) has been with a view to preserve peace in South Africa. Sir Philip Wodehouse has declared his intention to secure peace, and he has taken the means which seem to him the most effectual to that end. Whether his views are correct is another matter.

Many who hail with delight the new and enlarged colonial policy of Her Majesty's present advisers, foreshadowed by the British Basuto Protectorate, will regret that the delay which has occurred in proclaiming the Basutos British subjects, has afforded to the President of the Orange Free State the opportunity of treating with apparent scorn the overtures of peace which emanated from Great Britain ; and at the same time has enabled the Cape colonists, whose sympathies, as fellow-sufferers from the aggressions of native tribes, have always been naturally enough on the side of the Free State, to express approval of the determination to expose for a month or two longer the Basutos to the just vengeance of the Burghers, now that they have gained "an indisputable ascendancy" over their sable enemies. I have always endeavoured to show that the putting into summary execution "the Imperial mandate to stay the wretched warfare" between the Boers and the Basutos, would be beneficial alike to the interests of the Free State and of this Colony, and I most gladly call in aid of my own feeble arguments the annexed extract from that able journal, the *King William's Town Gazette*, from which I always quote with pleasure, whenever I have the opportunity :—

The Free State war, which is to be so abruptly concluded, was of a nature the most inimical to our native policy. Each reverse that the Boers received—and we maintain that they *did* receive reverses, their tremendous victories notwithstanding—more than effaced a colonial enactment for the governance of the natives. It gave to the natives exactly what they require to make good warriors—it gave them pluck. . . . To reduce all our arguments to a little sentence : the Free State war was making the white man look ridiculous. This sort of thing would not pay the colonists, although the closing of the courts and the repudiation of debts suited the Free State book admirably. If it were for this reason alone, we should welcome with pleasure the plan of annexing Basutoland. Not that this is the great desideratum. We are only regarding it as the first approach to the annexation of the Free State. To the colonists who have been so complaisant as to permit the Staters to get into their books, this notion will be peculiarly acceptable. If we know that a man is insolvent, if there is a certainty that the most judicious arrangement of the estate will not result in a dividend that will pay the expenses of winding up, we yet like to get the books into our hands, and investigate the actual returns of receipts and disbursements. Although Sir George Clerk obligingly set the Free State on its legs, by granting it independence, he did not destroy its actual reliance upon the Colony from which it was peopled. It was the old story of parent and son—threats of a summary disposition of property, leaving but one coin to the expectant heir—and yet a liberal allowance made. Since its establishment as a Republic, the Free State has been living upon the paternal curse, although apparently absolved from all connection. This being the case, we claim to have some voice in its affairs. If two or three journeymen carpenters get out of work and initiate a war, it is their concern that they do not get their bones broken ; but it is our look-out that they shall not imperil the funds entrusted to them for a far different purpose. If they warred properly, beat their adversaries, and made money out of the transaction, we should have no objection to their indulging their bellicose propensities; but when they only disgrace their colour by their conduct of squabbles, and rob their creditors under the pretence that they are effecting wonders, then it is time that more enlightened people should control them.

While the *Advertiser and Mail* cannot be accused of being backward in showing sincere sympathy with our neighbours of the Free State, it very properly stigmatizes " the fulsome and pot-valiant address to the President from the district of Winburg, requesting His Honour again to become a candidate for the presidency, and assuring him that they in such case are prepared to stand by him, and defend their rights with their lives, even to the taking up of arms against a 'foreign power,' if need be ;" and, in common with the *Friend of the Free State*, strongly condemns " a further and unlimited supply of bluebacks to *assist* the public," and the dishonest and wicked proposal of " closing the civil courts for seven or ten years for Free State debts, and the entire repudiation of all colonial ones ;" it appears no very easy matter to decide which is the more absurdly ludicrous idea of the two—that of, in the language of the editor of the Free State *Friend,* " stirring up the unsophisticated farmers to cross bayonets (if need be) with the British infantry," or that of the repudiation of debts and denial of justice to civil suitors.

The special Cape Town correspondent of the *Port Elizabeth Telegraph* finds fault with what he calls the "disreputable *modus operandi* used to accomplish" the British Basuto Protectorate ; but, if it be the "thin end of the wedge" for the annexation of the Orange Free State to the British Colonial Empire, many will not join in the unmeasured abuse of Sir Philip Wodehouse " as a scheming autocrat or despot," but, on the contrary, will award to him his just meed of praise for having been instrumental in promoting the welfare and progress both of this Colony and the Free State. Surely, the popular avowal of such silly and dangerous doctrines as those above referred to within the Orange Free State is evidence of its misgovernment, and it does not require much argument to prove that the extension of British rule to that State would be attended with advantage to all parties concerned—the Free-Staters themselves, the colonists of the Cape and Natal, and, last not least, the aboriginal tribes ; and it behoves the press of South Africa to labour with its moral influence speedily to bring about this " great desideratum." Under all the circumstances then of this case, it is cheering to find that the belief with respect to the wish of the Orange Free State to " be incorporated with the British Empire," of the *Zuid-Afrikaan*, an influential organ of the opinions of the inhabitants of Dutch descent in the West, to which allusion was made in my last letter, is corroborated by the report in the columns of the *Great Eastern*, which consistently advocates the cause of the Basutos, " that the annexation of the Free State is the popular cry of the day among both the English and Dutch."

It is to be expected, as the *Friend*, writing from Bloemfontein says, "that fierce denunciations of Sir Philip and his policy will be heard in the Council Chamber, and that it will be assuredly maintained by some that he is the *schuld van alles ;*" but perhaps, after a natural ebullition of feeling, the President may yet be empowered by the Volksraad to meet Her Majesty's High Commissioner in April next, in a truly amicable spirit, for the purpose of discussing the "just claims of the Free State," so long as it remains an "independent" Republic, to the favourable consideration of Great Britain, and at the same time of preparing the way of uniting, by some system of annexation or federation, the colonies of the Cape and Natal with the Orange Free State and Basutoland, as dominions of the British Crown under the protection of the British flag.

Saturday, 20th February, 1869.   COLONIST.

P.S.—It is often much easier to censure the mode in which a particular policy has been carried out, than to devise a practical substitute for what has been done. Perhaps, without sufficient consideration, I presumed, with no bad motive, to venture an opinion that the declaration of the Basutos as British subjects ought to have been simultaneous with the commencement of the negotiations with the Free State; but it has occurred to me that His Excellency may be able satisfactorily to explain that, before the future boundaries of Basutoland are settled, he cannot formally proclaim the proper limits of the *new* British territory, and that the interests of Her Majesty's *old* subjects of the Cape of Good Hope and Natal may be seriously affected if Her *new* subjects, the Basutos, have not sufficient land whereon to live. It is said that the Governor is very soon to hurry over the Karroo to the scene of the negotiations with President Brand, for the purpose of finally carrying out the good intentions of Her Majesty's Government, and it is earnestly to be hoped that, notwithstanding the difficulties which beset his mission of future peace to South Africa, the efforts of Sir Philip Wodehouse will be crowned with success.

THE BASUTO QUESTION.

SIR,—Although you " imagine that the public are becoming pretty well tired" of the Basuto question, I cannot help thinking that, after your truly practical comments of this morning, it will be a matter of regret with very many of your readers that you do not more frequently, in your editorial column, discuss this important and interesting subject. It seems to me that few will be found to differ from you, that President Brand erred when, in his reply to Sir Philip Wodehouse, he apparently relied upon the opinion " that the proposed annexation of Basutoland was a breach of Sir George Clerk's convention with the Free State," the express words of which, as bearing upon this point, I must be permitted to quote :—

Article 2.—The British Government has no alliance whatever with any native tribes or chiefs to the northward of the Orange River, with the exception of the Griqua Chief, Captain Adam Kok, and Her Majesty's Government has no wish or intention to enter into any treaties *which may be injurious or prejudicial to the interests of the Orange River Government.*

In a former letter, I transferred into your columns the able arguments of the *Graham's Town Journal*, with a view of showing that there was no valid ground for the President's remark, that the communication of Governor Wodehouse, " that Moshesh and his tribe were in all probability to become subjects of the British Crown," had taken him by surprise. Whatever may have been the misgivings of the authorities of the Free State with respect to the good intentions of Sir Philip Wodehouse, they ought certainly to be removed by the conciliatory rejoinder of Her Majesty's High Commissioner, to what you do not inappropriately term " Mr. Brand's attempt to snub him." If the version of this despatch of the Governor given by the *Friend of the Free State*, received by yesterday's mail from the frontier, be correct, it will indeed, " although no threat is held out, be rather a delicate and difficult matter for His Honour longer to continue the war."

What could Sir Philip Wodehouse have said more than to " have assured the President that he wished to act fairly by the Free State, that in future Moshesh would have no voice in the matter, that all questions and disputes would be settled between the British Government and the Free State; but that His Excellency foresaw difficulties in the way, should the Basutos be cooped or penned up within too narrow limits, so that the tribe had not sufficient land on which to live with their families" ? However much many who are anxious, to see the humane policy of Her Majesty's Ministers with respect to the Basutos satisfactorily carried out, may regret that Sir Philip Wodehouse, placing too great reliance on the strength of his argument " with Mr. President Brand to stop the war which can lead to no good end," should not sooner have held the proposed conference at Burghersdorp with the representative of the Free State and the Chief Moshesh, it must be conceded to him that reason and justice are on the side of his argument, and that it could hardly have been expected that his overtures of peace should have been received in the way they have been. I may not be quite accurate in my dates, but I think it will be found that the great victory of Tanjesberg, which certainly was more decided than the usual battles of the Burghers, has had something to do with the opposition on their part to allow arms to yield to the negotiations for peace.

It is in vain, however, to attempt to conceal the fact that censure is freely bestowed on the delay which has taken place in the formal declaration of the Basutos as British subjects, particularly as they are likely to suffer from it, if it be true that " Moshesh will not permit his people to fight any more till he has seen or heard further from Sir Philip Wodehouse." As evidence *both* of the general feeling *against* the course pursued by the Governor, and *in favour* of my view of the case in his justification, I cannot refrain from quoting the opinion of a gentleman of learning and ability, as well. as great local experience on the frontier, who is a " born Colonist :"—

The Basuto difficulty becomes a very complicated affair. John Brand, if he studies the interests of the people he governs, should at once stop his guerilla warfare. He will find it more difficult to make civilians of his Boers than it will be for the Governor to make loyal subjects of the Basutos; *but the sooner His Excellency is on the spot the better.*

That Sir Philip Wodehouse is evidently intent upon acting fairly by the Free State may be gathered from the annexed paragraph from the *Friend* of the 21st February, which certainly does not appear to be a bad way of compromising a difficult matter :—

THE BASUTO LINE.—We hear that a gentleman recently from Aliwal North has learnt that Sir P. Wodehouse purposes declaring the old line to be *the* line of the Free State; but that the farms already disposed of, or granted in the so-called conquered territory, will still be held by the purchasers or grantees—but under British titles, and under the same conditions of occupation as previously; the purchase money owing and still unpaid on the said farms to go to the Free State Government as compensation for the expenses of the war. This, if true, seems to be rather an equitable arrangement. The purchasers and grantees, we are convinced, for the most part, would not object to accept British titles to their land.

I had written thus far when your telegrams from Burghersdorp and King William's Town, of the wonderful successes of the burghers, rather startled me. They may be exaggerated, and seem a little inconsistent with the subjoined statement of the *Friend* :—" But few Basutos, it is rumoured, will be found in the Teimie, and the cattle are said to be removed from thence to the Double Mountains," but they must have some foundation to rest upon. The " serious complications" you anticipated appear to have arrived, and the result may perhaps be the annexation of Basutoland to the Republic of the Orange Free State, rather than to the British Colonial Empire. If this be so, it is to be feared that the remnant of the tribe of Moshesh will fare badly, and the prestige of Great Britain in protecting the cause of the aborigines, and in checking their hostile propensities towards the British Colonies in South Africa, will have received a shock. In the absence of precise information it is vain to indulge in speculations, but there can be no harm in expressing the hope that the conference at Burghersdorp may yet be attended with beneficial results to all parties concerned—the Cape, Natal, the Free State, and the Basutos. Perhaps *now* even Natal may fail in gaining the prize of Basutoland, which by right of conquest will belong to the independent nation of the Free State, or otherwise I would put in a claim on behalf of the Cape of Good Hope for this slice of new territory, if annexation was not so unpopular in Cape Town, because I feel disposed to agree with the *Graham's Town Journal*, that there are many good reasons why the land of Moshesh and his tribe should be annexed to this Colony instead of to Natal.

Tuesday, March 3.   COLONIST.

THE REPUDIATION OF DEBT BY THE FREE STATE.

SIR,—In the leading article of your Second Edition, published yesterday for transmission to England per mail-steamer *Norseman*, you correctly argue that the great " successes on the part of the Free State, in its struggle with the Basutos, are likely seriously to embarrass the negotiations which the Governor has signified his intention to open ;" and who can tell but that they

II

may ultimately end in the abandonment of the humane policy of Her Majesty's Government, and in the strangling in its birth of the British Basuto Protectorate? It is true that you seem to have arrived at the conclusion that "out of apparent evil good springs, and that the circumstances which have arisen will doubtless advance the confederation of the various Colonies and States of South Africa," which, in the opinion of many, cannot fail to be a "source of blessing to the members of the union, and which will also exercise a highly beneficial influence on the civilization and social development of the native tribes of South Africa." Some, however, much as they desire this happy consummation, may think that you are too sanguine in your expectations, *now* that Thaba Bosigo, the famed irresistible stronghold of Moshesh, is in the hands of the triumphant Burghers, and that, so far from the "extinction of the Free State as an independent power" being an accomplished fact, the South African Republic, under the auspices of President Brand, again elected to his high office, now that laurels deck his brow, will long continue a terror to all those who dare to encroach upon its territory gained by the right of conquest. If the report be correct that the old Chieftain, whom, it is supposed, the "deserving French Missionaries" have taught to be peacefully inclined, is dead, further complications may perhaps arise in keeping in subjection the alleged more warlike propensities of his sons, that is to say, if they have any warriors left to fight; and new difficulties to the Free State, "in holding the country which they have conquered," may be probably also accompanied with disadvantages to the neighbouring British Colonies of the Cape and Natal. At any rate, without despairing that the forthcoming conference at Aliwal North may be attended with good results, my present communication with your readers is prompted by the dread that a Republican form of Government is likely to remain for some time longer at least on our border, although many Britishers as well as Africanders within the Orange Free State are evidently yearning to become again loyal subjects of Her Majesty, Queen Victoria.

The *Burghersdorp Gazette*, in the extract you have given from it, states: "It is greatly to be feared that at the approaching session of the Volksraad in the Free State, one or two iniquitous measures will be carried, either the entire repudiation of debts away out of the Free State, or a further closing of the Civil Courts for ten years, with an immense issue of bluebacks. The latter is the popular scheme, and, as far as the action of the Free State goes, there is grave apprehension that it will succeed." There seems to be good ground for the fear thus entertained, if the representations of a correspondent, a "Free Stater," in the columns of the *Friend*, be founded on fact, viz.:—

Many of our unsophisticated boers, at the instance of some unprincipled men among us, are signing memorials; one, urging upon the Government to make no end of bluebacks; another, praying the Raad for the total repudiation of all foreign debts, and the staying of all Free State debts for ten years to come; a third asking the Volksraad to keep the Civil Courts closed for seven years still, after May next; and these memorials, credible persons say, are eagerly and numerously signed, and that there is not the least use to endeavour to convince the Boers that they are doing wrong.

My chief object is, through the medium of your columns, to invite the attention of the Port Elizabeth Chamber of Commerce, for the Cape Town institution is forbidden to tread on the dangerous ground of politics, to the *Fifth* Article of Sir George Clerk's Convention, the Magna Charta of the Independent Republic, which is in the terms following:—

Her Majesty's Government and the Orange River Government shall, within their respective territories, mutually use every exertion for the suppression of crime and keeping the peace, by apprehending and delivering up all criminals who may have escaped or fled from justice either way across the Orange River, *and the courts, as well the British as those of the Orange River Government, shall be mutually open and available to the inhabitants of both territories for all lawful processes.* And all summonses for witnesses directed either way across the Orange River shall be countersigned by the magistrates of both Governments respectively, to compel the attendance of such witnesses when and where they may be required, thus affording to the community north of the Orange River every assistance of the British Courts, *and giving, on the other hand, assurance to such colonial merchants and traders as have naturally entered into credit transactions in the Orange River territory during its occupation by the British Government, and to whom in many cases debts may be owing, every facility for the recovery of just claims in the courts of the Orange River Government.* And Her Majesty's Special Commissioner will recommend the adoption of the like reciprocal privileges by the Government of Natal in its relations with the Orange River Government.

It is submitted that the spirit, if not the letter, of this treaty will be infringed by the denial of justice on the part of the Free State to colonial creditors in shutting the doors of their courts of law to civil suitors, and thus hindering "lawful processes" for the recovery of just debts. Although the *Friend* expresses a hope "that the good sense and right feeling of the majority of the Raad will prevail, and that these memorials, and those who affix their signatures to the same, will be treated with the contempt they so richly merit," it may be just as well for Sir Philip Wodehouse, after other important matters are settled, to bring to the notice of the legal mind of Mr. President Brand this point of law, or rather equitable construction of the Articles of Convention.

With respect to "the entire repudiation of debts" to outsiders, the Volksraad, after calm deliberation, will never dream for a moment of adopting so suicidal a policy; but the mere popular approval of these silly memorials above referred to, is calculated to shake the credit of the Free State at a time when they want to borrow money. As it is well put by the *Worcester Courant*, "capitalists will naturally argue, that if there is a talk of repudiation now the national debt is comparatively small, this talk might assume a more serious aspect as the debt be-

came larger; and therefore it would be imprudent to invest their money in Free State debentures."

In my too-oft repeated letters to the editor of the *Standard*, I do not aim at originality, but my object has earnestly been to endeavour to excite discussion on the important and now "uncomfortable relations" between this Colony, the Free State, and the Basutos, by collecting the opinions and condensing the arguments of others, and by giving extracts from the ably-conducted press of the Eastern Province, British Kaffraria, and the Free State, which might otherwise have escaped the notice of your numerous country readers, and which I believe calculated to throw light on this interesting subject of the British Basuto Protectorate, which has not altogether, according to my ideas, been fairly handled in Cape Town.

Thursday, March 5.   COLONIST.

The Gunpowder Question.

Sir,—In my last letter, under a false impression that Thaba Bosigo had fallen into the hands of the victorious burghers, and that even the veteran chief Moshesh was no more, I despondingly imagined that Basutoland, instead of becoming British territory, would be annexed to the Orange Free State; and therefore I ventured to suggest that the South African Republic should, during its probably lengthened career of independence, in the spirit of the Articles of Convention of Sir George Clerk, "give every facility for the recovery of just claims in the courts of the Orange River Government" to the colonists of the Cape and Natal, who have had commercial dealings with them. The *Argus*, however, of this morning says, "Information received yesterday from Aliwal North, of a thoroughly trustworthy character, gives a different complexion to the war news from the Free State," and this has probably determined the Governor to accelerate his departure from Cape Town, for it is currently rumoured that His Excellency proposes to start on Wednesday next, in a spider with a pair of horses (relays of course being provided on the road), *via* Beaufort West, Richmond, and Murraysburg, for the scene of the proposed conference with the Lieutenant-Governor of Natal, President Brand, and the new loyal subject of the Queen of England, Moshesh. The position, then, of Sir Philip Wodehouse does not seem, after all, to be so embarrassing as it has been represented to be, and there is yet reasonable ground of hope that he will at once be enabled satisfactorily to carry out the main and good object of Her Majesty's Government—" the restoration and maintenance of general peace" in South Africa. Indeed, the conclusion of the *Argus*, which writes with authority as follows :—" The frontier police are moving towards Basutoland to meet Sir Philip Wodehouse, who is without delay to proceed thither. Perhaps, after all, the settlement may be arranged without any great difficulty. The Free State may fairly claim some increase of territory in consequence of recent successes, and the burghers may possibly be content with a moderate portion in consideration of the peace and quiet on the border, which may be expected to follow the proclamation of the protectorate," appears to be a solution of the problem, not inconsistent with the alleged communications of His Excellency to his private correspondents at Bloemfontein. Of course, it remains to be seen what effect the conciliatory rejoinder of Her Majesty's High Commissioner to the rather warlike reply of Mr. President Brand, coupled with the fact, brought prominently to notice, that the stoppage of the supply of ammunition can easily be managed, may have produced on the deliberations of the Volksraad. Is it not probable, as well as desirable, that the President may still be instructed to listen to reason in the coming negotiations, and not to oppose the peaceful wishes of Her Majesty being carried out, at the same time that he is commissioned to endeavour to make as good a bargain as possible with respect to the addition of territory to the Orange Free State, or compensation out of the military chest for the laudable purpose of redeeming the obnoxious blue-backs, the offsprings of the long war?

My object earnestly being to make the British-Basuto Protectorate as popular as possible with the readers of the *Standard*, and to attempt to remove the prejudice which has been excited against it in Cape Town, I prefer, even at the risk of again subjecting myself to the harmless ridicule of the editors of the *Argus* and their literary and witty correspondents, to pursue my matter-of-fact course of quoting largely from the ably-conducted Frontier press, so peculiarly conversant with this and like questions, rather than to borrow its ideas and information, and clothe them in my own feeble and less convincing language. *The Graham's Town Journal*, in referring to the last despatch of Sir Philip Wodehouse above mentioned, which is said to "be penned in conciliatory language," and "the instruction given to the Port Elizabeth Civil Commissioner concerning the stoppage of the gunpowder permits," in its own amusing and terse style writes thus:—

> The conciliatory despatch and the hostile instruction were intended to go together, and unitedly to produce an exactly definite effect. They resemble in relation and purpose the constituents of a seidlitz powder. The conciliatory despatch is the carbonate of soda, and the hostile instruction is the tartaric acid of His Excellency's diplomacy. In his view of the case it was necessary that both should be taken together. He very likely thought that his polite style of letter writing would be misunderstood unless accompanied by a certain sharpness of action.

The *Great Eastern*, which, many will rejoice to see continuing in its sphere of usefulness with *renewed* vigour, instead of succumbing to difficulties, smartly defends Sir Philip Wodehouse against a severe attack made on him by the *Graaff-Reinet Herald*, for " his arbitrary act of interference," as it is called, of " interdicting any further supply of ammunition to the Free State," in the annexed passage from its leader of the 29th of last month :—

Our Graaff-Reinet contemporary has not handled this subject with his usual ability. Possibly, stopping the supply of ammunition may be disastrous to certain traders in this Colony, but the first consideration of High Commissioners and Colonial Governors is not trading, but government. It is by no means an unusual thing for rulers and governments to adopt a policy which is calculated to check currents of trade, divert them, or stop them altogether. The peace of this Continent is of vastly more consequence than the profits arising from the selling of gunpowder and lead, for stopping the sale of ammunition to the Free State. We are exceedingly glad that Sir Philip Wodehouse has resorted to it. The Free State cattle-lifters thought nothing of stopping the legitimate trade of this Colony, when they saw that they could avoid debt and live without work by declaring war and shutting up their Law Courts. Hundreds of our enterprising, industrious, and honest fellow-countrymen who live in the Free State are compelled to sit with their arms folded and watch—without having the power to prevent it—their properties grow " small by degrees and beautifully less," to provide supplies for a mob of boisterous cowards who ridiculously call themselves a Grand Army. The steps taken by Sir Philip Wodehouse, on the instructions of the Imperial Government, will do more good for the trade of this Colony, for the Free State, and for South Africa generally, than anything that has been done on the other side of the frontier border during the last quarter of a century. It is not easy to estimate the fearful losses which the Cape mercantile community have sustained by this rumpus with the Basutos. The trade which was growing so rapidly and conducted so satisfactorily between the respectable firms in the Free State and our Colony has been utterly destroyed, and the amount of debt due to our merchants is frightfully large. Instead, therefore, of censuring Sir Philip Wodehouse for taking decided steps to put a stop to the war, he should be thanked—most certainly by the merchants and traders—and that too most heartily.

Even the *Eastern Province Herald*, which so fairly sympathizes with our neighbours of the Free State in their struggle with the Basutos, begins to see that, if the closing of the Courts of Law within that State be the natural consequent of the prolongation of the war, the stoppage of the transmission of gunpowder from Port Elizabeth northward of the Orange River will not be such a bad thing after all. As far as my memory serves me, it uses rather strong language in saying something about the Free-Staters becoming greater thieves than the Basutos, if they continue to shut the doors of their Courts of Law against the just claims of Port Elizabeth, whence they draw all their supplies ; and I only regret that I have not the opportunity of giving the extract *in extenso*, for the benefit of your readers.

It is earnestly to be hoped that the President of the Republic will no longer be in antagonism with the representative of Her Majesty, and that the restoration of peace, on terms satisfactory to both the former combatants in the war, will alike render unnecessary the restriction in the granting of permits of gunpowder and fire-arms at Port Elizabeth, and the denial of justice at Bloemfontein to colonial creditors. It is true that this question seems to be presented rather in a different light in the subjoined extract from an able article on the Basutos, *communicated* to the *Great Eastern*, which appears in the *Argus* of this morning :—

The repudiation scheme of roguery is still gaining ground, and *if it is not a wily but unmanly scheme to compel the Cape Colonists to get the Free State annexed*, it is the most shameful piece of rascality ever heard of in our days. It is to be hoped that a body of men will be found in the country who will most strongly protest against this iniquitous method, as well as against the unjust proceeding of continually closing the Law Courts, thereby giving freedom to rogues and ruin to honest men.

Surely the Free State authorities will be hard indeed to please, and will sacrifice the interests of those committed to their rule, if they do not gladly accept the terms about to be proposed by Sir Philip Wodehouse, according to the following statement of the *Graham's Town Journal*, which cannot fail to recommend itself as an equitable compromise to all unprejudiced persons :—

The *Friend* puts forward some details which explain what His Excellency is supposed to mean by fairness towards the State. Moshesh is to be nobody. In any contract he is not to be a highly-considered personage. The British Government is not about to be guided by Basuto policy or to avenge Basuto wrongs. Basutoland under the British is not to be an old foe with a new face ; but an old foe restrained by a powerful hand. Then as to the boundary line. The line before the so-called conquest is to be the frontier, but the farms sold or granted last year are to remain the property of purchasers or grantees, and are to be held under British title, the purchase money to go to the Free State Government.

Very many of the Queen's subjects at this end of the Colony will join with me in sincerely wishing that signal success may crown the efforts of Her Majesty's High Commissioner on his mission of permanent peace to South Africa ; and, if I were not afraid of bringing down on my devoted head the dire anathemas of the able editors of the *Argus* and *Advertiser and Mail* for unnecessarily meddling with politics, I would suggest that, *before* His Excellency takes his departure from Cape Town, there shall be some expression of public opinion, in accordance with that of the *Graham's Town Journal*, " that the best plan of removing difficulties from the path of the Free State Government, in relation to the pending negotiations, is to make the Free State people favourable to the intentions of the British Government," and that some loyal demonstration should also be made, with the view of strengthening the hands of the Queen's Representative in establishing on a sound and equitable basis the British Basuto Protectorate, which all "Her Majesty's abandoned subjects" within the Orange Free Republic cannot but fondly hail as the first step towards the extension of British rule to that land, which was once the Sovereignty.

Saturday, 7th March, 1868.   COLONIST.

The Orange Free State.

Sir,—The *Argus* and *Advertiser and Mail* appear to look at the recent victories of the burghers over the Basutos through a different medium—the *one* sanguinely hopes and wishes that there is nothing in them seriously to embarrass the proclamation of the protectorate by the Queen's representative, and the reasonable settlement of the boundaries of Basutoland; the *other* rather exultingly wonders "how His Excellency the High Commissioner will accept this new, and to him, very unexpected issue of affairs, and what he will do with it." The weight of the evidence, however, seems to establish that the capture of the Kieme, Letsea's stronghold in the ceded territory, was a decided success, and may materially affect the coming negotiations for peace; but it is hard to see how it can change the good intentions of Her Majesty's Government to put an end to the wretched war. Without doubt the booty seized was large, and will go a long way towards reconciling the Boers for the dangers and discomforts of the commando, and may perhaps encourage them to fight on, *now* that Moshesh exhibits the white flag, and his warriors, if not panic-stricken, feel desirous of suspending hostilities at their *new* Queen's command.

If the editor of the *Friend*, with his great ability and local information, finds it "somewhat a matter of difficulty to form a clear estimate of the situation in which the Free State is placed," surely persons at a distance must at the present moment indeed feel puzzled in predicting, with any certainty, the probable result of the conference at Aliwal North, which, when I last addressed you, I erroneously believed, from what I heard, was to be hurried on a week. It may be admitted that there exists much difference of opinion amongst the Free Staters themselves with respect to the contemplated British Basuto Protectorate. Some regard it as "the next best thing to federation which could have happened to them; that it will have the effect of restoring peace and tranquillity to their border without the necessity of a further issue of bluebacks, or the closing of the civil courts and the repudiation of colonial debts." Others loudly deprecate "the interference of the British Government, under the firm conviction that the Basutos are all but crushed," and that the South African Republic "could now, unaided, dictate a satisfactory peace with them, or drive them over the Drakensberg;" and so far from believing that the Basutos are likely to be better neighbours when they become British subjects, they ridicule the notion that Queen Victoria will be able more efficaciously to restrain the thievish propensities of their sable enemies than their respective chieftains, Moshesh, Letsea, Makwai, Molitzani, or even Bushuli, if he be not dead. Many will feel inclined to agree with me and the *Friend of the Free State*, that they who take a sanguine and favourable view of the *new* native policy of Her Majesty's Ministers have much the best of the argument, but, unfortunately for the cause of the immediate restoration of South Africa, even some of those who hail with delight the interposition of the Crown of England in affairs northward of the Orange River, are "not a bit sorry for the Basutos, and believe that they richly deserve all that they are likely to get."

In taking up the *Standard* and the *Argus* of this morning, it struck me as remarkable, and a singular coincidence, that in the columns of *both* journals the reasonable expression by Sir Philip Wodehouse, of " astonishment at the Orange Free State continuing hostilities, destroying the crops, &c., after he had notified the fact that the Basutos were about to become subjects of the Queen," appeared in immediate juxtaposition with the announcement that President Brand had appointed " a day of thanksgiving to Almighty God for the success of their arms against the Basutos." His Honour is doubtless most sincere in his laudable wish that the country over which he rules should solemnly proclaim their pious gratitude to the Giver of all Good ; but there will be some who will entertain the idea that the character of the Free State for sound religious feeling would have commanded more general respect if it had not needlessly continued the work of slaughter and the destruction of food, *after* the Queen of Great Britain and Ireland had authoritatively declared that she was anxious to restore peace to South Africa, and prepared to do justice to both the combatants in this long-protracted war, so disastrous in its consequences to the British Colonies of the Cape and Natal, as well as to the aborigines of the land. It has been urged, in justification of the scorn with which the peaceful overtures of Her Majesty's High Commissioner have been treated, that the South African Republic of the Orange Free State could not lose the opportunity of showing its *independence*, and that it is entitled, by the law of nations, to be the sole arbiter of its own will with respect to the punishment of its enemy—the Basuto nation ; but, as usual, I prefer on this point to borrow the sentiments and language of one better qualified to speak on this subject—the *Friend :*—

This line of argument is very well in theory—but in theory only ; for it is a notorious fact that England withdrew her sovereignty from this State of her own free choice, and can resume it again at any time, for anything we can do to prevent it. The geographical position of this State, surrounded by British possessions, will always prevent it being independent, except in name. The last act of the Governor of the Cape is proof sufficient of this. Finding that we are continuing the war against his clearly expressed wish, he has at once stopped our supply of ammunition at Port Elizabeth. No more permits are to be granted to Free Staters by the magistrate there. We agree with the *Graham's Town Journal*, that this is an unwise and impolitic step on the part of His Excellency, calculated to awaken bad feeling, without effecting any good, for we have an abundant supply of ammunition of every kind in our magazines at present—probably sufficient to finish the war, even if it last some months longer. We merely allude to this fact here, to prove that our boasted independence is but a mockery and a delusion, as it has ever been. Granted then, that we are not independent of the British Colonies, would it not be better policy for us to endeavour to act in a conciliatory manner towards the High Commissioner, by giving effect to his wishes, and thus to gain the friendship and good will of our neighbours?

Perhaps, after all, *now* that even the *Advertiser and Mail* thinks that the Free State has achieved all the success which it had desired, or could reasonably desire, and that the lowest estimate of the booty seized, £30,000, will go far indeed towards paying the expenses of the war, *which must now be considered as at an end, all the avowed objects of it having been accomplished;* President Brand may approach the conference at Aliwal North in a true spirit of conciliation and good will towards Great Britain, and that a friendly alliance may be formed between the Great Powers of South Africa to pave the way for "the restoration of British authority over the Free State," which your able contemporary last mentioned "believes will be an unquestionable benefit."

It here occurs to me to notice the fallacious reasoning of those who unjustly charge the honest supporters of Sir Philip Wodehouse, in carrying out the Imperial mandate of protecting Basutoland, with "vindicating arbitrary and despotic measures, at utter variance with the fundamental principles of British freedom." What has His Excellency the High Commissioner of the Queen done, that it is to be accounted a sin in any of Her Majesty's loyal subjects to sympathize with him and to wish him success in the important but difficult task which has been confided to him, "the restoration and maintenance of the general peace of South Africa?" Where is the act of tyranny which has been perpetrated by Earl Derby's Government? Moshesh and his tribe petition the Queen of England to extend her regal way over Basutoland, and, in her desire to be consistent in promoting the cause of the aborigines in South Africa, Her Majesty has been graciously pleased to grant their prayer.

It may be thought and argued that the British Basuto Protectorate is "the thin end of the wedge," the first step towards the Orange Free State ceasing to be an independent Republic; but no one, much less any representative of the opinions of Her Majesty's Ministers, has said or even dreamt, that such re-annexation to the British Colonial Empire of the territory, which was once the Sovereignty, a happy event which many hope and believe is not far distant, will ever be effected in any other manner but "justly and constitutionally, with the consent of the people." Of course, "if the abandoned subjects of Her Majesty within the Free State do not follow the example of Moshesh, and pray for the Queen's protection, they will continue to suffer from the want of order and good government, which now prevail northward of the Orange River. The only fear is that, if they do petition the Queen and the Imperial Parliament for the restoration of British rule to the land in which they live, unless they are supported by the sympathies and co-operation of the Cape people and Parliament, some opposition may be made by the authorities at home to the extension of British territory in South Africa, against which there exists a strong prejudice in the Mother Country, chiefly on the score of the cost of previous Kafir wars, which are not likely to occur again. It behoves then all who hope and desire to see the same British flag waving at Bloemfontein and Thaba Bosigo, constitutionally to agitate the question of federation or annexation of the Orange Free State to this Colony, particularly if Natal should succeed in annexing Basutoland, which the *Graham's Town Journal* clearly dreads, when it so strongly argues against the Cape Frontier Police being employed for Imperial or Natal purposes. It is therefore under all circumstances satisfactory to learn that action has already been taken *within* the Free State in this direction, and that a memorial, to be signed by the subjects of the Free State Republic, addressed to the Governor of the Cape of Good Hope, is in course of circulation there, pressing upon His Excellency to consider the subject of federal union of the South African States; and it seems probable that a similar memorial will issue from the Cape colonists on the Eastern Frontier. Perhaps, instead of making any appeal to Sir Philip Wodehouse on this point, it would be the more legitimate and effectual course for the Free State people to petition the Queen, and to endeavour to put forward unanswerable reasons why the resumption of the sovereignty, the *first* step *either* to annexation to this Colony, *or* to the grand federation scheme, would be attended with solid advantages to all parties concerned, the Free State, Basutoland, and the colonies of the Cape and Natal.

Wednesday, March 11. COLONIST.

The Annexation of the Orange Free State.

SIR,—At the risk of being deemed tedious, I cannot refrain from referring in terms of honest praise to the spirit and tone of your able leading article of this morning, the main practical purport of which may be said to be the encouragement of the people of the Cape, Natal, and the Free State, to "unite their energies in striving to bring all South Africa under one flag." You clearly appear to wish to see "commenced and put into fair train, the steps necessary to bring the Free State again under British rule," and want to be informed whether anything has been done in this direction. The petition to the Governor, to which you allude, praying for His Excellency's favourable consideration of a Federal union with the British colonies in South Africa, had already, on the 6th of this month, obtained about one hundred signatures, and it was expected to be numerously signed. A correspondent, however, of the *Friend of the Free State*, " Federation," considers this appeal from the people of the State to Sir Philip Wodehouse " a breach of etiquette," and counsels rather agitation, by means of public meetings, revival of annexation committees, and memorials to the President and Volksraad. In corroboration of his opinion, he quotes the reply of Sir George Grey to an address from Aliwal North, so far back as 1858, in which he said :—" The question of a union between the Colony and the Free State, to which you advert, shall receive my careful attention. But such a union, upon whatever terms it may be based, can only be brought about by the Colonial Parliament and the Volksraad of the Free State. Those bodies can *alone* give expression to the wishes of the inhabitants of the two countries, which I can then represent to Her Majesty's Government. In such a matter I can only advise and guide—with the most heartfelt desire that the decision arrived at may be for the lasting benefit of all South Africa." Doubtless there is some force in this objection, and " there are," as you say, " difficulties in the way of taking the initiative in matters of this kind," but it seems to me that if there be any truth in the statement "that the Hollanders constitute almost entirely the pro-State and anti-British section" within the Orange Free State, the best course would be for the Free Staters to petition the Queen of England to do for them what she has already done for the Basutos—to declare them British subjects, and it may perhaps turn out that such a petition to Her Majesty is more than a "mere rumour."

It may, and no doubt will, be argued, that the present moment, when the interference by Her Majesty's Government on behalf of Moshesh and his tribe has been misinterpreted and misunderstood, and has even produced angry irritation, would be inopportune to commence such an agitation ; but, it is thought, that " the prejudices which have been excited against anything British" will soon subside, and that a majority of the inhabitants of the Orange Free State will enlist themselves on the side of British rule and British protection. Some even entertain the opinion that Mr. Advocate Hamelberg, who is the most influential member of the Dutch party, is in favour of moderate measures—that he is entirely opposed to bluebacks, repudiation of debt, the denial of justice by closing the courts of law, and inclined to view favourably a British Federal Union. The large British party within the Free State " growl that Moshesh should have gained what is still withheld from them ; but the simple reason is, that he, untrammelled, gained by pertinacity what they never asked for, and have only yet to ask to gain. Had their application been before the Home Government with that of Moshesh, no doubt it would have met with the same favourable response as his." It cannot be denied that many, both in the Colony and the Free State, think "that the Government are commencing apparently at the wrong end of the stick by annexing Basutoland before the Free State;" but surely the first article of the Convention of Sir George Clerk, which, "finally transferring the Government of the Orange River territory to the representatives delegated by the inhabitants to receive it, guarantees, on the part of Her Majesty's Government, the future independence of that country and its Government," precludes Her Majesty *spontaneously* to restore the regal sway of the British Crown to the Republic of the Orange Free State, without the consent of the majority of the people of that State.

It is but natural, and was to be expected, that those of the Free State who "are anti-British as well as anti-Basuto" should oppose Her Majesty's High Commissioner in the satisfactory settlement of the boundaries of Basutoland; but there is also too much reason to fear that your prediction will be verified, "that the Free State policy will be to make Sir Philip Wodehouse's task as difficult as possible," with the view of "forcing upon his attention the fact that things would work much more satisfactorily and easily if the Free State were also British soil." The *Graham's Town Journal* conveys the same idea, when it says, that even they, "who are more or less anxious that the State should become British," "will object to the cession of territory to the Basutos as a matter of policy, hoping that by resisting the demands made by Sir Philip, and which he thinks to be essential, the British Government may be driven to settle the difficulty by including the Free State as well as Basutoland in the act of annexation." This crooked line of policy must, many will think in common with you, fail in its object. Her Majesty's High Commissioner, in carrying out the instructions of the Home Government, to throw the shield of Great Britain's protection over Moshesh and his tribe, must act with justice towards them, and with a due regard to the interests of the neighbouring Colonies of the Cape and Natal, not to mention the Free State itself, by such a "modification of the boundary as will ensure ample consideration of the claims of the State, without rendering permanent peace altogether unattainable;" but, at the same time, he cannot exceed his authority and reannex at present the Free State to the British Colonial Empire.

Without any disparagement of the bravery of the burghers, it may be taken for granted that an armed resistance to the will of Great Britain is entirely out of the question, and the idea of actual hostilities against Her Majesty's old subjects of the Cape, or new subjects of Basutoland, will never be seriously entertained for a moment by the President and the Volksraad, or the people of the Free State. Whatever then may be the opposition of the "foreigners who have become inhabitants of the Sovereignty since its abandonment," to the efforts of Sir Philip Wodehouse to restore peace to South Africa, it behoves the British party, at least, within the Orange Free State, and all Her Majesty's subjects at the Cape and Natal, not to thwart in any degree the establishment of the British Basuto Protectorate on an equitable basis, and to regard it as a stepping-stone, which it most certainly is, to the *further* extension of British rule and protection northward of the Orange River. No doubt, the representations from the people of the Free State, that they are tired of the want of order, good government, and credit under a Republican dynasty, and that they yearn " to be allowed to rest and live under the large folds of the flag of England," would be gladly conveyed by Sir Philip Wodehouse to Her Majesty's Government, and supported by his powerful recommendation to their favourable consideration.

While I admire the general tenor of your remarks, I must be permitted, before concluding, to join issue with you on the point that "Sir Philip Wodehouse's statement of the annexation question was a one-sided one." Without wishing in the least degree to detract from the merit of Mr. President Brand's clear historical account of the causes of the war, or to dispute its accuracy, I think you would not have accused " Sir Philip of overlooking more important truths than Mr. Brand," if you had borne in mind the exordium of his despatch of the 11th of February :—

I hope that my notice will not be misunderstood, if I abstain altogether from discussing or questioning the description of past transactions given in your letter. I have but one object in view, that of restoring peace and ensuring the future tranquillity and well-being of the British Colonies, the Free State, and the Basutos ; and I shall apply myself entirely to the endeavour to obtain the acquiescence of your Government in the course which I believe to be best fitted to promote its attainment.

In the despatch of the 10th March, written evidently under a natural feeling of annoyance, that " the appeal he had made to the President for the suspension of hostilities between the Free State and the Basutos" had not been listened to, but that, on the contrary, the war was being carried on more vigorously than ever, His Excellency does not profess to go into details of the causes of the war, but fairly and briefly argues in justification of the British interposition on behalf of Moshesh, on the ground that the old chief " had twice consented to spare the Free State at the request of this Government, whose intervention had been in both cases solicited in the most pressing terms by the Free State." It seems then to me that, under the circumstances, the Governor must stand honourably acquitted of the imputation that he has in an unfair and partial manner summed up the case between the Boers and the Basutos.

Saturday, 21st March, 1868.   COLONIST.

British Subjects.

Sir,—As public attention just now seems to be directed to the subject of the allegiance of the inhabitants of the Free State to the British Crown, a few remarks may not be considered out of place. The correspondent of the *Argus*—" A Friend of the Free State"—is right when he enunciates the general proposition, " Once a British subject, always a British subject." This is the general rule, but it has its exceptions. A natural-born subject of one country cannot throw off his allegiance to his Sovereign by swearing allegiance to the Sovereign of another country ; he cannot, by any act of his own, put off or discharge his allegiance to the former. But he can be discharged by the concurrent act of his Sovereign to whom his allegiance was first due.

The position of the Free State is somewhat analogous to the exception just mentioned. By the articles of convention entered into between Sir George Clerk and the representatives of the Free State, it was, amongst other things, agreed that the inhabitants of that State should be finally freed from their allegiance to the British Crown, and declared to be, to all intents and purposes, a free and independent people, and that their Government should be treated and considered a free and independent Government. There can therefore be no doubt that the inhabitants of the Free State, who were such at the time of the convention, and their descendants, were, by these articles, entirely absolved from their allegiance to the British Crown, and that they could not be accused of high treason if they refused to respect the terms of the Governor's proclamation. But does this apply to the President ? Should Mr. Brand persevere in the war against the Basutos, could he (as the correspondent of the *Argus* supposes) be indicted for high treason ? Would it not be presumed that the convention which frees the subject frees also the President, the source from which the subject derives his civil status, from his allegiance ? If the Government is to be free and independent, is it too much to infer that the President, who is the principal member of the Government, and to whom the Government looks for advice and aid, and without whose authority little can be done, is to be fettered and have his independence checked by his allegiance to Her Majesty ? Or would it not be more in accordance with the spirit of the convention to suppose that, inasmuch as the Government is to be free and independent, the President, the moment he accepts office, is, by virture of these articles, absolved from his allegiance ? It seems to be clear that those colonists who have emigrated to the Free State subsequent to the convention, are still bound by their allegiance as natural-born subjects. But that the President is equally bound, is not

I think, so self evident. I ask for information. I have no doubt but that your very able correspondent "Colonist," who has taken such an interest in the annexation of Basutoland, will be able to inform me.

March 25, 1868.   ANGLO-AFRICAN.

British Subjects in the Free State.

Sir,—In your columns of this morning, "Anglo-African" pays me undeservedly the compliment of appealing to me for information on the question put by "A Friend of the Free State" in the *Argus* of Tuesday last.

If Mr. President Brand should still continue the war against Moshesh and his people, who are now British subjects, would not he, together with all other British subjects taking part in the war, be liable to a charge of murder for every Basuto slain?

Your new correspondent, although he writes with becoming modesty and diffidence, appears to me to be master of his subject, and not to be far wrong when he somewhat qualified the legal position broadly assumed in your previous leading article, " that any subject of Her Majesty by birth, who shall bear arms against Basutoland or the Basutos, will commit an act of high treason." Although, fortunately for the peace of South Africa, there is no fear of actual hostilities between the Queen's Representative and the President of the Free Republic, and no probability that even the Volksraad will, to borrow an idea from the *Great Eastern*, "dare to touch" the Basutos, now that they have become British subjects, some further remarks on the " existing relations between the British Government and the Free State" may not be without interest to your readers. The general principle of law is that "*natural allegiance*" is such as is due from all men born within the Sovereign's dominions immediately upon their birth; it cannot be forfeited, cancelled, or altered by any change of time, place, or circumstance, *nor by anything but the united concurrence of the Legislature.*" It seems reasonable, and is fairly put by " Anglo-African," that the Articles of Sir George Clerk's Convention " entirely absolved from their allegiance to the British Crown" all who were inhabitants of the Sovereignty at the time of its abandonment in 1854, and it is also ably argued by this able lawyer, that the President, " the principal member" of this " free and independent Government," should be included in the exception, and not fettered by his loyalty to Her Majesty. But it occurs to me to make a quotation from a despatch of the Duke of Newcastle of the 14th of January, 1854, as not irrelevant to the point under discussion :—

There is, I believe, little doubt that no measure resting on the Queen's prerogative only for its authority could release them from the ties of such native allegiance ; an Act of Parliament would be required for that purpose. It is probable that the inhabitants of the future Commonwealth would generally prefer to retain the rights of British subjects rather than become wholly aliens, and subject to the ordinary incapacities of aliens within Her Majesty's dominions.

If, therefore, the Imperial Parliament has "not ratified the abandonment of the Sovereignty by a declaration of release from allegiance to the abandoned subjects of Her Majesty," you may perhaps, after all, be right in the interpretation you have put upon the meaning of the last words of the Governor's Basuto Proclamation, " And I hereby require *all* Her Majesty's subjects in South Africa to take notice of this my Proclamation accordingly." I must not, however, be considered to be doing more than throwing out this point for argument; for I feel constrained, much as I would wish otherwise, to go even further than " Anglo-African," and to doubt whether it is so " clear that those colonists who have emigrated to the Free State subsequent to the Convention are still bound by their allegiance as natural-born subjects." The legal authorities of decided cases, which are doubtless fresh in " Anglo-African's" memory, may be against me ; but I cannot help venturing an opinion that I have reason and common sense on my side on this point. If Her Majesty has been pleased, although unwisely, to recognize the entire independence of a Free Republic on the immediate border of her own Colonies in South Africa, it can hardly be expected that even her former subjects, who have become citizens of that Republic, should act in open defiance of their own legally constituted authorities, and treat their sable neighbours, the Basutos, with justice and moderation, instead of with determined hostility and vengeance. Suppose, for the sake of the argument, that the declaration by Her Majesty's High Commissioner of the Basutos as British subjects was detrimental instead of beneficial to the interests of the Orange Free State, and that the State was powerful enough to dispute the will of Great Britain, and waged war on that account, would those who have become naturalized citizens of the Republic, and fought under its banner, be guilty of high treason to the Queen of England, because they were once subjects of Her Majesty ? The principle, " that subjects of Her Majesty by birth cannot get rid of the allegiance they owe to her by the mere fact of being also citizens of an independent State," upon which you based the opinion above referred to, has been recently much discussed in England in consequence of the unsuccessful attempts of " American citizens," who have crossed the ocean to create discord in Ireland, and join in a wicked rebellion, to beard British authority with impunity in her criminal courts of justice. The refusal by the British Government of the application of Mr. Adams to allow prisoners to be tried by juries half composed of foreigners, induced President Johnson, with a view, as it has been said, of pleasing the Fenians in the

I

United States prior to an election, to suggest some modification and alteration of the laws of England and America which are identical on this point. The principle of international law herein involved has consequently been freely and ably argued by the English press, and, at the risk of again giving offence to the literary correspondent of the *Argus*, I quote *in extenso* a passage from the *Daily News*, which, in terse and clear language, explains my own ideas on this subject :—

We have chosen to deal rather with the intention of the different classes of Americanized foreigners than with any technical rules of international law. The subject is admittedly open for friendly discussion and negotiation, and the object of each nation should be rather to arrive at a satisfactory principle, which shall be fairly applicable to each, if the circumstances of each happened to be reversed, than to insist on extreme and sweeping views of national dignity. Such a moderate and just principle would, we conceive, be found to be in a regard paid to the true purpose for which naturalization is sought. *The country of birth may well consent to pass from the rights of allegiance over those who have left her for good and all, and who seek to meddle no further with her affairs. Even if a war were to break out, and such as these were to be taken in arms against their native land, they might rightly expect to be treated as true-born foreigners, when they had long ago renounced whatever rights or privileges belonged to their native inheritance.* But, on the other hand, when naturalization is merely colourable, when it does not withhold the citizen from taking part in the domestic conflicts of his native land, or when his allegiance is thrown off at the moment of war having actually broken out, then every overt act of hostility should in common sense be deemed treason. This principle would support every just and honest claim for immunity, and would be in perfect harmony with the amplest exercise of the privilege of political asylum. But it would maintain harmony among nations by preventing reckless men from invoking their protection in order to make them a base for hostile operations against their allies.

Whether it be high treason or not for the Free State to fight with the Cape Colonists, the British troops, or the Basutos, there can be no doubt that the sooner the country northward of the Orange River comes under the flag of England, the better for all parties concerned ; and I am therefore glad to see in your issue of this morning a suggested Petition to the Queen from the Free State, praying Her Majesty to do for the inhabitants of the land which was once the Sovereignty, what she has already done for the Basutos—"to extend her protection to them."

I cannot conclude without further suggesting that the colonists of the Cape and Natal should also appeal to their " own most gracious Queen," in support of the prayer of their brethren beyond the Orange River, not only for the sake of the Free Staters themselves, but for the selfish purpose of putting an end to bluebacks, repudiation of debt, closing of courts of law, and other evils, *ad infinitum.*

Thursday, 26th March. COLONIST.

115

THE PRESIDENT OF THE FREE STATE IN CHAINS!

SIR,—If the Basuto question, which properly continues to afford "discussions, arguments, and surmises" in the editorial columns of the Eastern Province press, is becoming dull to Cape Town readers, the *Standard's* sensational telegram from Graham's Town, upon which you so amusingly dilate this morning, appears calculated to create a demand for further comment upon the probable results of the intervention of Her Majesty's Government in behalf of Moshesh and his tribe. The numerous friends at this end of the Colony of the President of the Orange Free State, who recollect him at the Cape bar, and believe that he entirely coincides with the well-known sympathies of Sir Christoffel Brand, the Speaker of the House of Assembly, have been indeed startled at the idea that he should have been accused by the Hollanders of being "too English." Mr. John Brand was always much esteemed as a straightforward and high-minded gentleman, but he never attempted to conceal the strong bias of his mind in favour of the opinions formerly advocated by the *Zuid-Afrikaan*, and the fact of his voluntarily resigning the useful office of law lecturer and his practice at the bar for the Presidentship of the Orange Free State, seems at least to be presumptive evidence that he was more ambitious to become "a real South African patriot," completely independent of any allegiance to England's Queen, than a judge of the Supreme Court of the British Colony of the Cape of Good Hope. In his honest and anxious desire to "establish a Dutch Republic over the border," he, no doubt, sacrificed his personal interests; and, however unsuccessful his government may have been in controlling the rude elements of society northward of the Orange River, he was zealous and well-intentioned in the discharge of his duties; and no one, even if he questions the soundness of the argument of his late despatches to Sir Philip Wodehouse, can dispute that he was really in earnest in attempting to maintain the independence of the Republic over which he rules. He is about to return to his professional pursuits in this Colony, and may perhaps again take a seat in the Cape Parliament, convinced by bitter experience that it is to the interest of the State, in its geographical situation and dependent position, that it should cease to be *nominally* free, and that it should seek for true liberty, order, and good government "under the large folds of the flag of England." It is true that the *Friend of the Free State*, while taking favourable notice of the last part of Mr. President Brand's reply, declining to become again a candidate for the Presidential chair, "strengthen above all the good understanding which has thus far subsisted between the Government and inhabitants of the Cape Colony and Natal, and those of the Orange Free

State, and which I confidently trust will ever continue to subsist," does not give His Honour "credit for having done much, if anything, during his Presidential reign, to foster or cherish this feeling." It also seems to censure Mr. Brand for not openly avowing his sympathy with his predecessor, Mr. Boshof, on the subject of "federation with the British Colonies," and to believe that His Honour's idea of a union is far distant in prospect : that is to say, when the Queen's troops shall have taken their departure from the shores of South Africa, and the Colony of the Cape of Good Hope shall have ceased to be British.

This may be an unfair and exaggerated representation of the President's views, but when the *Friend of the Free State* writes in this fashion, and the *Tyd*, the organ of the Dutch element beyond the Orange River, puts forward as a fact that the "memorial in which the inhabitants of the Free State request a foreign Governor to annihilate their independence" by Federation, has "created a most unusual unanimity in the whole country, urgently requesting Mr. Brand again to allow himself to be nominated for the Presidency," it certainly is strange, if not "a thing too preposterous to be supposed for a moment," that the Hollanders should make him a "captive in chains" for his alleged British propensities, and his too great respect for the Queen's Representative. After the praise which has been bestowed upon the President of the Orange Free State, not only in Cape Town, but also by some portion of the Frontier press, for the determined manner in which he resisted the good advice of the representative of Great Britain to stop the wretched warfare, and for the ability with which, as the advocate of the burghers, he has made out a case against the Basutos,—it is not very surprising that some should be sceptical as to the truth of the rumour that he is to be charged with being "untrue to his country," and too ready to yield implicit obedience to the behests of Her Majesty's High Commissioner. If, in consequence of the Basutos being expected to attack Rouxville, there had been a report that all true-born Englishmen, aided by the "men of influence in the Free State, and the honest and industrious farmers who migrated over the River because their farms were too small for them on this side," were commencing a constitutional agitation to remove the President from his high office, because he did not at once accept the peaceful overtures of Great Britain, and willingly put faith in the assurance of her representative "that the just claims of the State would receive the fullest consideration," many might have thought that they could safely attach credit to it.

The *Eastern Province Herald*, evidently under a conviction that the recent victories at Tandjesberg and the Kieme have been most decisive and conclusive, argues "that it would have been a false step, injurious alike to the Free State and the

Basutos themselves," to have suspended hostilities at the bidding of Sir Philip Wodehouse; but it seems to me that you have, in common with so many of your contemporaries of the press, arrived at a just conclusion, " that the Boers' conquests are a little less complete than they would have us believe," and consequently that no great advantage has been gained by the prolongation of the war. Although the Free State authorities appear anxious to avail themselves of the legal axiom, that possession is nine points of the law, by ordering the grantees to occupy the conquered territory, the opinion is freely expressed in the columns of the *Friend*, that such occupation would be attended with danger, "before the Governor has been consulted, and preliminaries of peace agreed upon," and, if this be so, the burghers have not much improved the basis of negotiations with respect to the future boundaries of Basutoland by the *alleged* conquest of the territory ceded by Moshesh in 1866. As there is no smoke without fire, there must be some foundation for the intelligence from Aliwal North, and perhaps it will turn out, as the *Advertiser and Mail* suggests, that some complaints are about to be made against President Brand by some members of the Volksraad. As a day or two will put us in possession of the real facts of the case, it is vain to speculate much upon the point, but may not the report be a joke as a sort of set-off to the absurdity that an Englishman was to be charged with high treason for originating the federation memorial to Sir Philip Wodehouse? For my own part, I sincerely wish that Mr. President Brand is still a free agent, and that he will be empowered by the Volksraad to approach the Aliwal North Convention in an amicable spirit, and that after having agreed to the boundaries of the new British territory, he will, in the words of the *Graham's Town Journal*, " open up a negotiation for the full admission of the State to its old rights and privileges under the Sovereignty."

Saturday, 28th March, 1868. COLONIST.

BRITISH SUBJECTS.

SIR,—The question of the allegiance due to the British Crown by the inhabitants of the Free State has, since I last addressed you, increased in interest, and assumed, perhaps, a serious complexion. I observe from the *Mercantile Advertiser* of this morning, that certain three British-born subjects, residing at Philippolis, unsuccessfully pleaded that they ought not to fight against the Basutos now that the Governor's proclamation had declared the Basutos British subjects; and that Mr. J. M. Howell, when cited before the landdrost of Bloemfontein to show cause why he refused to go on commando, is alleged to have quoted from a letter of Sir Philip Wodehouse to the effect that it would ill become anyone who owed allegiance to the Queen to take an active part in hostilities against the new subjects of the British Crown. There is also a rumour that Sir Walter Currie had been authorized to use force, if necessary, to eject the Burghers from the conquered territory. If this order be put into execution, it may lead even to hostile conflict between the Free State and the Cape Colony, an event to be deprecated. The frontier press also hints, if I am not mistaken, that all British subjects caught in arms against the Basutos would be tried, if not for high treason, at least for a misdemeanour. With your permission, therefore, I wish to add a few remarks to my former communication on this subject.

Your correspondent " Colonist," in noticing the request for information, quotes from Kerr's Blackstone, which proves that natural allegiance cannot be forfeited by anything " *but the united concurrence of the Legislature,*" and the despatch of the late Duke of Newcastle, to which he refers, seems also to take for granted that " *an Act of Parliament would be required for the purpose of releasing from the ties of native allegiance*" all who were formerly subjects of the Crown of England. If this be so, and no action has been taken by the Imperial Parliament in the matter, my theory of the power of Sir George Clerk's Convention, entirely to absolve from allegiance to Her Majesty all who were inhabitants of the Free State, and their descendants, as well as President Brand, will fall to the ground, and the idea of " Colonist," with respect to those subjects of Her Majesty who have cast their lot in the Free State since it was declared independent, which appears to be founded on the reason and common sense of the argument of the *Daily News*, might be all very well for discussion in a Debating Society, but would not regulate the decision of the Supreme Court.

Not being conversant with the principles of International Law, I again intrude upon your columns with the view of inviting discussion on this important subject. Many of the rumours afloat with regard to the difficulties which beset the Governor in the coming Aliwal North Conference in the settlement of the future boundaries of Basutoland, are no doubt groundless, and I for one regret that violent leading articles should be written upon the assumption of the truth of facts, which all would deplore, but which are not proved. There is one report, however, to which allusion cannot do harm, but may do much good, and that is, " that the annexation of the Free State is contemplated," and if some of the Cape Town press would discuss this question in its editorial columns, they would, in my opinion, be conferring a benefit not only on the Free State, but also on the Colonies of the Cape and Natal.

Cape Town, 1st April, 1868.   ANGLO-AFRICAN.

"Annexation alone will make the State free."
—*Graham's Town Journal.*

Sir,—The editor of the leading organ of public opinion at Graham's Town, who has added to his well-earned reputation by having consistently supported the Queen's Representative in his endeavour to carry out the good intentions of Her Majesty's Government, to restore peace and tranquillity to South Africa, concludes an able article, which, deprecating the horrors of war with our neighbours, with whom we should be on the best of terms, and wisely counselling submission to the British Government on the part of "the authorities and people" of the Orange Free State, argues that the State must be weary of "a false and fruitless freedom," with the terse sentence, hereunto prefixed, which seems well worthy to be the theme of discussion by the Colonial press at the present moment. Whatever difference of opinion may exist as to the *modus operandi* of Her Majesty's High Commissioner in bringing "the Basuto nation within British jurisdiction," or however much you "may entertain a lurking belief that a different initiation of the new policy of Great Britain in reference to the border tribes might have averted the present ugly crisis," few, who have the interest of all parties concerned really at heart, will venture to dispute that you act with wise discretion in "willingly conceding that this is not the time to urge such views."

While the conduct of Sir Philip Wodehouse has been violently censured in Cape Town, it is gratifying to those who believe that he has been throughout actuated by the best of motives in the execution of the instructions of the Home Government, and honestly entertain the opinion that his clear and conciliatory despatches deserved better treatment at the hands of the President and Volksraad than they have received, to find that no "strong adverse feeling exists along the route by which he journeyed to the Free State," but that, on the contrary, he has been everywhere greeted with welcome demonstrations of loyalty to the Queen, and of respect towards himself as Her Majesty's faithful representative in the Colony. It seems to me, I confess, that the course of action pursued by His Excellency, which has been so severely assailed, needs no justification; at any rate I care not, after the able leaders of the *Argus* and *Standard* of this morning, as well as that of the *Graham's Town Journal* above referred to, further to argue this part of the case, at least at the present stage of the proceedings. I, for one, am sanguine that "the wise and liberal offer" communicated from Colesberg by Sir Philip Wodehouse to Mr. Brand, may yet effect a wonderful "change in the spirit of the dream" of the Volksraad, and that they may be induced to listen to reason, and to admit the soundness of the conclusion of the *Argus*, that "it would be much wiser of the Burghers to accept three hundred farms of fifteen hundred morgen each, under the protection of the British Crown, than to throw themselves madly on the points of British bayonets." Be this as it may, the Basuto Protectorate by Great Britain is an accomplished fact, and my object in intruding upon your columns is to urge that no time should be lost in taking practical measures to make it, as it has been correctly designated, "the thin end of the wedge"—the stepping-stone to the further extension of British rule and British protection northward of the Orange River—the resumption of the Sovereignty.

The loyal inhabitants of Colesberg, under the guidance of their respected Civil Commissioner, so long the British Resident in the Sovereignty, could not conclude their recent address to Sir Philip Wodehouse "without expressing their firm conviction that the re-annexation of the Orange Free State is necessary for the good and permanent peace and prosperity of its inhabitants, and for the commercial and social development of South Africa." Upon this point there is unanimity of opinion both in the Colonies of the Cape and Natal, and, but for the baneful influence of "the violent anti-English faction, known as the Hollander party, which the Orange Free State Government is not able to control," there is good ground to hope and believe that the majority of the inhabitants of that State might easily be brought to desire and to ask "to be allowed to live and rest under the large folds of the flag of England." Even the editor of the *Advertiser and Mail*, whom you have so properly rebuked for "pandering to un-English sentiments," by grossly exaggerating the weight and influence of the French Emperor's intercession in behalf of Christian missions in South Africa and in favour of Moshesh and his tribe, writes thus :—" If the Basutos, who were formerly the foes of Britain, are taken under British protection, is no offer to be made of a similar favour to be extended to the Free State, which was abandoned to its fate just on account of the formidableness of that Basuto hostility?" No one can deny that the *Argus* is quite right when it says, in the interesting summary of the Basuto question transmitted to England by the mail-steamer *Celt*, that "all the mischiefs and difficulties which have since arisen, have been the results of the fatal measure of abandonment by the British Government of the Orange River territory, and the establishment in its place of a free and independent Government, having nothing beyond friendly relations with Great Britain, for which, it must never be forgotten, the Cape and Free State colonists are not in any way or in any sense responsible." Under all the circumstances then, would it not be just and expedient to inaugurate a constitutional agitation within the Cape Colony, with a view of endeavouring to induce Her Majesty's Government to reverse this fatal policy of abandonment, and to act consistently in the further extension of British influence in South Africa by making, not only the Basutos, but also the Free Staters, British subjects? Of course the difficulty in the way is that the free and independent Republic has not implored, in common with Moshesh, to be placed under regal sway of England's monarchs, and so long as the Hollanders reign supreme beyond the Orange River, it is not likely that a petition to the Queen to resume the sovereignty will meet with the cordial approval of the Free Staters; but will not the fact of the English and Afrikanders on this side of the river joining in proving by well-adduced arguments that it is to the interest of both countries that they should live under *one* flag—that of England—go very far in persuading the majority of the people of the Free State to throw the Hollanders overboard, and to hail the hoisting of the Union Jack at Bloemfontein with joy equal to that lately evinced by the old Chief at the happy consummation of this event at Thaba Bosigo? Sir Philip Wodehouse with great propriety, while busily engaged in annexing Basutoland to the British Colonial Empire, declines " to discuss the expediency of re-uniting the Orange Free State with the Colony of the Cape;" but this is no reason why the colonists of the Cape and Natal should not respectfully request Her Majesty's High Commissioner, after having accomplished his present purpose, to bring the subject of the extension of British rule to that State to the favourable consideration of Her Majesty's Government. The Port Elizabeth Chamber of Commerce have already addressed the Governor at Aliwal North in terms of warm approval of the British Basuto Protectorate, and have expressed the opinion that "it would be a source of immense relief to this Colony, if in the course of the negotiations with Mr. President Brand, it shall so happen that His Excellency were to see his way to bring the Orange Free State again under British power, by annexation, federation, or otherwise." Why should not the Cape Town Chamber of Commerce, after the misrepresentation of the peaceful intentions of Her Majesty's Government, and the decided opposition to its policy in certain quarters, follow this good example? On a former occasion the petition to the Queen and Imperial Parliament against the removal of the troops, which *first* made its appearance in the columns of the *Standard*, and met with your editorial approval, was followed by local Parliamentary action and the support of the Governor, which produced successful results. Why should not a similar constitutional course be now adopted, and Her Most Gracious Majesty be invoked by petition to resume the Sovereignty—to extend British territory, and to increase the number of the subjects of the British Crown northward of the Orange River in South Africa?

Saturday, 4th April. COLONIST.

WE ARE NOT YET FREE.

Sir,—Mr. Josias Philip Hoffman, who, as the President of the Representatives delegated by the inhabitants of the Sovereignty to receive from Her Majesty's Special Commissioner in 1854 the Government of the Orange River Territory, and the *first* President of the Republic, ought to be a good authority, commences a sensible appeal to his fellow-burghers of the Orange Free State with the words, "We are not yet free." He reminds them that at the time he insisted "that it was a shame, if not an act of betrayal, that the British Government should desert them," and that he had in vain asked Sir George Clerk to "have them declared free," and "the King of Holland to recognise them as an independent people." He then appears emphatically to corroborate the opinion which has been maintained by your correspondent "Anglo African," with respect to the Free Staters being still British subjects, in the following passage :—

Boshof and Brand came here as British subjects, *without their having the right to speak of a declaration of freedom.* Such is the situation. Will you now, in your acknowledged independence, take up arms against the British Government? Then you are *rebels*, and can be punished as such. Look, then, to what you do. Your President, the Hon. Mr. Brand, has already told you that he is a British subject, and who, then, will help you? * * * Present, then, without delay, memorials to the Volksraad, and implore them to do their duty, either to secure your independence, which, if they cannot do, to have you annexed again to the British Crown. To remain as you are is perilous.

Many who reflect that Blackstone and the late Duke of Newcastle both held that natural allegiance to the Crown cannot be forfeited except by an Act of the Imperial Legislature, will be led to conclude that the former Ministers of Her Majesty, who "sacrificed the Sovereignty, including large Colonial and British interests, to a wretched, short-sighted policy of expediency, did contemplate the possibility of the measure being again reversed, *as they stuck at requesting Parliament to ratify the abandonment by a declaration of release from allegiance to the abandoned subjects of Her Majesty.*" If this view of the case be correct, has not a good opportunity arrived for the reversal of this fatal policy, by annexing the Orange Free State, as well as Basutoland, to the British Colonial Empire?

A correspondent, "Patriot," in the columns of your contemporary this morning, puts several grave questions, which I must leave to others, more conversant with the principles of international law, to answer, but to the *fourth* question, "If the Basutos, who are foreigners, are worthy of protection, are the British subjects and their property in the Free State not worthy of the same? and more especially, is not this Colony's property in that State worthy of the first and best act of protection"? I most unhesitatingly give a reply in the affirmative, and add, let no time be lost in making every constitutional effort to induce the Queen of Great Britain to throw her shield of protection over her *former*, as well as her *new* subjects northward of the Orange River. If something be not done in this direction, complications may arise ; and the fair name of England be tarnished, and her prestige in South Africa even receive a shock, at the hands of the violent Hollander party in the Orange Free State. The *Graham's Town Journal* properly remarks :—" That, under the circumstances, a deputation of Englishmen from Bloemfontein should have come down to Aliwal North to wait upon His Excellency, is perfectly natural. The Englishmen in the Free State are in a most perplexing and painful position. They may well say they have a divided duty. Their difficulties will command the sympathy of the whole colony. It is to be hoped that His Excellency will know how to meet their case." To me it seems that Her Majesty's High Commissioner would do well *at once* to cause it to be made known that, if any decided movement were taken by the inhabitants of the Free State to express their desire to be relieved of their *nominal* independence and " false and fruitless freedom," and to become again, if they have ever ceased to be, British subjects, His Excellency would exert his influence to induce the Home Government to see this reasonable desire put into execution with as little delay as possible. Although it is said that the Governor does not feel that he can treat with the inhabitants of the Free State while negotiations are going on with their Government, it is to be hoped that the report is true that His Excellency had promised to forward to the Imperial Government a petition in favour of annexation, which had been presented to him by a deputation chiefly of Englishmen. Perhaps there may be a fair prospect of the prayer of such a petition being granted, if it be only from the dread of the necessity of equipping a military expedition from England, although not quite on so large a scale as that required to bring King Theodorus to his senses, for the purpose of protecting the rights of British subjects at Bloemfontein.

Tuesday, 7th April, 1868. COLONIST.

BRITISH SUBJECTS IN THE FREE STATE.

SIR,—The idea to which I ventured to give expression at the conclusion of my last letter, has been anticipated and amplified by the *Graham's Town Journal*, which playfully indulges its imagination by predicting that " Theodorus in the North of Africa may find his double in John Brand in the South," and that it may be deemed necessary to march a " little British army," under the command of Sir Percy Douglas, across the

Orange River, "to the rescue of another company of captives." Although official information has not yet been received that the eight English gentlemen who dared to visit Aliwal North for the purpose of "asking Sir Philip whether he could not annex the Republic" have been committed to the gaol of Bloemfontein, on a charge of high treason, it does not seem unlikely that even the very remote possibility of a *second* Abyssinian expedition to the Trans-Gareipian territory may *at once* induce the House of Commons, the guardian of the interests of the tax-payers of England, to present an address to Her Majesty, favourably to receive and to grant the prayer of the petitioners of the Free State, who were formerly, and long to be again, under the protection of the English flag. A British subject, writing from Philippolis, directs attention to the anomaly of Englishmen being punished by fine and imprisonment for refusing to wage war with the Basutos after they had been proclaimed British subjects, and wisely suggests, in the event of no change immediately taking place in the Republican dynasty of the Orange Free State, the appointment of a British Consul to protect the rights of those who still owe allegiance to Queen Victoria.

The opinion before submitted in your columns, that Her Majesty's ministers, who, through the instrumentality of Sir George Clerk, carried out the fatal policy of abandonment of the Sovereignty, *purposely* abstained from formally releasing the Queen's subjects from their allegiance by Act of Parliament, appears to be confirmed and supported by the annexed statement of the *Great Eastern*, no mean authority on any point connected with this subject, to which it has so long and consistently devoted its attention:—

The conditions of the Convention were never meant to do more than *permit* certain subjects of Her Majesty to manage their own affairs, and, although Sir George Clerk included therein a stipulation that the inhabitants should be formally absolved from their allegiance, the Home Government clearly showed their intention of making it merely a *permissory* document, by positively refusing to fulfil the stipulation. . . . For all the Convention can effect to the contrary, the Free Staters are at this moment merely a set of British subjects, who have been permitted to run riot for the last fourteen years, to the great discomfort of all decently-organized communities in the neighbourhood, and who may be lawfully brought under British control at any moment when the British Government may deem it expedient.

If this be a correct view of the case, am I very far wrong in attempting to get up a constitutional agitation *even* in Cape Town, for the purpose of inducing, not by arbitrary dictation, but by convincing arguments, the people of the Orange Free State to ask the Queen of England to grant to them the same boon she has just conferred on Moshesh and his tribe—British rule and British protection ? There must be some great advantage in being a subject of Her Majesty, or the wily Chiefs of the aboriginal tribes of Southern Africa would not all be so eagerly anxious " to be allowed to rest and live under the wide folds of the flag of England." Your readers will recollect that Mr. President Brand, in his despatch to Sir Philip Wodehouse of the 31st of January, wrote thus :—

Had Moshesh adhered to the treaty of Thaba Bosigo, as Molappo has to the treaty of Imperani, of the 26th of March, 1866, by which he became a subject of the Free State, and as Paulus Mopeli has to the treaty by which he became a subject of the Free State, his people would now be enjoying the blessings and prosperity of peace, and the Government of the Free State would not have been compelled to take up arms and prosecute a costly war, which we all most sincerely deplore.

It will also strike many as a very singular coincidence that, about the time the President was in his speech to the Volksraad saying " I have satisfaction in being able to state that Captains Molappo and Paulus Moperi have conducted themselves during the Basuto war as faithful subjects, and that I continue to receive the most satisfactory reports from their commandants in regard to *their fidelity and thankfulness at being able to enjoy blessings of peace in tranquillity and rest as Free State subjects,"* Molappo should be himself most desirous of and engaged in becoming a subject of the Queen, and to be enrolled under the banner of Sir Walter Currie at Thaba Bosigo. The anti-British influence of the Hollanders, which has succeeded in preventing the Volksraad from treating Her Majesty's representative with proper respect, and in compelling them to decline his offer of friendly negotiation, may prevail for a time in checking the majority of the people of the Orange Free State from following the example of Moroko, Molappo, and other chiefs, and appealing for Great Britain's intervention in their behalf, but this is no reason why the counter-influence of the loyal subjects of Her Majesty within the Colonies of the Cape and Natal should not be set at work to urge upon their neighbours northward of the Orange River, both English and Afrikanders, to unite in petitioning, as Moshesh has done, for the favour he has received at the hands of the Queen.

Sir Philip Wodehouse, who must be pleased with his reception throughout the country districts *en route* to Aliwal North, in returning thanks to the Burghers at Hanover for their hearty welcome, is reported have said :—

Many of you here present no doubt have relations and connections in the Free State, and very naturally you look to the result of my mission. The sole wish of Her Majesty's Government is to establish peace throughout these districts, and we thought that this object could be best attained by taking the Basuto tribe under the protection of the British Government. *I am aware that an opinion exists, and, no doubt, many here assembled share in that opinion, that it would be to the interest of the Free State were that country brought under British rule, and annexed to the colony.* Such is not now my intention. You must know that the Basuto nation has for the last four years been earnestly praying Her Majesty to take them under her protection, and any move in the same direction in regard to the Free State must necessarily emanate from the people of that State. *But, as yet, no request of that kind has been made, and naturally the British Government will not take the initiative in such a matter.*

It may then, I think, be taken for granted, from the reasoning of the best authority as to the inclinations of the Home Government, that, if the *independent* Trans-Orange Republic be weary of its nominal freedom, and seeks for true liberty and good government under the salutary influence of the British Crown, it is only to ask to be annexed to the British Colonial Empire, and its request will be granted.

In the further extension of British rule northward of the Orange River, the Cape and Natal are no less interested than the Free State itself, and they ought, therefore, *all* to join in well-organized efforts to bring this happy event about. Although after the insult on the Queen's Representative on the spot, it is not probable that the commission deputed to confer with His Grace the Duke of Buckingham in England, and to protest against the policy of Her Majesty's Government with respect to the Basutos, will receive a very favourable hearing, would it not be as well that some action should be taken to approach Downing-street, *through the proper official channel*, with the view of making it known that it is the general opinion of the colonists of the Cape and Natal, as well as of many in the Free State, that the annexation of Basutoland, although good in itself, is only a half-measure—a step in the right direction, which must be followed up by the resumption of the Sovereignty? However much the good intentions of the Home Government with respect to the *partial* extension of British rule beyond the Orange River may have been misunderstood in the Western Metropolis, there can be little doubt that the vast majority of the inhabitants of the Cape, Natal, and the Free State, would rejoice and be content if "England only were to fulfil her bounden duty by maintaining her rule over *all* South Africa."

Saturday, 11th April, 1868. COLONIST.

THE PROTEST OF THE FREE STATE AGAINST THE BRITISH GOVERNMENT.

SIR,—The *Advertiser and Mail*, goaded by the *Standard's* taunt that "it was pandering to un-English sentiments," retorted that your "turning round and commending only the intervention of Sir Philip" on behalf of the Basutos, when you saw that it was backed by irresistible power, was a very un-English sort of proceeding indeed; but your leading article of this morning is an able defence against this grave accusation, and affords satisfactory proof that you are prepared to support the Queen's Representative against the existing Dutch prejudices of Cape Town and Bloemfontein. It is one thing to have found fault with the delay in issuing the Proclamation in the *Government Gazette* declaring the Basutos British subjects, and another *now* that the annexation of Basutoland to the British Colonial Empire has been accomplished, in a captious spirit to raise objections to what has been done, and to sow the seeds of discontent with a measure of Her Majesty's Government, which, it is admitted by all, is for the good of South Africa.

Your contemporary, better versed in literature and science than in international law, in his laudable desire " to advocate fair-play between the weak and the strong, and to do justice even to the helpless Free State as much as to America or France," takes, it is submitted, rather an exaggerated view, and does not quite fairly represent the case, when he writes :— " What the Free State protests against, and is justly indignant at, is that its independence as a State—that independence which was forced upon it by Sir George Clerk in 1854—is now deliberately ignored, and that ' Sir Philip Wodehouse is carrying out a despotic intervention in defiance of its independence, contrary to the law of nations, and backed only by the law of might.'" In what manner has the independence of the Free State been ignored by Her Majesty's High Commissioner? What act of Sir Philip Wodehouse justly merits the oft-used and popular epithet of "despotic and tyrannical?" How has the law of nations been infringed and might exercised against right? The ill-advised resolution of the Volksraad, to treat with contempt the Representative of Great Britain *on the spot*, who had declared his readiness " to give the fullest consideration to the just claims of the State," and to send a protest to England against the matured policy of Her Majesty's ministers, may, it is thought, be ascribed to the influence of Mr. President Brand and Mr. Advocate Hamelberg in the debate on the question of British intervention at the extraordinary session. I have in vain searched the speeches of these two lawyers for any argument, founded on the principles of the law of nations, to prove that any wrong had been done to the Free State by the interposition of the Queen of England to restore peace to South Africa. The burden of their song was that " the Governor was tampering with their rights"—" that he was the cause of their difficulties with Moshesh"—" that the acts of treachery of the Basuto chief justified the prolongation of the war ;" but the *two* main grounds of their complaint seem to be, as formally expressed in the resolution, " the acceptance of Moshesh and his people as British subjects, and the annexation of his country to the British territory, *and* the assertion of a right to prohibit our State being supplied with ammunition from the Colony, both alike in conflict (as it was alleged) to the spirit and letter of the Convention" of Sir George Clerk.

1. The *Argus*, in its leader of Saturday last, clearly showed, by historical references, that it was " not, as has been asserted, contrary to received international maxims and laws, for one nation to step in between two belligerents, and offer a protec-

torate to one of them on certain terms;" and thereon correctly founded the argument that "no one could doubt the right of the English Government to annex Basutoland even while at war with the Free State," provided it could be shown that a protracted and wretched border warfare between the Boers and the Basutos was detrimental to the interests of the British Colonies of the Cape and Natal. Of course, in such a case, Great Britain ought to act with even-handed justice and equity, and not forcibly " snatch away any territory fairly gained in war by the Free State." But Sir Philip Wodehouse has never assumed arbitrarily to fix the future boundary line between the Orange Free State and Basutoland, and has throughout "invited negotiation" at Aliwal North, for the purpose of amicably settling the knotty points with respect to the so-called " conquered territory"—*not*, in reality, in possession of the burghers.

It is true that Mr. President Brand, not only in his despatch to Sir Philip Wodehouse, but also in his opening speech to the Volksraad, states that "the conquered territory has been cleared," but it is reported, on the other side, that Sir Walter Currie finds a great many Basutos still in occupation of the lands which they have cultivated, and are alleged to have deserted; and it appears also that the destruction of the crops, which in many places are standing in luxuriance, has not been carried to the alarming extent anticipated.

While it cannot but be gratifying to all who naturally sympathize with the weaker against the stronger party, or, as the *Argus* amusingly puts it, who espouse the cause of the " little 'un," in a street fight with " a big fellow," that no principle of international law has been seriously abrogated in the establishment of the British Basuto Protectorate, I cannot help submitting to your readers that there is some sound practical common sense in the view taken of this matter by the *Great Eastern*, in the annexed extract from its late leader, commenting on the debate in the Volksraad :—

A great deal was said about the power and dignity of the State having been insulted by Sir Philip Wodehouse's proceedings, and also about the injustice of infringing the Convention of the 23rd February, 1854—the President quoting *American* authorities on international law. This would be very fine and very proper, if in any sense the Free State could really and lawfully be considered an independent State—although even the Great Powers have already arrogated to themselves the right to annex, dictate to, or treat as they please, all such *little* powers, as by their misconduct endanger the peace or prosperity of their neighbours. International law does not apply to such pettifogging principalities, or diminutive democracies, any more than civil law to street *games*, or schoolboys whose heads may be knocked together by the policeman or schoolmaster, whenever they disturb the peace by evincing precocity in swearing or fighting.

Upon the whole, then, it does not seem that the point, or principle, of the law of nations, involved in the Queen of England having consented to make Moshesh and his tribe British subjects, *at their own request*, is so difficult or important as to require the carrying out the suggestion, made by Mr. Advocate Hamelberg, "of appealing to another Power to arbitrate between the British Government and that of the Orange Free State," and it is to be hoped that the great sticklers for the independence of the Republic will yet see the folly of dreading any communication with Her Majesty's High Commissioner, lest "he should place a halter round their necks." If Sir Philip Wodehouse has erred in this matter at all, it is that he has been too scrupulously cautious and timid to intermeddle in any way with the boasted, though nominal, independence of the Orange Free State, and too slow to proclaim aloud that "annexation is the only panacea for the many ills of that State."

2. After your convincing leader of this morning, your readers will not require me to argue the point as to the alleged breach of the Convention by the Governor not granting permits for the transmission of gunpowder and fire-arms to the Free State. It would indeed be superfluous to enlarge upon your text, "that it would be monstrous to suppose that the Governor of a British Colony would allow a neighbouring power to purchase arms and ammunition in his country for the purpose of carrying on a war with British subjects." Whatever difference of opinion may exist as to the want of diplomatic tact on the part of Sir Philip Wodehouse in having been too straightforward in exposing the weakness of the Free Staters, by referring to his ability to stop their supply of gunpowder, when they had plenty of it in store in their magazines, there can be no doubt that he was perfectly justified in exerting the power given by the local legislature of restricting the transport of the deadly weapons of war northward of the Orange River, to be used by the Burghers in defiance of the good intentions of Her Majesty's Government to stay further bloodshed in South Africa, which he had been commissioned by Her Majesty's Government to put into execution. I cannot conclude without expressing my gratification that the Governor should have called attention to the breach of the Convention by the closing of the Civil Courts against colonial creditors, as it is a proof of His Excellency's sympathizing with the mercantile interests of the Eastern Province, and will encourage agitation on the part of Port Elizabeth, Graham's Town, and King William's Town, for the annexation of the Orange Free State to the Queen of England's colonial dominions.

Tuesday, 14th April, 1868.　　　　　　　　　　　　COLONIST.

THE ANNEXATION OF BASUTOLAND.

SIR,—The *Advertiser and Mail*, after having the other day properly quoted, in evident terms of approval from Sir Philip Wodehouse's reply to the loyal address from Colesberg, "that

K

it would be an evil day for the Colony if there should cease to
exist in the minds of the community a diversity of opinion on
public affairs," in its sub-leader of this morning, without
commenting much on the further correspondence on the Basuto
question just published, writes as follows:—"*Every* dispassionate and impartial critic must feel that President Brand has
the best of the argument." I venture, however, to submit that
many will be found to differ *toto cœlo* from this judgment, rather
dictatorially delivered from the editor's chair, and not hesitate
in awarding the palm of praise, both in clearness of style and
soundness of reasoning, to Her Majesty's High Commissioner.

On one point, it seems to me that there cannot well be much
difference of opinion on the part of those who really wish well
to all parties concerned—the Colony, the Free State, and the
Basutos—and that is that it is to be greatly regretted that the
Volksraad did not empower the President to meet Great
Britain's representative at the proposed conference at Aliwal
North, to settle, after all that has been said and done, the *only*
real point at issue—the boundary line between the Orange Free
State and the new British territory, Basutoland. Can any one
who calmly and without favour or prejudice, carefully reads this
"lengthened correspondence," doubt the soundness of the
conclusion of the *Argus*, that "it contains matter which should
have been the subject of negotiation," and that "there are
disagreements on matters of fact which nothing but verbal
discussions could settle, and statements which nothing but the
hearing of witnesses could sift?" Suppose Mr. President
Brand had met Sir Philip Wodehouse, and proved to his entire
satisfaction all the allegations of his despatch of the 2nd of
April, he might perhaps have succeeded in establishing an
equitable title to the so-called "conquered territory," but more
correctly defined as "disputed territory." If the treaty of
peace concluded at Thaba Bosigo on the 5th of April, 1866, by
which Moshesh ceded to the Orange Free State the territory
annexed by Proclamation of Commandant-General Fick, could,
under all the circumstances attending the commencement of
the *last* war, be deemed fairly binding on the old chief, Great
Britain's agent would probably have felt himself compelled
either to give up the whole extent of land to the Orange Free
State, or to grant compensation for such portion of it as was
retained for the necessary support of Her Majesty's new
subjects, the Basutos.

Surely it would not be to the interest of the Free State itself
to take away from Moshesh and his tribe, their rich arable
lands, and compel them to indulge their "thievish propensities"
by depriving them of the means of growing their own corn;
and the treaties with Letsea and Molappo, "who were permitted
to continue to dwell in portions of the territory annexed by
Commandant-General Fick," afford the best evidence that even

the Volksraad did not covet all the good land of their sable neighbours. His Excellency says in his despatch of the 4th of April: "It has been my endeavour, in carrying out the instructions of Her Majesty's Government, to obtain the best possible information as to the actual, not the past, state of the country, and to make such overtures to your Government *as were, in my judgment, fair to all concerned, and likely to prove permanently beneficial.*" The opinion is pretty generally entertained that Sir Philip Wodehouse was right when he stated in his despatch of the 11th of February—

I believe that even among the most intelligent inhabitants of the State an impression prevails that the cession of territory demanded from the Basutos is in excess of what true policy would dictate, inasmuch as it would deprive the tribe of a great quantity of land best suited to them, and coop them up in comparatively barren tracts to a degree that would render thieving almost inevitable and necessary for their very existence. I think, therefore, that I may fairly suggest, as deserving of the most serious consideration of your Government, whether the true interests of the State do not point to such negotiations with a friendly power, on the subject of a modification of the boundary, as will ensure ample consideration of the claims of the State, without rendering permanent peace altogether unattainable.

Of course, however, if Mr. Brand controverted this opinion, and established by evidence that " the Basutos, if restrained from crossing the boundary line fixed by the treaty of Thaba Bosigo," would not suffer, but still have land enough to live upon, His Excellency's valid objection to "the first exercise of British authority having for its object the ruin of the people, who had just become British subjects," would have been removed. Great Britain certainly has no interest in the large extent of territory in Basutoland, except in so far that, if " the Basutos be confined within a tract insufficient for their support," it may be very difficult, even under British control, to restrain them from being troublesome to their neighbours of the independent Free State. It will be recollected that, from the very beginning of the discussion of this question, I have always argued that the Free State could not hope much to improve the basis of negotiation by refusing to suspend hostilities, when Sir Philip Wodehouse made that reasonable request, stating at the same time that he was prepared to "give the fullest consideration to the just claims of that State" on terms of friendly alliance with Great Britain ; and the result has proved that I was not very far out in my calculations. While Mr. President Brand has on several occasions authoritatively declared that the "conquered territory" has been cleared by the forces of the Free State, he does not venture to gainsay the statement made by Sir Philip Wodehouse in his despatch of the 4th of April: —" I learn from sources, on which full reliance can be placed, that Mequatling, Platberg, Tanjesberg, Maguaisberg, and indeed almost all the places of strength within the territory you claim, are again occupied, and command to a certain extent all the country not positively held by the Free State commandoes." Whatever equitable claim, then, the Orange Free State may have to the disputed territory, it cannot with any justice now avail itself of the popular legal maxim "that possession is nine points of the law," although it has been foolishly urged on by bad counsel to continue fighting, after the Basutos had laid down their arms at the bidding of their new Queen's representative at the Cape, for the express purpose of being enabled to do so. The *Advertiser and Mail* also reports that "it is against the armed intervention of His Excellency" on behalf of "his new ally, Moshesh," "that the Free State Government has determined to appeal to Her Majesty the Queen," but is this a fair and accurate representation of the case?

The resolution of the Volksraad does certainly in a formal manner put forward that the Convention has been violated " by the acceptance of Moshesh and his people as British subjects, and by the annexation of his country to the British territory, as well as by the prohibition of the supply of ammunition from the Colony," and therefore determines to treat Her Majesty's High Commissioner with contempt, and to go direct to England with a protest against the British Government. But is not the real ground of complaint the non-accession to the Orange Free State of the " conquered territory?" Does any one believe, who has well digested the correspondence, that, if Sir Philip Wodehouse had adopted Mr. President Brand's suggestion " with respect to the boundary line described in the treaty of Thaba Bosigo, and with his aid had ejected all the Basutos out of the 'conquered territory,' and given the Orange Free State permanent and undisturbed possession of it, the protest against the Basutos having been proclaimed British subjects would have been persisted in by the Volksraad?" But has the Free State set the right way to work to substantiate its claims for the rich land of its neighbours which it so much covets?

Does not the *Argus* put the case in a proper light when it says:—" They may have a splendid case against the British Government or its agents, but they refuse to state it. They may be able to lay claim to half, or two-thirds, or the whole of what is called the conquered territory, but they refuse to do it?" How can the British Government be expected to decide on the merits of this question so well as their accredited representative, who has the means of " more accurate information" on the spot? So long as justice is done both to the Free Staters and the Basutos, it must be a matter of perfect indifference to England what the future boundary line between the Orange Free State and Basutoland is to be. It will not, however, require even a reference to Her Majesty's Attorney-General in London for His Grace the Duke of Buckingham to decide that the British Basuto Protectorate is not " a treaty which may be injurious or prejudicial to the interests of the Orange River Government," within the meaning of the second article of Sir George Clerk's Convention, and that "the freedom" which has been granted "to the Orange River Government to purchase their supplies of ammunition in any British Colony or possession in South Africa, *subject to the laws provided for the regulation of the sale and transit of such ammunition in such British Colonies and possessions*," cannot be made to apply to the case where that Government desires to carry on war against the Queen's new subjects, the Basutos, in opposition to the humane policy of Her Majesty's Government. Although many will not concur with your contemporary in admiration of the logic of Mr. President Brand's despatches, few will withhold their cordial approval of his conclusion that "the Government of the Free State has not the remotest idea of coming into hostile collision with, or taking up arms against, the British Government, *with whom it is anxious to be at all times, and remain on the best and most friendly terms;*" and perhaps, after all, when the Volksraad again meets, they may yet see the wisdom and expediency of entering into friendly negotiation with Her Majesty's High Commissioner on the knotty points in dispute. Even the *Volksblad*, which on this question, to my mind, contrasts so unfavourably with its rival, the *Volksvriend*, that so well argues that "the annexation of Basutoland to the British Crown may be reasonably regarded as only the beginning to the end," the extension of British rule "to the Free State, utterly incompetent of self-government," seems to admit that "there may be difference of opinion as to whether the Free State authorities were wise or not in continuing their defiant attitude after the apparently reasonable proposal of the 300 farms was made by the Governor." There can be no doubt, also, that many of those in Cape Town who were sceptical about the good intentions of Her Majesty's Government towards the Free Staters as well as the Basutos, now openly avow their regret that the equitable offer made by Sir Philip Wodehouse from Colesberg was not at once accepted by the Volksraad, under the firm and honest conviction that a British title to land is of far more marketable value than an Orange Free State title, and that an opportunity has been lost of realizing a considerable sum of money towards the redemption of the obnoxious bluebacks, the offspring of the long-protracted war.

Saturday, 18th April, 1868.　　　　　　　　　　COLONIST.

THE ANNEXATION OF THE ORANGE FREE STATE.

SIR,—The temperate and well-argued letter of a "Free State John Bull," which you have transferred from the *Eastern Province Herald* into your columns of this morning, seems calculated to convince even those in Cape Town, who under the influence of Dutch prejudices, which ought not to be revived, still have doubts and misgivings as to the good intentions of Her Majesty's Government towards South Africa, that British intervention on behalf of the Basutos is not a very violent infringement of the law of nations. If it could be taken for granted that the war which concluded with the treaty of peace at Thaba Bosigo was a just one, Great Britain would, no doubt, be disposed to pay respect to the title of the Orange Free State to the land ceded by Moshesh under the first article of that treaty, *provided* the former inhabitants of that portion of Basutoland were not ejected from the land of their birth, and compelled to seek for shelter and their means of livelihood in the British Colonies of the Cape and Natal. A difficulty might perhaps arise even then, that the Basutos, as in the case of Molappo, who was considered by Mr. President Brand to be so contented with his lot, would refuse to remain under a Republican form of Goverment, and " pray to be allowed to rest and live under the large folds of the flag of England."

The *Advertiser and Mail*, which cannot get rid of its all-absorbing idea that "might is exercised against right," concludes that " the disposal of the conquered territory will be left in abeyance, pending the reference to Her Majesty's Government in England," but it appears to me that the view taken by the *Argus*, that " Sir Philip Wodehouse cannot call back the Basutos from the disputed territory, nor can he allow the Boers to assail them, while in pursuit of lawful occupations" within that territory, is more correct. This knotty point as to the boundary line will, after all, have to be decided on the spot, and the sooner the notion of sending a deputation to England is given up, the better for all parties ; for the plan which has been suggested by your last-named contemporary, " that each party should remain in its present position, pending the appeal, the commandoes in their entrenchments, and the Basutos in the localities from which they have not been driven," is likely to result in mischief and a renewal of hostilities. It will not surprise many to hear the statement in your telegram, that the decision of the Volksraad has caused dissatisfaction in the camp at the Tieme, for there can be no doubt that if the representatives of the people had listened to reason, and not adopted the suicidal policy of rejecting amicable negotiations with Her Majesty's High Commissioner, by this time the question of boundary would have been satisfactorily arranged, and a *mixed* population of burghers and Basutos would be peacefully occupying the "conquered territory." Perhaps, however, out of evil good may come, and this fresh proof of the inability of the Republican dynasty to promote the interests of the Orange Free State may hurry on the extension of British rule to that State. It must be admitted that the British Government erred most grievously in abandoning the Sovereignty and discarding the inhabitants as they did, through the action of their representative, Sir George Russell Clerk; and to put things straight again it may be necessary to have recourse "to a somewhat exceptional policy;" but it seems to me absurd to contend that because we have committed one egregious act of folly, we are not to retrace our steps on being convinced that the general interests of South Africa would be jeopardized by pursuing the same downward course any longer. The sooner, therefore, the Orange Free State is annexed to the British Colonial Empire again the better, and no time ought to be lost in bringing this happy event about. The Convention has been over and over again broken, and the Burghers have proved themselves utterly incapable of governing themselves, and it remains then simply for the British Government to tell them so plainly, and without much parley to proclaim the country British at all hazards. Things seem to be approaching a crisis, and all persons attached to British interests ought to waive minor points, and support Sir Philip Wodehouse in his arduous task of carrying out the humane policy of the Home Government to benefit South Africa as a whole. The anomalous position of British subjects within the Free State affords an additional reason for action on the part of the Queen of England's representative to extend Her Majesty's regal sway northward of the Orange River, and your telegram of this morning affords cheering evidence that the Governor of the Cape will do his best with the British Government in this direction.

A correspondent of the *Friend of the Free State*, "Patriot," in allusion to the injunction contained in the *Government Gazette* "to all Her Majesty's subjects in South Africa," to pay attention to the Basuto Proclamation, puts the question, " Who are the British subjects now residing in the Orange Free State ?" and answers it by the annexed extract from a despatch, dated 14th January, 1854, from the late Duke of Newcastle to Sir George Clerk, which has been before quoted in your columns :—" With respect to the question of the allegiance of the inhabitants who may have been born in British dominions, either within or without the Sovereignty, there is, I believe, little doubt that no measure resting on the Queen's prerogative only for its authority, *could release them from the tie of such native allegiance. An Act of Parliament would be required for that purpose. But for the reasons already adverted to in my despatch of November 14 last, I do not consider it necessary to apply to Parliament on this ground.*" As it is now rather late in the day to ratify and confirm, by enactment of the Imperial Legislature, the Convention of Sir George Clerk, which *professed* to make " the inhabitants of the Orange River Territory *free*," would it not be well that some steps should be taken to request Sir Philip Wodehouse to suggest to Her Majesty's present Ministers the introduction of a *short* Act of Parliament, to annul, as far as possible, what has been done—to resume the Sovereignty, and to restore to their natural allegiance to the Queen of England "Her Majesty's abandoned subjects in South Africa?"

Thursday, 23rd April, 1868. COLONIST.

THE GOVERNOR AND THE FREE STATE. ANNEXATION OR FEDERATION.

SIR,—It has been the fashion in Cape Town to quarrel with the *modus operandi* of Sir Philip Wodehouse, and even to accuse him of gross "tyranny and despotism" in his dealings with the Orange Free State, in carrying out the instructions of the Home Government to establish the British Basuto Protectorate. Some who lead public opinion in the Western metropolis must, it is thought, have been anxious to prevent the respectable Dutch inhabitants of this end of the Colony from duly appreciating the humane and peaceful policy of the Queen's present ministers towards South Africa, or they would not have laboured so hard to make Her Majesty's Representative at the Cape, entrusted with the execution of that policy, as unpopular as possible by too readily assuming the truth of sensational telegrams, now proved to be inaccurate, and founding thereon violently written articles to his prejudice. I have throughout attempted to argue that the despatches of Sir Philip Wodehouse, which contrast more favourably than ever with those of Mr. President Brand, *now* that it is self-evident that "the war was not nearly at an end, nor the so-called conquered territory cleared of Basutos," afforded the best evidence that he was determined in a conciliatory spirit " to give the fullest consideration to the just claims of the Free State," and the pertinent extract from the *Graaff-Reinet Herald*, in your issue of this morning, more than corroborates my view of the case.

It seems to me also that the *Graham's Town Journal* has satisfactorily proved that "His Excellency has brought to the task set him by the Imperial Government an admirable calmness of mind and an inexhaustible store of patience," and that he has almost entitled himself for the future to bear the motto of "*Sauviter in modo, fortiter in re*," whatever difference of opinion there may be as to his official courtesy or diplomatic tact in other past transactions. Some will now begin to think that even the delay in issuing the Proclamation declaring the Basutos British subjects, which *at once* so happily produced the desired effect of staying the bloody hand of war, was prompted by a wish on the part of Sir Philip Wodehouse to negotiate on friendly terms with the President of the Orange Free State, as to the future boundaries of Basutoland, *before* he formally declared it British territory. It appears, however, needless to dwell further upon the merits or demerits of the particular course of action adopted by the Governor, as it requires no great foresight to predict that there must be in Cape Town, as there has already been in the Eastern Province, a strong reaction of public opinion in his favour. May it not be taken for granted, without argument, that "the peaceful subjugation of Basutoland to British authority is a happy event to the Orange Free State—the best thing that could happen to it short of its own annexation? That the Government of the State do not see this, is greatly to be deplored." But the subjoined paragraph from the columns of the *Friend of the Free State* affords some cheering hope that " a change will come o'er the spirit of the dream" of the councils of the Orange Free State as soon as the eyes of the people thereof are opened to see their real interests :—

THE PROTEST AND REACTION.—From all quarters we learn that great dissatisfaction exists among the intelligent of our Boers in regard to the resolution of the Volksraad to having nothing to do with His Excellency the Governor. Mr. Daniel Groblaar, the godfather to this (Mr. Hamelberg's) resolution, was surrounded by a crowd of Boers on the market last Saturday, who one and all denounced the resolution. Something more will come out of this.

Although it may take some time at Bloemfontein to counteract the baneful influence of the anti-British Hollander party, the prevailing opinion throughout the Colony must be, that when Sir Philip Wodehouse was prepared to apportion onehalf of the " conquered territory" to the burghers in farms of 1500 morgen each, and to settle down the Basutos as peaceful British subjects on the other half, the Volksraad ought to have immediately authorized Mr. President Brand to accept this reasonable and equitable compromise. As was well pointed out by Sir Philip to the ten annexationists who waited upon him at Aliwal North, the purchase price of the 800 farms sold at public auction with guaranteed British titles, would have gone far towards relieving the pecuniary difficulties of the Free State, while it is very much to be feared that the sale proceeds of the 222 farms advertised for sale on the 29th April next, *with Orange Free State titles*, will not amount to a sufficient sum to redeem the obnoxious bluebacks. Although the *Zuid-Afrikaan* (most inappropriately, I think,) applies to Her Majesty's High Commissioner the Latin aphorism, " *Quos Deus vult perdere prius dementat*," and appears to laugh at the idea of his having gained any advantage from his long journey in the spider, there can be little doubt that he will soon return to Cape Town with laurels on his brow, having satisfactorily accomplished his mission of peace by the annexation of Basutoland to this Colony, instead of to Natal, as was first contemplated. It being admitted, then, that the British Basuto Protectorate is an accomplished fact, how can it be turned to better account for the good of South Africa than to regard it as a stepping-stone to the extension of British rule to the Orange Free State in some shape or other ?

The editor of the *Friend of the Free State* concludes an interesting account of what occurred at Aliwal North on the 30th March, by saying, "the deputation took their leave highly gratified and satisfied with the interview with His Excellency, *and convinced that the first step had been taken towards remedying the mischief and annulling the foolish and criminal act of Sir George Clerk*," and it is to be hoped that no time will be lost in taking further steps to obtain the great desideratum—the resumption of the Sovereignty, which Her Majesty's Special Commissioner abandoned. Notwithstanding the "persistent advocacy of federation" by the *Argus*, many practical men will concur with Sir Philip Wodehouse, that "annexation was practicable and might be managed in time, but what was termed 'federal union' presented insuperable difficulties; in fact was almost impossible to work out;" and it is submitted that it would be quite feasible to provide for "the domestic legislation, such as the making of roads, or the construction of public works, and the passing of measures affecting the physical well-being of the people of the Orange Free State," without giving it a *separate* Government or Parliament; but the form of the Constitution to be granted to the Sovereignty seems of secondary importance to its being again placed under the protection of the British flag. His Excellency may be right, but I venture again diffidently to submit the opinion that he has been a little too scrupulous about laying himself open to the charge of interfering with the independency of the Trans-Orange Republic, by declining formally to receive the memorials which were presented to him from Bloemfontein and Philippolis. Of course, in the absence of instructions from the Home Government, he had no power to give effect to the prayer of these memorials; but, surely, the earnest representations of the Queen of England's abandoned subjects of their desire to be restored to their natural allegiance to Her Majesty, if, indeed, they can be said to have ever *legally* forfeited it, might have been received by Her Majesty's High Commissioner without giving offence to any one. Under existing circumstances, when a foreign influence is at work northward of the Orange River to prejudice British interests, I confess I cannot see why one so well qualified to give an opinion on the subject as Sir Philip Wodehouse should not have *spoken out* as to the expediency of extending British rule to the Orange Free State—but perhaps it would have been contrary to the law of nations to have tampered even with the nominal independence of the South African Republic. His Excellency will, however, doubtless keep his promise of conveying to Downing-street the wishes of the memorialists no longer to remain independent of England, and, perhaps also, it would be as well for all the inhabitants of the

Orange Free State, both English and Afrikanders, who are weary of their "fruitless freedom," simultaneously to make a *direct* appeal by petition to the Queen of Great Britain to do for them what Her Majesty has already done for Moshesh and his tribe—to declare them British subjects. The colonists of the Cape and Natal would also, it is again suggested, best show their sympathies with their neighbours of the Free State in joining in petitioning the Queen to extend her regal sway over that State as well as over Basutoland.

Saturday, 25th April, 1868.   COLONIST.

THE FREE STATE-BASUTO DIFFICULTY.

SIR,—Many will fully sympathize with your leading article of Tuesday last, which so justly appreciates "the wisdom, firmness, as well as forbearance of the Representative of the Queen of England" in his proceedings since he reached Aliwal North, and considerately expresses the "hope that His Excellency will, before his departure, have succeeded in so convincing the Free State people of his desire to do them justice, that they will make some effort, by petition or otherwise, to be again received as British subjects." Few also will dissent from the idea you seem to suggest that the deputation to England shall change its purpose, and seek rather the entire cancellation of Sir George Clerk's Convention, which professed to make the inhabitants of the Orange River territory free and independent, than complain on insufficient grounds that any of the articles of the said Convention had been infringed, either by the British Government or their accredited agent at the Cape. The evidence that "the people of the Free State are more reasonable than their President and representatives," to which you allude this morning, is so strong as to have given rise to a rumour that the Volksraad will soon re-assemble to rescind their absurd resolution to treat Her Majesty's High Commissioner with contempt, and to consent to an amicable negotiation with him as to the extent of "the conquered territory" which is finally to be annexed to the State. It remains to be seen whether the last proposal of an armistice and a temporary boundary line, which should be respected by both parties until a reply to the protest could be received from England, has met with a favourable reception; but there can be little doubt that the *Graham's Town Journal* is quite right in its conclusion "that the wisest course for the Bloemfontein Government to adopt would be to request His Excellency to revert to his former offer." The proceeds of the sale of the three hundred farms with British titles would very probably have realized a respectable sum towards the redemption of the bluebacks; while the Orange Free State would have had its border guarded by the occupation of the "conquered territory," converted into

British territory by the purchasers of these farms, who might fairly, under the circumstances, have looked to the British Government, the vendor, to guarantee them peaceful possession of the land sold, as well as to protect them against any aggression from Her Majesty's new subjects—the Basutos. Whatever, then, may be the ultimate decision on this knotty point of boundary, the main portion of the former territory of Moshesh and his tribe is now part and parcel of the British Colonial Empire in South Africa, and, although I was in error in assuming that Basutoland had already been annexed to this Colony, it appears probable that the Cape Parliament will, when the matter shall have been formally submitted to them for discussion by the Governor, sanction such annexation. As the High Commissioner intends for the present to make temporary arrangements for the government of the new British territory, it is submitted that the Colonial Legislature would act wisely in agreeing to and proposing some equitable terms upon which Basutoland might be annexed to the Cape; for, if the Imperial Parliament had reason and common sense on their side, when they objected to the continuance of British Kaffraria as a *separate* British Colony in South Africa, it can scarcely be argued that British Basutoland will long be allowed to remain in a similar position. Taking then, for granted, that Basutoland will ere long share the fate of British Kaffraria, and become incorporated with the Cape, the question arises—Is not the annexation of Basutoland to this Colony a step in the right direction, and does it not, in the natural course of things, lead to the further extension of British rule and protection northward of the Orange River?

In your editorial Summary, written for transmission to England by the mail-steamer *Saxon*, you sensibly remark that " the Free State itself is evidently anxious to terminate the state of almost anarchy into which a succession of native wars has plunged it"; but you must excuse me if I express the fear that your remedy for the grievances under which " Her Majesty's abandoned subjects" are now labouring, is too far distant in prospect, and rather theoretical, when you suggest " that the Queen's Ministers should select a man," to succeed our present Governor, " *capable of conceiving a policy and organising a plan of confederation, having within it a power of extension which may embrace, before the century closes, all that is contained within the two sea-boards of Southern Africa.*" I confess, I think Sir Philip Wodehouse much more practical, when he candidly avows the opinion " that federation is not feasible under the present circumstances of South Africa," and gives a decided preference to the other alternative—annexation.

The *Friend of the Free State*, while it does not despair that the day will come when the Orange River territory and Basutoland will " form one united and flourishing Colony under the rule of a Lieutenant-Governor appointed by the Queen of England, assisted by a local council," is evidently indifferent about the form of the Constitution to be granted in lieu of the existing Republic, provided the British flag be again hoisted at Bloemfontein. It cordially endorses the opinions of the *Graham's Town Journal*, before quoted in your columns, that " the State must be weary of its false and fruitless freedom," and that " annexation alone will make the State free," and earnestly urges upon the inhabitants of the Orange Free State to " go as humble suppliants to the foot of the throne, admitting that their self-government had proved a curse to themselves and their neighbours, and praying to be re-admitted into the family of British Colonies."

The *Port Elizabeth Telegraph* warmly approves of the idea of the people of the Free State petitioning the Queen to become British subjects, and " begs to assure its contemporary that the request, if necessary, will be well backed up from this side of the Orange River." The representatives of the Cape people in Parliament need not, *on the score of economy*, throw obstacles to the annexation of the Orange Free State to this Colony ; for a country which can, notwithstanding the continued warfare with the Basutos, export wool from Port Elizabeth to the extent of about £350,000 per annum, must have great natural resources, capable of being made available, to pay the expenses of its Government. At present, in its unsettled position, the Free State consumes, it is believed, about *one-fourth part* of the imports into Algoa Bay, and there can be little doubt that the restoration of peace, order, and good credit to the country beyond the Orange River, would materially augment the customs dues at Port Elizabeth, as well as raise a revenue from the quitrents on the land, which is good, and at present only partially occupied. It is therefore to be hoped that the people of Cape Town will not be slow to see that " the interests of civilization, humanity, and commerce alike demand" the extension of British rule northward of the Orange River, and that they will take part in a constitutional agitation to convince, by friendly argument, their neighbours of the Free State that it is to their interest again to be placed " under the wide folds of the flag of England." As a preliminary step to a petition to the Queen, humbly praying Her Majesty to resume the Sovereignty, I would suggest that an address be presented to Sir Philip Wodehouse on his return to Cape Town, congratulating and thanking him on his successful accomplishment of his mission of peace, and requesting him to use his powerful influence with the Home Government further to carry out their liberal policy of extending British influence in South Africa, by annexing the Orange Free State as well as Basutoland to Her Majesty's dominions on this continent.

Saturday, May 2, 1868.   COLONIST.

ARE FREE STATE BURGHERS BRITISH SUBJECTS?

SIR,—The *Advertiser and Mail* quotes the Letters Patent of the 30th January, 1854, abandoning the Sovereignty, and the Royal Proclamation of the same date founded thereon, and intimates that the question whether the Burghers of the Free State can still be considered subjects of the Queen after the publication of these documents, will be submitted to the highest legal authorities for opinion. It will be recollected that Her Majesty's High Commissioner, when directly interrogated upon this point by the *first* President of the Free State, Mr. Hoffman, who accompanied the Bloemfontein deputation to Aliwal North, replied that the natural-born subjects of the Queen of England still owed allegiance to Her Majesty, and appeared to convey the impression that they were still justified to approach the foot of the Throne of Great Britain by petition for the maintenance of their rights and the redress of their wrongs. No doubt, at first sight, the express words in the Proclamation, "We do hereby declare and make known the abandonment and renunciation of our dominion and Sovereignty over the said territory and the inhabitants thereof," appear conclusively to decide the question put in the negative. The trite legal maxim, "The King can do no wrong," does not necessarily imply that every act of the King's Government is "of course just and lawful." Queen Victoria *professed* by Letters Patent to confer coercive ecclesiastical jurisdiction on the Bishop of Capetown, but the Privy Council decided that Her Majesty had not the legal power to do so, having already parted with her authority to make laws for the Cape of Good Hope by having granted independent representative institutions to this Colony. Blackstone lays it down that "natural allegiance, which is due from all men born within the Sovereign's dominions immediately upon their birth, cannot be forfeited, cancelled, or altered by any change of time, place, or circumstance, *nor by anything but the united concurrence of the Legislature.*"

The late Duke of Newcastle, at the time, in a despatch to Sir George Clerk, *expressly* declared that an Act of Parliament would be necessary to release the former subjects of Her Majesty from their natural allegiance, but I believe it will be found, on a reference to his despatches in the Blue-book, that he hesitated to apply for such an Imperial Act of Parliament, because he believed that the inhabitants of the Orange River Territory, who were natural-born subjects of the Queen of England, would be unwilling to forego and be deprived of "the great variety of rights which they had acquired by having been born within the Queen's legiance." Of course an authoritative decision upon this point is of the utmost importance at the present moment in our relations with the Orange Free State.

It is true that the editor of the *Friend* and the other gentlemen deputed to convey to Sir Philip Wodehouse the memorials in favour of a British Federal Union, have not yet been committed to prison on a charge of high treason, but it is reported that even official threats have been thrown out that they, who dared to agitate for the substitution of a Monarchical for a Republican form of Government northward of the Orange River, shall suffer for their rash act. It would be a great consolation to those attached to British interests in the Orange Free State to know .that, although they had been apparently abandoned by the Convention of 1854, they were *in point of law* still British subjects, and that the all-powerful arm of Great Britain would be raised in their defence, if they became the victims of any act of unjust tyranny for venturing to treat Her Majesty's Representative with becoming respect, and making known to him the wishes of a large number of the inhabitants of the land which was once the Sovereignty, to be again placed under the protection of the British flag. Notwithstanding Sir Philip Wodehouse has done all in his power to prevent the necessity of " keeping commandoes in the field during the winter," which must entail cost on the Free State and hardships on its subjects, the President seems determined not to accept the proposed armistice, and has issued " instructions to the different Landdrosts to commandeer another batch of 500 men to relieve those at present doing nothing in the field." Of course, if the burghers are British subjects, they ought to refuse to go out and fight with Her Majesty's new subjects, the Basutos, and thus it is very material to have the knotty point herein attempted to be argued finally settled. It is a matter of regret that Her Majesty's High Commissioner is not sufficiently instructed, or the most simple plan to get rid of all difficulties would be to issue a Proclamation, similar to the Basuto Proclamation, declaring the Free Staters British subjects, and the Orange Free State British territory, a consummation which would be hailed with delight by all the Englishmen and Germans, as well as by the Afrikander boers, who were not under the baneful influence of the anti-British Hollander party.

Wednesday, May 6.   COLONIST.

The Return of the Governor.

Sir,—The *Advertiser and Mail*, while it is compelled to praise Sir Philip Wodehouse for " the wonderful amount of cool self-possession, calmness of temper, and quietude of tact in all his dealings, alike with the Free State and the native tribes, ever since his departure," and to admit that " he honestly meant to deal fairly with all of them, and to settle affairs amicably on a permanent basis of peace and justice," authoritatively declares that "his mission has proved beyond all question an unmitigated failure." Many will be bold enough to dispute the soundness of this conclusion, and even feel themselves justified in predicting good results to Southern Africa in consequence of His Excellency's presence at Thaba Bosigo personally to receive from Moshesh and his tribe their grateful allegiance to the Queen of England, who has been pleased to declare them subjects of Her Majesty. It cannot be denied that "nothing has been determined as to the territorial boundaries of this British annexation," but is not this the fault of the President and Volksraad rather than that of Her Majesty's High Commissioner? "The civil, but short note with which the Governor bade the Free State good-bye," speaks volumes on this point. The plain English of it seems to be, even if the Duke of Buckingham should most graciously receive the deputation in Downing-street, and grant them all they want—"the conquered territory," the burghers of the Free State will not be so well off, as if the equitable compromise of the Queen's Representative at the Cape, to sell three hundred farms in that territory with British titles, and to give the proceeds of the sale to the bankrupt exchequer of that State, had been accepted. The dictum of your contemporary, who has throughout opposed the British intervention on behalf of the Basutos, that "upon His Excellency rests the responsibility of the chronic and guerilla warfare which must still continue, and the serious inconvenience which must result to colonial merchants from the continued closing of the Free State Civil Courts," appears to be unjust, and to be founded on the fallacious assumption that the disputed territory has been conquered. I venture to think that it will be found to be the general opinion of the British party northward of the Orange River, which includes all the English, Germans, and many of the Afrikander Boers, that Sir Philip Wodehouse would have acted wisely if he had proclaimed at once, as the boundary between the Orange River State and Basutoland, the Warden line, approved of both by Sir George Grey and himself, on the reasonable ground that "the so-called conquered territory can neither be cleared, occupied, nor governed" by the South African Trans-Orange Republic. It seems to me also that it is unfair towards His Excellency to charge him with the responsibility of the denial of justice to colonial creditors, when he has in his despatch to the President directly condemned the conduct of the Free State in this respect, as being an infringement of Sir George Clerk's Convention, and when there exists a report, to which some credence is attached, that the vote of the Volksraad declining to have anything to do with the High Commissioner, may partially be ascribed to the desire on the part of some of the representatives of the people to prevent the enforcement of civil process within the territory of the State for the recovery of just debts, as well as of the claims of the Republican Government for quit-rents in arrear.

Some rather loudly maintain that the statement made by Mr. Adderley in the House of Commons, proves that the annexation of Basutoland to the British Colonial Empire has been unauthorized by the Queen's Ministers, but it is diffidently submitted that Sir Philip Wodehouse is not the man to act beyond the instructions from Downing-street, and that perhaps it may turn out that the discussion on this point has not been quite fully or accurately reported. On the other hand, the *Graham's Town Journal*, with its usual practical good sense, infers from these remarks of the Under-Colonial Secretary, that if "the Volksraad were to pass a vote in favour of a return to British rule, and the majority of the people in this Colony would unite to recommend to the British Government a favourable consideration of that vote," a "ready compliance" would be given in England to the reversal of the fatal policy of the abandonment of the Sovereignty. Under existing circumstances, I care not to argue further whether the Governor has been justly or unjustly condemned for his line of conduct, when all seem agreed that his motives were good. The address, which has been well signed in Cape Town, affords evidence that even in the Western metropolis, so far removed from Basutoland, public opinion is not wholly against His Excellency, and the press of the Eastern Province may fairly be said to be decidedly in his favour. Swellendam also, perhaps under the influence of that public-spirited gentleman, Mr. John Joseph Barry, who is justly esteemed a good authority on Free State matters, has joined in this address, the main purport of which may be said to be the appreciation of the good intentions of Sir Philip Wodehouse towards our former fellow-colonists beyond the Orange River, and the expression of an opinion that it would be to their real interests if the Orange Free State, together with Basutoland, were made part and parcel of Her Majesty's Colonial dominions in South Africa.

I cannot refrain from making, according to my old bad custom, a quotation from the *Graham's Town Journal* on this point:— "On the Free State side, events are being shaped towards the inevitable end of British supremacy. The commandoes are unpopular. Meetings are held in almost every ward for the purpose of censuring the course taken by the Volksraad in the British and Basutoland question; and in several cases the same meetings declare in favour of a return of the State to the old allegiance. The Volksraad was about to sit in regular session, and the *Friend* anticipates that memorials from all sides, protesting against the protest and denouncing the deputation, will cover the table." This, coupled with the rumour that Mr. Advocate Hamelberg was not indisposed, if unsuccessful in his

L

mission to England to get all "the conquered territory," to demand of the British Government to resume the Sovereignty on certain terms, affords good ground for believing that there is a growing opinion within the Orange Free State itself, that the Union Jack should be again hoisted at the fort of Bloemfontein. Indeed, the *Great Eastern*, in allusion to Sir Walter Currie's sojourn under the Tieme, amusingly says:—" The gallant Knight had not been encamped a week before the Free State Army admitted that they would rather drink his health than fight him. There appears to have been orders issued that these visits were not be kept up, but, orders or no orders, Sir Walter's tent has always been full of visitors, and, if he is not out of the country before the next election takes place, we shall have to look out for another Commandant for our Mounted Police Force. They will take Sir Walter to the President's chair 'nolens volens.'" Upon the whole, then, I hope that I have succeeded in showing that the long journey of Sir Philip Wodehouse has not been so fruitless as has been represented, and, if it only produces the great desideratum of the extension of British rule over the Orange Free State as well as over Basutoland, his name will long be gratefully remembered by all who have the welfare and progress of South Africa at heart.

15th May, 1868. COLONIST.

The Address to the Governor.

Sir,—Although there is not much to object to in the general tenor of your remarks in this morning's leading article, it cannot fail to strike many that you somewhat under-value the efforts so energetically made by Sir Philip Wodehouse "for giving effect to the instructions of Her Majesty's Government with regard to the reception of the Basutos as subjects of the British Crown." Some, no doubt, will join with you in regretting that the boundary line between the Orange Free State and Basutoland has not been permanently fixed; but certainly those in Cape Town, who cannot help their natural sympathies with their former fellow-colonists beyond the Orange River preventing them from duly appreciating the good intentions of the Queen's Ministers to put an end to the Basuto war, ought not to blame His Excellency for this conciliatory act of forbearance in not declaring the limits of the new British territory. The *Advertiser and Mail* repeats that the Governor "deserves not applause, but censure, for the practical encouragement he has given the Basutos to continue their systematic depredations on the Free State farmers, pending the settlement of the boundary question, which, by his own consent, has been referred to the decision of the Imperial Government in England;" but, surely, this is unjust towards His Excellency after the rejection by the President and Volksraad of his reasonable offer of an armistice and a provisional line to be respected alike by the Free-Staters and the Basutos. It could hardly under the circumstances be expected that the first act of the Queen's Representative towards Her Majesty's new subjects, the Basutos, should have been their forcible expulsion from the disputed territory, of which they still hold partial possession, notwithstanding the oft-repeated assertion that it has been conquered and cleared by the Free State Army, particularly as it would be difficult to procure for them a suitable habitation without some inconvenience to the neighbouring Colonies of the Cape and Natal. It seems to me, however, that Sir Philip Wodehouse does not stand in need of any advocate to defend him against the accusation of your contemporary, so persistent in condemning him, and that the subjoined extract from his despatch of the 14th of April to His Honour the President, cannot fail to secure the verdict of public opinion in his favour:—

I shall be very glad to find myself in a position to enforce upon the Basutos the absolute necessity of abstaining from all depredations, to see the country open and safe for all peaceable individuals, and to witness the revival of commerce throughout these regions; *at the same time, I see no prospect of obtaining these benefits, while the Basutos have before them the spectacle of a hostile camp at the Tieme, in the midst of their most valued possessions.* And it is in the hope that your Government, participating in my desire for tranquillity, and recognising the cost and hardships which will be entailed on the State and its subjects, by keeping commandoes in the field during the winter, will be prepared to entertain the following proposal, which I make upon the express understanding that its acceptance shall not operate to the prejudice of any representations which it is intended to submit to Her Majesty's Government in opposition to my views. I have to propose. . . . With this temporary arrangement I believe that acts of violence and dishonesty could be effectually checked.

While I am glad to see that you "cordially endorse the address to the Governor," and think you right in saying that it was intended "not simply in the light of a personal compliment to His Excellency," but also "as a manifesto of the views which those who sign it entertain in regard to the Free State itself," you must forgive me for suggesting that you are rather unjust towards "the framers of the address" in the forced construction you put upon its last paragraph. They could scarcely be ignorant that, if "the British Standard is to be hoisted in Bloemfontein as well as in Thaba Bosigo," the people of the Free State must *take the initiative* in "the expression of the general will" in favour of this happy event; but, as memorials praying for "the extension of British rule to that unhappy land of chronic war and insolvency" had been already presented to Her Majesty's High Commissioner at Aliwal North, and the prospect of further agitation in this direction within the Free State itself was not very remote, and as also Sir Philip Wodehouse had been at the Cape for more than six years, the period usually allotted to Colonial Governors, and there was a rumour that he is not to remain here much longer, they desired to express the opinion that his being instrumental, before he ceased to be Governor of this Colony, in the annexation of the Orange Free State to the British Colonial Empire, would not be inconsistent with his "useful and honourable career in South Africa." Whatever fault, however, may be found with the sentiments or language of the address, it is thought that few will regret having signed it, if it be only on the account that it has elicited so good a reply. This clear and conciliatory document, while it will encourage the British party within the Orange Free State to join with the colonists of the Cape and Natal in agitation for the *speedy* reversal of the short-sighted and mischievous policy which severed the Free State from this Colony, must also convince the people of that State that Sir Philip Wodehouse is really sincere in endeavouring to obtain for them, through the medium of the British intervention, " a substantial return for the exertions they have made, and the losses they have sustained during this melancholy strife with the Basutos."

The *Volksblad* may, perhaps, be disappointed in observing that the alleged "palpable mis-statements" of this address have been endorsed by Mr. Frank Reitz at Swellendam, and regret that the signatures to this "verbose document" of so many respectable Dutch farmers, who have relations and friends northward of the Orange River, are calculated to remove the prejudice which unfortunately exists in the minds of the majority of the Boers against the Queen's representative "for having meddled in the Free State and Basuto quarrel at the time he did;" but the more the Basuto difficulty is discussed the more will it appear that Sir Philip Wodehouse has reason, justice, and equity on his side. Some clamour loudly against the employment of the colonial forces—the Mounted Frontier Police—in Basutoland, and it is to be feared that the complaint will be re-echoed within the walls of Parliament; but may it not be fairly argued that, when the police could be moved at little or no expense, without danger to the security of the property of the district they left, it would have been unwise and inexpedient at a moment when it is not yet quite decided whether the Queen's troops are to be removed from the shores of South Africa or not, to have drawn too largely upon the Imperial Military chest; and also that Sir Walter Currie and Mr. Bowker, who naturally sympathise with the Burghers, were less likely to come to extremities in the discharge of the delicate duty of protecting Moshesh and his tribe in the so-called "conquered" territory than British officers eager for an opportunity of proving the military prowess and discipline of the troops under their command? The hospitality of the popular Commandant in his tent under the Tieme may have been exaggerated by the *Great Eastern*, but there is clearly no fear of any hostile collision between the Boers and the Police. It remains to be seen whether the reported movement in the Volksraad to rescind their absurd resolution not to treat with Her Majesty's High Commissioner at the Cape, has been successful; but it would not be very surprising, after the tone and tenor of Mr. President Brand's last despatch, to find that the *Argus* is right in predicting " that the Government of the Free State already repents of the obstinacy with which it has refused to enter into negotiations with the Governor for the settlement of the Basuto difficulty;" and if this be so, the day is not far distant when British rule will be extended over the Orange Free State as well as over Basutoland.

Saturday, 16th May.   COLONIST.

The Governor's Speech.

Sir,—Although it may be gathered from the general scope and tenor of your leading article of this morning, that you intend to express approval of the speech of the Governor at the opening of the last session of the third Cape Parliament, which, if report speak truly, was well received by all parties, you rather unjustly withhold praise "from the concluding portion of the address which relates to the Basuto question." While you cannot condemn its spirit you seem to suggest that it is wanting in substance. I venture to submit that many will dissent from your idea "that the gist of his statement is to be found in his promise to produce the instructions on which he has acted and the subsequent correspondence," and experience no difficulty in arriving at the conclusion that there is quite sufficient material information within the four corners of this statesmanlike document to justify the formation and recording of an earnest opinion that Sir Philip Wodehouse has well performed his duty in the endeavour "to give full effect to the benevolent intentions of the Government of Her Majesty." How can the blue-book throw much light upon this subject, when we already know that Her Majesty's Ministers " have come to the conclusion that the peace and welfare of Her Majesty's possessions in South Africa would be best promoted by accepting the overtures made by Moshesh towards being received under the authority of the Queen, and that they left to the discretion of Sir Philip the time and manner of accomplishing the measure, and the terms on which he should communicate on the subject with the Free State, which they supposed would be glad to see a new order of things, calculated to give them freedom from the depredations of the Basutos ?" Can any one now doubt that there is no foundation for the outcry which has been raised in Cape Town, grounded on the reported statement of Mr. Adderley in the House of Commons, that His Excellency has exceeded his instructions from Downing-street? The *Argus* aptly remarks: "The speech wound up by a reference to the annexation of Basutoland and the negotiations with Mr. Brand, made in singular good taste;" and it is thought that this opinion will find very many adherents, not only in the colonies of the Cape and Natal, but within the Orange Free State itself. I have before attempted to combat the arguments of that portion of the Cape Town press, which contends that "the mission of the Governor to Aliwal North and Basutoland has been an unmitigated failure;" and I confidently submit to your readers that the part of his speech which sums up the "reasons for being content with the results of his recent journey," more than corroborates my view of the case. The Governor also graphically, but in a conciliatory tone, describes "the evils of the delay which must inevitably result" from the Government of the Free State having sent a protest to England, instead of negotiating with him on the spot; and, notwithstanding the contempt with which he has been treated by the Volksraad, declares his "willingness to proceed with the necessary negotiations." I, for one, cannot help expressing regret that "this utterance from the gubernatorial chair" had not been delivered at an earlier period, so as to have been before the Council of the Free State in the recent debate, when perhaps it might have had the good effect of the new proposals for negotiation with His Excellency in Cape Town having been submitted in a more reasonable shape. The report of the debate on the 6th of this month, which was received by to-day's post, is most interesting, inasmuch as it affords convincing evidence that there is a strong reaction of feeling northward of the Orange River in favour of British intervention for the purpose of restoring peace to South Africa. Dr. Neebe puts the case in a nut-shell when he says:—" The welfare, nay, the very existence of the State, depends upon entering into amicable arrangements with the British Government. I therefore urge that we should meet His Excellency. We must make the best of our bad case. Where are we to get the money to continue our ruinous course any longer? It is perfect folly to talk about our honour, and in the meantime ruin the country." It is true that Mr. President Brand sticks to his text that "the conquered territory" has been cleared of Basutos, and strongly argues in support of sending a deputation to England; but it will strike many who are anxious that British rule should be extended to the Orange Free State, that the annexed extract from one of his reported speeches is very significant at the present moment:—"*Even if a portion or the whole of the public were opposed to a deputation being sent, and in favour of the Governor being met, it would be our duty to act against the public, if this be most advisable.* As far as he understood, the spirit of the people was for a protest and deputation being sent. *We cannot obtain gunpowder, but we have enough to carry on a years' war.*" I confess my total ignorance of the constitution of the Volksraad, but if it be, as I have heard stated, of a permanent nature, so as not altogether clearly to reflect the present opinions of the people of the Orange Free State, some will think that Her Majesty's High Commissioner ought not to be too scrupulous about receiving the respectful petitions of the subjects of the Queen of England beyond the Orange River, who have not yet been legally deprived of their natural allegiance, except through the official channel of the Free State Parliament. Doubtless, it is often in good taste to exclude politics from public dinners, but the fact of the toast of Sir Philip Wodehouse having been proposed at the President's dinner by the mover of the resolution in the Volksraad, which so strongly denounced Sir Philip's line of conduct, does convey to my mind an impression that the Queen's representative is not after all so very unpopular within the Orange Free State. This also reminds me to advert to a statement made by the Volksblad the other day, "on the best authority," "that the courtesy and cordiality with which His Excellency was received at different country towns, stood in no connection with his intended policy in reference to the Basuto question," and in contradiction of this erroneous assumption, to refer your readers to the sensible address, which appeared in the *Argus*, from the leading men of the Dutch-speaking community of the division of Albert, which expressly recognizes in terms of approval the efforts of Her Majesty's High Commissioner to settle on a permanent peaceful basis the relations between the Boers and the Basutos. It is often easy to indulge in criticism, even when it is undeserved, and I may perhaps lay myself open to censure on the present occasion; but I cannot help remarking that the "weak point" of the Governor's address seems to me to be his laboured justification of the employment of the Frontier Police. Surely it needed no argument to prove that "the reception of the Basutos as British subjects," so essential for the future peace of South Africa, was a "colonial question." The absence also of any hostile collision between Sir Walter Currie and the Free State commandoes in the conquered territory, speaks for itself in favour of British troops not having been marched to the Orange River, and, when the Mother Country has so long been, and still is generous towards the Cape of Good Hope in affording military aid, it can hardly be expected that the representatives of the Cape people would grudge some trifling colonial expenditure even upon an "Imperial question." While I generally approve of the remarks of the *Argus* upon this speech, I cannot admit the soundness of its conclusion that, because His Excellency was silent "with regard to the resumption of the Sovereignty," that therefore there is to be "no Parliamentary discussion on the question."

It seems to me that the Eastern Province especially will be grievously disappointed if there be not a debate this session as to the justice and expediency of speedily annexing the Orange Free State as well as Basutoland to the British Colonial Empire.

21st May, 1868. COLONIST.

The Governor's Speech.

Sir,—In my last letter I presumed to question the soundness of your criticism on that part of the speech of the Governor which referred to the recent "transactions which have taken place between the President of the Orange Free State, the Basuto Chief Moshesh, and himself," and I attempted to argue that enough had been already disclosed to raise a fair discussion upon the merits of the conduct of Her Majesty's High Commissioner in this important matter, without the need of further information from Blue-books. The subject is involved in no great mystery. The Queen's Ministers resolved to put an end to the wretched war between the Boers and the Basutos, not only, perhaps, for the purpose of pleasing Emperor Napoleon, who pleaded the cause of "the deserving French missionaries," but also in order to maintain the consistency of Great Britain in her treatment of the aboriginal tribes of South Africa ; and they came to the conclusion that the only way to attain the desired end was the conversion of Moshesh and his tribe, at their own request, into British subjects. They left entirely to the discretion of their accredited agent at the Cape "the time and manner" of making the necessary arrangements, and, so far from anticipating any opposition to the accomplishment of their peaceful purpose, they fully expected that the Orange Free State would, to repeat the words of the Governor's Speech, "be glad to see a new order of things, calculated to give them freedom from the depredations of the Basutos." The foolish perverseness of the President and Volksraad, in declining to meet the Queen's Representative at Aliwal North, in order to settle the boundary line of Basutoland, is the sole cause of the difficulty, which may, however, now soon be dissipated, if the people of the Orange Free State will only induce their representatives to retrace the false step they have taken, and rely upon the earnest assurance of His Excellency, that "he looks forward to the day when he may yet have an opportunity in negotiation of satisfying the Government of the State of the sincerity of his feelings for them." In the first "hurried notice" of the concluding portion of the address which relates to the Basuto question, at the opening of Parliament, you merely intimated your opinion that "it did not say much," but in your leading article of this morning, penned after mature reflection, you carry your censure much further, when you assert, that you "are very certain that what the thoughts of the Governor are upon the Basuto question are not conveyed by the language of the Speech." You must forgive me for venturing to make the remark, that some of the readers of the *Standard* will deem it rather inconsistent, after your having on more than one occasion imputed to Sir Philip Wodehouse a want of diplomatic tact, now to compare him either with a Metternich or a Talleyrand, for it certainly is a libel upon Lord Brougham to charge him with having said that "language was given to statesmen to conceal their thoughts." There will be many, I think, who will conscientiously differ from you on this point, and fail to discover any ambiguity in the language of Sir Philip Wodehouse on this or any other occasion, and who will most willingly give him credit for the sincerity of his able speech, which happily concludes with the declaration that he "shall be most glad to be instrumental in giving full effect to the benevolent intentions of the Government of Her Majesty" towards both the combatants in this long protracted and fruitless war—the Burghers and the Basutos. In my last letter I also gave utterance to the idea that His Excellency had entered into too laboured a vindication of himself for having employed the Frontier Police upon a "colonial question," which clearly, as he says, "has a more important bearing on the interests of these countries than anything that is now passing around us," but I find that you seem this morning to advance the argument that the furtherance of "the cause of civilization and Christianity" is "entirely and distinctly" a matter of "Imperial policy," in which, according to your view at least, the colonists of the Cape of Good Hope have no concern, and about which they ought to be indifferent. I confess that I cannot go along with you in this mode of reasoning, and sincerely hope that all the representatives of the people of this Colony, who are not prepared to sacrifice at the shrine of Retrenchment all other considerations affecting the future progress and prosperity of South Africa, will adopt the more just and liberal opinion of Sir Philip Wodehouse that "the reception of the Basutos as British subjects" is an "Imperial question," "mainly, almost exclusively, because it is a colonial one," and that they will act accordingly. Looking at the question through an economical medium in a colonial point of view, you say, "The Parliament can hardly take action in a matter in which it is only indirectly concerned, and, although its police may have attended as an escort to the Governor, the military force and the strong arm of Great Britain will defend the territory the Imperial Government has taken under its protection." Is this judgment altogether sound ? May it not be argued that, after the experience of the case of British Kaffraria, it can hardly be expected that Basutoland, as British territory, can long remain under the separate, absolute, and distinct Government of Her Majesty's High Commissioner? Would it not then be prudent for the Cape Parliament to be wise in time, and propose some equitable terms to the Imperial Government with respect to the annexation of Basutoland to the Cape? If Natal were so anxious to gain the prize of the rich lands of Moshesh and his tribe, why should not the Cape put in a claim for them, particularly as it may be fairly inferred, from the Governor's Speech, that "there are ample means" within Basutoland to "support a system of Government suitable to the condition of the people of that country?" The production in Parliament of the instructions on which the Governor has acted, and the subsequent correspondence " for information only," will not affect much good, unless it lead to a debate in both Houses opening up the whole question of the further extension of British rule northward of the Orange River. British-born subjects within the Free State have already very properly refused to take up arms against the new subjects of their lawful Queen, but, if the Free State Government dare to punish them for disobedience to the commando law, will the British Government demand reparation, or organize a military expedition for the rescue of the citizens of the South African Republic? The most simple and practical solution of the serious complications which may arise out of this difficult and puzzling question, is the hauling down all Republican flags in this part of Africa, and the hoisting up of the Union Jack in their stead. Sir Philip Wodehouse, who unhesitatingly has declared his opinion "that the severance from this Colony of the Free State was a misfortune for both communities," is right perhaps in saying that "a proposal for their re-union must manifestly emanate from the people of the Free State, and must take the form of an unmistakable expression of the general will;" but, under the circumstances, in order to counteract the influence of the Hollander party beyond the Orange River, it is again submitted that there ought to be some decided expression of public opinion at the Cape, both within and without the walls of Parliament, to encourage the British party within the Free State to take the initiative in agitating for the resumption of the Sovereignty by Queen Victoria.

Saturday, 23rd May, 1868.   COLONIST.

THE ANNEXATION OF THE ORANGE FREE STATE.

SIR,—As a sort of set-off to the arguments with which a portion of the Cape Town press has laboured in endeavouring to prove that the long journey of Sir Philip Wodehouse to and from Basutoland has been entirely fruitless, and that his mission of peace was "an unmitigated failure," I cannot refrain, even at the risk of again exposing myself to ridicule in the columns of your contemporaries on account of my inveterate habit of making copious extracts from the newspapers of the Eastern Province, from quoting almost *in toto* the leading article from the *Somerset and Bedford Courant*, which cannot, I think, fail at the present moment to be interesting to your numerous readers in the country districts :—

Without stopping to inquire for what purpose His Excellency left Cape Town for Thaba Bosigo, these good people cry out "Failure unutterable." This may be all very well as a stroke of party policy. It may suit a certain class of writers to go hap-hazard against His Excellency, that they may satisfy the particular weaknesses of a few of their readers; but what is the real case? In the first case, His Excellency never intended to annex the Free State; in the second, he did intend to annex Basutoland; and in the third, annexation was not his work at all, as he acted in accordance with the text of his instructions. The party who most strongly opposed the Governor will have most cause to regret that opposition. The blundering obstinacy of the Happy Family at Bloemfontein is the very best point in His Excellency's case, should he recommend the renewal of British protection to the Free State. His Excellency can justly say, " I went to the spot; I met the Chief; I wanted to meet the President; the former complied; the latter, in opposition to the wish of, I am sure, a majority of his people, refused ; I want the power to compel either discussion or annexation." The Home Government is not slow in supporting those of its servants who may be deemed worthy of support, and we have had several causes of late to lead us to believe that Sir P. E. Wodehouse stands well with the authorities at Downing-street. His Excellency said that federation seemed impracticable, but he did not express his views upon the annexation of the Free State. He is far too wary a diplomatist for that. But His Excellency invariably judges popular feeling aright, and if the current of opinion three months back may have halted before it reached annexation, and split on federation rocks, it assuredly does not do so now. For annexation, pure and simple, there is a general outcry rising. We detect its first symptoms in the addresses presented from the Western Province towns, in the tone of the press of the Colony, and in the actions of the Free Staters themselves. The *Friend* takes up the subject *con amore*—as a friend should—and there can be no doubt that it represents the intelligence of the country. . . . We shall not defend the Basutos for their actions, although we certainly will express a belief that it is more than probable that a considerable portion of the stock they have "stolen" is as much their own as De Klerk's or any one else's. But the Governor has done something. The Boers followed up the spoor of the missing stock, and traced it over the boundary—but no farther. Then there was a dead halt ; the circumstance were reported to the President, who does not send a commando to punish the " lifters," or take one of his Armstrongs to the front, or " demand satisfaction" in due form, of Moshesh, but—writes to the Governor. What would Mr. Brand have done had this happened a few months back ? There would have been a pot-valiant, spitfire, bombastical hullaballoo. A force would have marched into Basutoland Proper, as some people call the country beyond the '66 line, cattle would have been taken in hundreds, some half-dozen of Moshesh's people would have been shot, and a great Free State victory would have been announced, and President Brand would have led off the Old Hundredth, while his "dear friends" divided the spoil. But there is now none of this delightful excitement. The President simply writes to the Governor. But the only party in the State whose word is worth the breath, cries, " We are not free." That party, a minority in present power, but a majority in intelligence, cannot " free" the State. The Home Government alone can do that, and the Home Government will be in the main moved by what may reach it from South Africa. We think therefore the time has come when those who desire annexation should give vent to their complaints against the present disastrous mismanagement of Free State affairs. His Excellency was equal to his late mission, but there is a power at his back the force of which was not brought to bear, rather from reticence, than dubiousness. True, the Free State question is not one that should go to the country, as the common term is, but it is one upon which both the Colony and the State are competent to speak. And now is the time to do it. When we see men differing so widely upon other subjects, writing so cordially on this, the great question of the day for us, we cannot shut our eyes to the growing conviction that Messrs. Howell, Barlow, White, and their friends have justice with them. And if His Excellency support the prayer for annexation, he will do "something" besides what he has already done. We hardly entertain the conjecture that he will oppose it. He has not travelled the length and breadth of South African civilisation blindfold, nor, once convinced, will he willingly retract.

A careful perusal of the late debate in the Volksraad will, it is thought, lead many to the conclusion that the reply, as reported, of Mr. Adderley to Mr. Miller's question in the House of Commons, which has been alleged to be ambiguous in meaning, and upon which it has been plausibly although erroneously argued by the opponents of the British intervention for the purpose of putting an end to the Basuto war, that Her Majesty's High Commissioner has exceeded his authority, has had the effect of "reviving the hopes of the Hollanders and Mr. President Brand," and has prevented the rescinding of the original resolution of sending a deputation to England, which, it is now said, will be in Cape Town in time to take departure by the mail-steamer on the 19th of June. A copy of the protest has been at last forwarded to His Excellency, and may perhaps be published in the promised bluebook, but if it be confined to the two alleged breaches of Sir George Clerk's convention, viz., the reception of the Basutos as British subjects, and the stoppage of the supply of ammunition by Sir Philip Wodehouse, it cannot have the effect of changing the wise determination of the Queen's Ministers to restore peace to South Africa, by granting the oft-repeated prayer of Moshesh. As the main purpose of this visit to England, however, of the two delegates of the Volksraad is to complain of the extension of British influence northward of the Orange River, ought not the colonists of the Cape and Natal, not only on account of their own interests, but also for the benefit of the Orange Free State itself, to take some action *in the contrary direction*, so that the land which was once the Sovereignty, may, in common with Basutoland, be again subject to British rule under the "wide folds of the flag of England?"

Thursday, 28th May, 1868.   COLONIST.

British Rule for South Africa.

Sir,—Your sub-leader of this morning, which brings to prominent notice the fact that Moselikatse, the chief in whose dominions the South African gold-fields are situated, has intimated his anxiety to become a British subject, and which also directs attention to the alleged cruel treatment of natives, and even the existence of slavery in the Transvaal regions, seems eminently calculated to excite the sympathy of Great Britain with the agitation already commenced within the Colonies of the Cape and Natal, as well as the Orange Free and Transvaal States, in favour of substituting the regal sway of Queen Victoria for the Republican Governments now in existence beyond the Orange and Vaal Rivers. *A propos* to the subject of annexation, which, as you rightly say, is now " being taken up on all sides," I must ask permission to transfer to your columns two pertinent extracts from an able letter, evidently from the pen of an old Cape colonist and traveller, which appears in the London *Standard* newspaper of the 11th of April last, received by to-day's mail-steamer :—

The abandonment of the Vaal River country, under a degrading treaty, was a disgrace to Great Britain, and that the abandonment of the Orange River Sovereignty was a fearful evil, could be proved by the misery and anarchy consequent thereon, at which any one possessed of a spirit of humanity must shudder. . . . . The ill-advised abandonment of the ceded territory led to the expenditure of millions of money, and the surrender of territory to republicans on our border was inexplicable to the aborigines in our neighbourhood, and led to the extinction of many tribes. Anybody who has read the history of the Cape Colony must be convinced how much the colonists were opposed to such a step; but this opposition was all in vain, for Sir George Clerk carried out the scheme with a determination worthier of a better cause.

And again :—

Independent of the tribes already enumerated, we have on the border the so-called republics retarding trade and civilization. Having said thus much, it may be naturally asked, what is to be the remedy for the evils arising from heterogeneous masses of races under separate governments? I emphatically reply a federal union or general confederacy under the flag of our beloved Sovereign. When this has been formed, and then only, under a good Providence, will the southern promontory of Africa flourish, and the riches of her soil be brought to light, consisting as they do of various, both useful and valuable, minerals. Then, too, only will an end be put for ever to the burden which her South African colonies have been to the mother country ; and, on the contrary, by their wool, wine, and other products they will largely contribute to the commerce of the United Kingdom.

The writer in England of this letter, in which the arguments in justification of the course pursued by Her Majesty's Ministers in granting " the exceptional concession to the Cape of Good Hope" with respect to the military defence of the Colony are very clearly put forward, adds the following postscript, which needs no comment beyond the sincere expression of a wish that he may be proved to be right in his reasonable anticipations :—

Simultaneously with the closing of the preceding writing, a steamer arrives from the Cape bringing the important intelligence of the annexation of Basutoland to the Colony by Sir Philip E. Wodehouse, with the concurrence of Her Majesty's Government, and staying the suicidal war between the Basutos and the inhabitants of the Free State. This step I sincerely trust is a prelude to sundry annexations and the general confederacy. I have, with every well-wisher of South Africa, long contended for unity with a prosperous future.

Although, however, there is not much difference of opinion as to the justice and expediency of the resumption of the Sovereignty by the Queen of England, it is to be feared that, unless the people of the Free State take the initiative in urging, through the medium of the Cape Parliament, their desire to be placed under the protection of the British flag, the Home Government will not take much trouble on their behalf. The British-Basuto Protectorate was forced upon Her Majesty's Ministers at the earnest entreaty of the Chief Moshesh, and it was wise on their part to intervene for the preservation of the general peace in South Africa ; but, unless the subjects of Her Majesty beyond the Orange River shake off the trammels of the Hollander influence, and speak out decidedly in favour of British rule, it may be some time yet before the flag of England waves at the fort of Bloemfontein. It is to be hoped, then, that the Orange Free State will soon take the hint of Sir Philip Wodehouse, and " give expression in some unmistakable form to the general will" in favour of its re-annexation to the British Colonial Empire, and that the colonists of the Cape and Natal will not be backward in sympathizing with and supporting their former fellow-colonists in their struggle for a change of dynasty and a complete return to their natural allegiance to the British Crown.

Saturday, 30th May, 1868.   AFRICANUS.

THE ANNEXATION OF THE ORANGE FREE STATE.

SIR,—The congratulatory address to Sir Philip Wodehouse on his return to Cape Town from Basutoland, which was intended not only as a well-merited compliment to the High Commissioner in carrying out the good intentions of Her Majesty's Government to restore peace to South Africa, but also as an expression of public opinion in favour of the re-annexation of the Orange Free State to the British Colonial Empire, has received the signatures of many Dutch-speaking farmers, who have relations within the Free State, and is generally approved of by the Eastern Province press. The *Graham's Town Journal* says " that it is a very excellent address—one to which the great majority of the colonists in these parts would very gladly sign their names." In commenting upon it, the editor further writes :—

It is not the English alone who see in the annexation of Basutoland the best remedy, if not an infallibly perfect one, for the evils the State suffers from. The Dutch see this quite as clearly, and make no secret of their approbation. We do not say that this opinion is universal. But we do say that it is the opinion of the majority. We know what is thought of the case on the frontier. The addresses from Aliwal North, Colesberg, Burghersdorp, town and district, Graaff-Reinet, Murraysburg, Victoria West, and Swellendam show what the prevalent opinion is in the interior districts, both Eastern and Western ; while the Cape Town address speaks the mind of the capital. The *Friend*, we repeat, should give the news of the Colony expression through its columns. The people of the State would also see from these addresses of the Cape people that they are anxious for a reunion with their brethren over the Orange. They would see too that this anxiety is in no sense akin to a lust for conquest, or a mere extension of territory, and increase of power, *but a desire after an honest union for mutual advantage.*

The *Great Eastern* concludes a leading article, in which it warmly approves of the Governor's policy throughout with regard to the Basuto question, and quotes at length and praises the address, with the subjoined passage :—

We join with them most cordially in the hope that His Excellency may be instrumental in the annexation of the Free State. If Sir Philip Wodehouse can effect that, he may well be forgiven for all sins of omission and commission with which he has been charged by the parties in conflict in the colony.

The *Port Elizabeth Telegraph*, in allusion to the clear coincidence of opinion between His Excellency and the gentlemen who had appended their names to the document to which he was penning an answer, namely, " that the severance of the Free State from this Colony was a misfortune for both communities," writes as follows :—

The proper course, therefore, for the annexationists in the Free State to adopt is, first, to cast their eyes about them for a pro-annexation candidate for the next presidency, and having secured his election in succession to Mr. Brand, to endeavour to procure a declaration from the Volksraad in favour of the incorporation of the Free State with this Colony on a federal basis, and then to obtain sympathetic petitions from the Burghers, and so be in a position to approach the British Government with a request for reunion that shall at least be entitled to receive its most careful and respectful consideration. Notwithstanding his reticence upon that point, we may be pardoned if we cherish the expectation of finding in His Excellency's later correspondence with the British Government some reference to a question that must necessarily, we should imagine, have forced itself upon his attention during his journey to and from Thaba Bosigo ; the more so since he cannot have failed to notice the anxiety felt in most of the colonial towns and districts through which he travelled that one of the results of his intervention in Transgariepian affairs might be that a way for the ultimate re-union of the Free State with this Colony might be opened up. We earnestly call upon the pro-annexationists in the Free State to be up and doing. They admit, what all true friends of their country have long since felt, that there can be no real—that is, permanent—security for life or property in any part of the Free State while it continues a separate territory. Such being the case, it behoves them to make an united and determined effort to procure the annexation of their fine country to this Colony. Cape colonists, at least the thinking portion of them, desire that they should at once take the initiative in this important matter, and, if necessary, they may rely on every possible assistance being afforded them from this side of the Orange River.

Some attempt has been made in Cape Town to show that Sir Philip Wodehouse has been " despotic and tyrannical" in his mode of converting the Basutos into British subjects, but the *Graaff-Reinet Herald* seems to me conclusively to answer this when it says:—

The Free State would neither have the profits arising from the sale of 400 farms on the Caledon, sold under British titles, nor accept a provisional boundary line pending the appeal to the Throne. They would have nothing but a persistence in a foolish and wasteful war, which it was well proved they had no power to terminate. *If ever there was a case for arbitrary interference, surely this was one. But the intervention (for it was nothing more) never was arbitrary. From first to last, it was conciliatory. In its terms it respected Free State rights, and desired to negotiate on a fair representation of Free State claims.* Such negotiation the Free State Government considered to be degrading to its dignity, and would not consent to.

Whatever difference of opinion, however, there may exist as to the inconsistency of the Volksraad in declining to treat with the Queen's Representative on the spot as to the boundary line of the new British territory, it may be taken for granted, without argument, that the annexation of Basutoland, if it be not a stepping-stone to the further annexation of the Orange Free State, will only be a half-measure, and involve the British Government in serious complications on questions affecting the rights and duties of British subjects northward of the Orange River. Indeed, much of the opposition to the hoisting of the flag of England at the mountain of the Chief Moshesh—Thaba Bosigo—may be ascribed to the fact that it was not simultaneously hoisted on the fort at Bloemfontein. The Free Staters did not relish the idea of "being left out in the cold," while the Basutos were admitted into the family of British Colonists. It is to be hoped, then, that the Free State deputation will not succeed in prevailing upon His Grace the Duke of Buckingham to recall his wise resolution to make the Basutos British subjects, but that he will go further in the same direction, and confer the like boon upon the inhabitants of the Orange Free State.

Your readers will observe that Mr. President Brand is reported to have said in the debate in the Volksraad, on the 18th of last month, "There is still time for the deputation to go, *for it appears that no certain instructions were sent from England to Sir Philip Wodehouse to accept Moshesh and his tribe as British subjects.* If delay took place in the deputation not reaching Cape Town for the 4th of June steamer, they might take advantage of the delay by meeting the members of the Cape Parliament, and perusing the blue-books containing the correspondence between the Governor and Moshesh. He himself was curious to learn the nature of this correspondence." Upon this, it has occurred to me to suggest that, perhaps after all it is not very improbable that the Rev. Mr. Vandewall and his companion will not reach Downing-street, for when they find from the inspection of the bluebooks, that the Governor, in his speech at the opening of Parliament, gave an accurate view of the purport of his instructions, under which he has acted, when he stated that "Her Majesty's Government had come to the conclusion that the peace and welfare of Her Majesty's possessions in South Africa would be best promoted by accepting the overtures made by the Chief Moshesh towards being received under the authority of the Queen, and *that they left to his discretion the time and manner of accomplishing the measure, and the terms on which he should communicate on the subject with the Free State,* which they supposed would be glad to see a new order of things, calculated to give them freedom from the depredations of the Basutos," they will make the best of their way back to Bloemfontein, and endeavour to persuade the President and Volksraad to come to terms with Her Majesty's High Commissioner on the only material point at issue—what extent of the so-called "conquered territory" shall be annexed to the Orange Free State. The Governor, not only in his replies to the addresses, but in his speech to the assembled Cape Parliament, reiterates his anxiety and willingness to "proceed with the necessary negotiation ;" and, if the Free State consults its interests, it will at once give up further proceedings on the protest, and endeavour to make out an equitable claim for as much land as possible, if not by right of conquest, by cession of Moshesh under the terms of the treaty of Thaba Bosigo.

Wednesday, 3rd June, 1868.   COLONIST.

THE ANNEXATION OF THE ORANGE FREE STATE.

SIR,—It is as I anticipated; the Blue-book relative to the reception of the Basuto nation as British subjects has not thrown much new light on the question, and certainly does not support the conclusion, nor gratify the wish of those who so eagerly caught at Mr. Adderley's ambiguous statement in the House of Commons, as proving beyond doubt that Her Majesty's High Commissioner at the Cape had greatly exceeded his instructions.

The *Advertiser and Mail*, while it actually recommends the Free State Government at once to accept the last proposal of Sir Philip Wodehouse, and thus show signs of beginning to relent in its opposition to the British Basuto Protectorate, complains "that the settlement of the boundaries between the Free State and Basutoland, instead of being an integral part of the arrangement, is now as undetermined as ever." But is it just to lay the blame, which fairly attaches to the President and Volksraad, upon the Governor ? It will be recollected that at the time His Excellency incurred public censure for not being more prompt in action, and delaying the issuing of the proclamation declaring the Basutos British subjects which, when it did make its appearance in the *Government Gazette*, immediately produced the salutary and much desired effect of staying hostilities on the part of the Free State army. Can anyone doubt that, if Mr. President Brand's reply to the *first* despatch, in which Sir Philip Wodehouse said, " I most earnestly hope that this communication may have the effect of inducing your Government to suspend hostilities with those who are now, in all probability, about to became the subjects of a Power actuated by the most friendly sentiments towards the Free State, and whose endeavour it will be, in carrying into effect this measure, to give the fullest consideration to the just claims of that State, and to take every precaution against the renewal of those disorders on the border which have led to such repeated complaints and have ultimately caused the present war," had been favourable, and the white flag of truce, which Moshesh proffered, had been respected, His Excellency would have deferred the formal promulgation of Basutoland as British territory, until he had been enabled by negotiation with some person, duly authorized by the Volksraad, accurately to define its proper limits? The Duke of Buckingham states in his despatch to the Governor :—

> I am glad that the prolongation of your term of Government enables me to entrust the negotiation of this matter to you, as you have given so much attention to the position and to the relations of the native tribes, and I trust that it may be in your power to effect an arrangement which will conduce to the advantage of British interests in South Africa, to the good of the native tribes concerned, and above all, to the preservation of peace.

May it not be inferred from this, that the *speedy* termination of the wretched war between the Boers and the Basutos was the main reason of Her Majesty's Government having come to the conclusion of accepting the " repeated offers made by the Chief Moshesh, that he and his people, with their territory, should be received under the authority of the Queen?" It is true that the majority of the Volksraad, under the joint influence of the lawyers, Mr. President Brand and Mr. Advocate Hamelberg, have protested against the recognition of the Basutos as British subjects, on the ground that it is an infringement of the *second* article of Sir George Clerk's Convention, which disclaims " any wish or intention on the part of Her Majesty to enter into any treaties to the north of the Orange River, which may be injurious or prejudicial to the Orange River Government ;" but this point has already been decided by the British Government against the Free State, and will not, I think, bear argument. When, therefore, Sir Philip Wodehouse, baffled in his earnest attempt to make " the settlement of the boundaries" of the new British territory " an integral part of the arrangement" for accepting the overtures of Moshesh, which had been left to his discretion, found that his appeal for the suspension of hostilities between the Free State and the Basutos had been made in vain, and that the war was being prosecuted with vigour, how could he act otherwise than at once make the formal announcement that the shield of British protection had been thrown over Moshesh and his tribe, and show his determination to carry out the good intentions of Her Majesty's Government to restore peace to South Africa? Whatever fault, however, may be found by others in Cape Town with the *modus operandi* of the High Commissioner in this matter, I care not further to dwell upon the vindication of his conduct, which has already received so largely the verdict of public opinion in the country districts in its favour; but I am content to take the annexation of Basutoland to the British Colonial Empire as an accomplished fact, not likely to be in any degree disturbed by the efforts in England of the delegates of the Volksraad, and to argue upon its probable result in the reversal of the policy of the abandonment of the Sovereignty, in which both the Colony and the Free State are alike deeply interested.

It would seem that the *Advertiser and Mail* rather exults that the Blue-book does not touch upon "the ultimate annexation of the Free State to the Colony," but, although it somewhat rashly assumes "that the Imperial Government have never dreamt of it at all," it is confidently submitted that the further extension of British rule northward of the Orange River cannot fail to command the favourable consideration of the Queen's Ministers, evidently alive to the advancement of British interests in South Africa, if proper representations from the Colonies of the Cape and Natal, as well as from the Orange Free State, be only made on the subject. The Natal press generally, I am glad to find, supports the annexation of Basutoland to Her Majesty's colonial dominions as a stepping-stone to the annexation of the Orange Free State, and your readers will forgive my transferring to your columns an extract from a leading article of the *Natal Witness*, so much in point :—

Without taking the interests of the natives into consideration at all, the certain degradation of a large body of British subjects is quite a sufficient ground for urging on the Government the policy and the necessity for their re-annexation. The anomalous position of the Free Staters has already become conspicuous. They are British subjects, liable to the consequences of resisting an encroachment on the constitution under which they live, and yet left destitute of the protection of the country to which they owe their primary allegiance. The injustice, as well as absurdity, of supposing such a state of things can be allowed to continue, without producing the most disastrous, expensive, and demoralizing results, is too obvious to admit of argument or to need demonstration. But there is also a commercial allegiance which our neighbours owe, and which it is desirable they should not repudiate. The Cape and Natal merchants will experience not a little inconvenience if such a repudiation should take place. And yet what are we to look for? Will it not follow, as a matter of course, that if the Free State persuades herself that she has been unjustly dealt with by the Cape or British Government, that she will very easily argue herself into the justification of a course of commercial repudiation that must be a grievous wrong to those who will suffer most by the policy that entails the injury upon them, without their having the slightest voice in the business? Nor need this repudiation, to be fatally effective, be put into the form of a solemn act. It is even now virtually in operation by the closing of the courts, the persistency with which ruinous policy is pursued by the Government rendering mercantile settlements all but impossible, and furnishing a plausible excuse for all defaulters. The brightest feature in the present prospect is the anxiety evinced, and now finding emphatic utterance, for the annexation of the Free State by the people themselves. Sir Philip or the home authorities do not seem to have taken this probability into account; but it can hardly be imagined that the unsatisfactory position of the Free State can be allowed to continue as it is, or to become as much worse as it must inevitably become. If, as seems to be the prevalent feeling and opinion, the Free State should resume its old status among the British South African Dependencies, then the question arises as to whether any demonstration or movement in Natal can or should be made to secure this end. The Cape Colony is far more deeply interested than we are; but, irrespective of any immediate claims that are in danger of being jeopardized, there are the general interests of commerce to be considered, and all the advantages that will accrue from the promotion of peace and the consolidation and expansion of the commerce of this part of the South African continent.

I cannot conclude without expressing a hope that Mr. Wollaston will succeed in the appointment of a Select Committee of the House of Assembly to consider and report upon the Basuto " question, principally as affecting the interests of this Colony in its relations with the Free State, and the progress of civilization in South Africa," as this will afford an opportunity of all those interested in this important colonial, as well as Imperial question, to be heard in the Cape Parliament.

Saturday, 6th June, 1868. COLONIST.

THE ANNEXATION OF BASUTOLAND TO THE CAPE.

SIR,—In your sub-leader of Saturday last, in which you briefly review the despatch of the Duke of Buckingham, containing the instructions to Sir Philip Wodehouse with respect to the recognition of the Basutos as British subjects, and more especially refer to the "interesting letter" with which the Blue-book concludes, you say, that " Moshesh is quite right in the view he takes, and that you are disposed to recommend the Cape Parliament to have as little to do with him as he desires to have to do with them." You must permit me, even in your own columns, to express a doubt whether the advice you tender to the representatives of the Cape people be altogether sound, and to submit the expediency of the portion of the Governor's Speech having reference to Basutoland and the Free State, which has so important a bearing on the interests of South Africa, claiming its just share in the deliberations of the Colonial Parliament. The wishes of the old Basuto Chief are best described in his own words: " All that I have hitherto said, however, to prove to your Excellency that neither myself nor the tribe have any wishes to be annexed to the Colony of Natal; that we would rather become a portion of the Colony of the Cape of Good Hope ; and, that, above all, we should like to depend upon the High Commissioner alone, in case it should be practicable." The very thing which Moshesh says he would most like, was suggested by Sir Philip Wodehouse himself to Her Majesty's Secretary of State for the Colonies, and how does the Duke of Buckingham meet the proposal ?

If Her Majesty's Government had merely entertained the question of a closer alliance with the Basutos by the appointment of a British agent, or by some other means not involving Sovereign rights, it would have been right that the tribe should continue to be under the control of the Governor of the Cape Colony in his capacity of High Commissioner; but as their recognition as British subjects and the incorporation of their territory are now the matters under consideration, Her Majesty's Government have to decide in what manner these important matters can be best carried into effect, and they feel no doubt that the best and most obvious arrangement would be the annexation of Basutoland to the Colony of Natal.

Moshesh gives many good reasons for preferring the Cape to Natal, and, as the British Government have clearly determined not " to establish an isolated protectorate in the midst of Africa over a barbarous people, and to maintain the same by force of arms in case of need," does it not follow that the only practical measure is the annexation of Basutoland to the Cape Colony ? Although on the map the Basutos are next-door neighbours to, and seem naturally to belong to our enterprising sister Colony, a mountain barrier, extending along the whole mutual frontier, and, except at one or two points, almost inaccessible, practically cuts off all communication between Basutoland and Natal, whilst, as Moshesh says, "there is nothing to hinder any trade which may spring up between Basutoland and the Cape Colony—which trade, as everybody well knows, has now been going on for many, many years." After a careful perusal of your leading article of this morning, in which you properly bring to task the Eastern members for their want of punctuality in attending to their Parliamentary duties, and refer to Mr. Wollaston's motion for a select committee, I find—you must forgive me for saying so—some difficulty in deciding whether you have, or have not, changed your opinion as to the policy of the Colonial Parliament meddling with the Basuto question. It is true that you do not seem to disapprove of the sound reasoning of the Governor's Speech in answer to the objection, which has been mooted, that the reception of the Basutos as British subjects is " an Imperial and not a Colonial question," and that you positively admit that " the Colony has a most direct interest in an equitable, peaceable, and permanent settlement of the question," and also that it is clearly the intention of the Queen's Ministers that " Basutoland should in futuro be governed by some Colonial agency," and you even shrewdly hint that its annexation to Natal might be prejudicial to the interests of the Cape ; but then, on the other hand, you appear to be overwhelmed by the dread of expense, and are desirous of throwing the entire responsibility of "advancing the cause of civilization and Christianity" with Her Majesty's new subjects —the Basutos—on the "Imperial Government." At the risk of being deemed presumptuous, I venture to give a decided opinion that the history of the compulsory annexation of British Kaffraria to this Colony by an Act of the Imperial Legislature, coupled with the *express* dissent of the Duke of Buckingham from the opinion of Sir Philip Wodehouse in previous despatches, "that if an opportunity should offer for establishing closer relations with the Basutos, it would be right, with reference to our general policy, to bring them under the control of the Cape as High Commissioner, rather than under that of the Natal Government," ought to induce our Colonial Legislators to be wise in time, and at once to take action in Parliament with the view of proposing some equitable terms for the annexation of Basutoland to this Colony. While I cannot wholly coincide with the opinion you apparently entertain, that there is some mystery and ambiguity in the public despatch of Her Majesty's Secretary of State for the Colonies, there can be no doubt that the production, before a Select Committee of the House, of the despatches of Mr. Cardwell, Lord Carnarvon, and Sir Philip Wodehouse, to which you refer, cannot fail to throw light upon "the circumstances and reasonings which brought about the decision of Her Majesty's Government," in which not only this Colony and the Free State, but all South Africa, are so deeply interested. I, for one, therefore sincerely hope that the *Norseman* may bring to Table Bay a good freight of Eastern members in time to support Mr. Wollaston in the Assembly, on the 18th instant, in his reasonable attempt to obtain the fullest investigation and discussion of this important subject, and that the Select Committee will, after considering the Basuto "question, principally as affecting the interests of the Colony in its relations with the Free State and the progress of civilization in South Africa," report in favour of the annexation of Basutoland to the Cape of Good Hope as a preliminary step to the annexation of the Orange Free State.

Tuesday, 9th June, 1868.　　　　　　　　　　　COLONIST.

Mr. Wollaston's Motion in re "Basutoland and the Free State."

Sir,—When I last addressed you, somewhat in doubt whether, in your editorial capacity, you really intended to support Mr. Wollaston's motion for a select committee "to consider and report upon the Basuto question generally as affecting the interests of the Colony in its relations with the Free State, and the progress of civilization of South Africa," I little anticipated that your Cape Town contemporary, who has so

consistently throughout supported the policy of Her Majesty's Government of receiving the Basuto nation as British subjects, would oppose all " Parliamentary discussion" on this interesting topic during the present session. The *Argus* says, " We shall give our reasons for thinking, first, that the resolution of the honourable member for Fort Beaufort is of too vague and general a character, and secondly, that any interference with the question is just now inadvisable." The first objection can readily be removed by adding to the resolution such words as to convey the "definite instructions" of the House upon what points it seeks and desires the suggestions of a select committee, and, in fact, the *Argus* has already supplied *three* good points for the consideration and report of the committee:—
1. The propriety of annexing Basutoland to this Colony ; 2. The extension of British rule and protection to the Orange Free State ; 3. The desirability of the Cape Parliament occupying the position of being a mediator between the Home Government and the Free State. I venture to suggest a *fourth* point, upon which a select committee might be consulted, viz., whether, in the event of the people of the Free State taking the initiative in declaring their weariness of their nominal independence and "fruitless freedom" under a republican form of Government, and their wish to be permitted " to live under the wide folds of the flag of England," there ought to be any objection on the part of the Cape Parliament to the annexation to the land which was once the Sovereignty to the British Colony of the Cape of Good Hope. With respect to the second objection, " that Mr. Wollaston and the House would do well to wait until the Home Government has definitely announced its policy" on the Free State-Basuto difficulty, a question which, it is admitted, " must ere long come in some shape before the House," it seems to me that this objection is grounded upon the fallacious assumption that the Colonial Parliament is called upon to " *legislate*" on the mere " anticipation" that the deputation from the President and Volksraad of the Orange Free State will be of no avail in changing the wise determination of Her Majesty's Government to grant the oft-repeated prayer of " the Chief Moshesh, that he and his people, with their territory, should be received under the authority of the Queen ;" whereas, in truth and in fact, all that is asked for by the honourable member for Fort Beaufort is " *a committee, with power to take evidence and call for papers, to consider and report*" upon a question which, Sir Philip Wodehouse rightly tells us, "may in the future, perhaps, have a more important bearing on the interests of these countries than anything that is now passing around us." Surely, if " the transactions which have taken place between the President of the Orange Free State, the Basuto Chief Moshesh," and the Queen's Representative at the Cape, were of sufficient importance to claim so large a share

of the Governor's Speech, they are worthy of discussion at least by the representatives of the people of this Colony in Parliament assembled. If the constitutional practice, borrowed from the House of Lords and the House of Commons, of voting an address in reply to the opening speech of the Representative of the Crown had not become obsolete at the Cape of Good Hope, some notice must, ere this, have been taken both in the Legislative Council and the House of Assembly " of that portion of His Excellency's speech having reference to Basutoland and the Free State." If the Volksraad of the Trans-Orange Republic protests against the recognition, by the Queen of England of the Basutos as British subjects, as an infringement of Sir George Clerk's Convention, and sends delegates to Downing-street for the express purpose of inducing Her Majesty's Ministers to retract their "benevolent intentions" towards Moshesh and his tribe, and to retrace the wise step of extending British influence in South Africa, are the representatives of the loyal people of this Colony in Parliament assembled not to give utterance to any opinion on this point? Does not the present session afford a fitting opportunity to our colonial legislators to record their cordial sympathy with the opinion, so well lately expressed by Sir Philip Wodehouse, "that the severance of the Free State from this Colony was a misfortune to both communities," and thereupon to recommend to the Mother Country a reversal of the fatal policy of the abandonment of the Sovereignty? After the able letter from "A Frontier Man" in your columns of this morning, it would be a work of supererogation further to pursue this question, and I cannot hope by any arguments of mine to strengthen the position taken up by him, that no time ought to be lost in making known to the Imperial Government "what is the opinion of the Cape Parliament in regard to the distinct and separate existence of the two Transgariepian Republics as independent States." Your readers, therefore, must allow me to take for granted that that opinion would be against the continuance of these two Republics, and in favour of "the British flag waving supreme in South Africa."

The *Graham's Town Journal* makes the following sensible and practical comments on the recent proclamation of President Pretorius in its last leading article :—

By the advance of its frontier on all sides but the south, the Transvaal puts itself into possession of the most considerable part of the recent gold-fields, claims authority over several native tribes and their lands, and secures a sea-port on the Eastern shores. This is a statement which, we think, will command attention. At present very little is known about the character of the gold-fields. Their extent and wealth may have been exaggerated, and it is equally possible that they may have been underestimated. The importance of the new acquisition of the Transvaal has, in this respect, to be established by facts. Should it turn out that the basins of the Zouga and Limpopo are rich in gold, the Transvaal will be considered so far lucky in its acquisitions. We do not see that any objections could be started to this extension of territory if it only included land and the wealth, or the means of the wealth, it contains. The growth of colonies is inevitable, and the Transvaal is the nearest Colony, or Colonial State, to the Gold-fields. But this acquisition of territory is also an extension of authority over the tribes at present occupying or claiming the annexed lands ; and it is not clear at all that these people are willing to be annexed, or that they have by their conduct entitled the Republic to force its authority upon them. One of the chiefs whose territory and people have been thus arbitrarily dealt with and appropriated, has lately made a direct offer of his allegiance to the British Government. This may be taken to be a decisive proof of his antipathy to a Transvaal connection. The chief we refer to is Matjen, in whose lands one of the Gold-fields is situated. . . . In connection with this step, there is another which has to be considered in order that its meaning may be rightly estimated. It is said that the Transvaal Government has been making persistent efforts to establish commercial relations with the United States. It is clear enough that the Republic has an eye to business. This is all right and fair. But we see in this free and independent action the seeds of future difficulties which can only terminate in the extension of British authority to the utmost limits of colonization in South Africa.

It is also reported that the Volksraad has instructed the Rev. Mr. Vandewall, who is said to be a citizen of the United States, that, in the event of his not meeting with a gracious reception by the Duke of Buckingham, he is to appeal to America, and it may so happen that Brother Jonathan, if his attention be directed to the South African Republics at the same moment, may be induced "by the temptation of rich gold-fields, with the super-added luxury of being, when he chose, a thorn in the side of John Bull," to make a strenuous effort " to gain a footing on the African continent." Enough, then, has been said to prove that the extension of the regal sway of the British Crown to the now-existing Republics of the Free State and Transvaal, is not only a colonial but an Imperial question, and to suggest the expediency of the Cape Parliament inaugurating a discussion with the view of encouraging the Imperial Government to progress in " the advancement of the cause of civilization and Christianity" in South Africa, instead of to retrograde at the bidding of the delegates from the Orange Free State. The *Port Elizabeth Telegraph* concludes a review of the Basuto Blue-book, which is very just and favourable to Sir Philip Wodehouse, by saying :—

> We understand that it is intended shortly to convene a meeting of the inhabitants of this town to give expression to the public mind in reference to British intervention in Transgariepian affairs, when we doubt not the important services rendered by our present Governor in connection therewith will be suitably acknowledged.

And it would not very much surprise me if that meeting passed a resolution requesting the Eastern members to support Mr. Wollaston in his laudable endeavour to obtain Parliamentary investigation and discussion upon the Basuto and Free State question in all its bearings upon the future welfare and progress of South Africa.

Saturday, 13th June, 1868.   COLONIST.

The Port Elizabeth Meeting.

Sir,—While many in Cape Town evidently sympathise with the Orange Free State delegates to Downing-street, and even predict that they will be successful in convincing His Grace the Duke of Buckingham, or his successor in office, that the Basuto Proclamation by the Queen's Representative in this Colony was a terrible infringement of the law of nations, it cannot but be gratifying to all who duly appreciate the benevolent intentions which prompted this step, that Port Elizabeth, the Liverpool of the Cape, at a public meeting, " which may be said fairly to have represented the community," has spoken out, in unanimous and cordial approval, " of the admission of the Basutos as British subjects," and of the conduct of the High Commissioner in giving effect to the instructions of Her Majesty's Government to restore peace to South Africa. If, upon the evidence as it then stood, this meeting felt justified in declaring " that, throughout the negotiation, His Excellency had endeavoured, by every means in his power, to secure the co-operation and friendly feelings of the Orange Free State Government," does not his despatch of the 13th of June, just published, which concludes by saying, "And I am glad to learn that the Volksraad have not the slightest doubt of the sincerity of my offers, as well as to think that all the evils which must arise out of the delay inseparable from sending a deputation to England will be chargeable, not to my refusal to aid in the attainment of the objects the Free State are now said to have had in view, but to my having been prevented from learning what would be expected, and discussing the means by which it could be accomplished," strongly confirm the opinion so well expressed in the second resolution ? The protest, which has at last seen the light, does not disclose any new point of law not previously argued, but many will agree with the *Argus* of this morning, that this rather long and laboured document does not fairly represent the facts, inasmuch as it " conveys the impression that Sir Philip had a definite and inflexible policy, which he has carried out at all hazards, and which he declined to alter, whether Mr. Brand and his Raad heard or forbore," whereas, in truth and in fact, to borrow again the language of your contemporary, " Sir Philip has, from first to last, invited friendly discussion on the question of boundary," which, after all, is the main, if not the only material, point at issue. Your readers may perhaps recollect that I have often used, as an argument in favour of the President being authorized by the Volksraad to meet Her Majesty's High Commissioner in amicable negotiation at Aliwal North, the probability of the bluebacks being partially redeemed by gold and silver coin out of the military chest, if the Free State could have established an equitable claim, irrespective of the natural rights of the original owners and occupiers to their native soil needed for their support, to the territory ceded by Moshesh by the treaty of Thaba Bosigo; and what does Sir Philip Wodehouse say on this point ? —" In the first letter which I addressed to you on this subject, on the 13th of January last, I stated expressly the intention ' to give the fullest consideration to the just claims of the Free State.' It seems almost needless to observe, that if those claims had been put forward in the shape of a demand for ' pecuniary compensation,' I should have been under the strongest obligation to give them the 'fullest consideration.' My rejection of them would have furnished ample ground for an appeal to Her Majesty's Government." Although I must again dissent from the opinion, "that the merits of this case are entirely with the Free State," which has been maintained by the much-esteemed editor of the *Advertiser and Mail*, to whom I most gladly tender an apology that I should for a moment have doubted that he was strongly in favour " of the extension of British dominion in South Africa," it seems to me that it would be a work of supererogation further to argue the case, as there is no good reason to expect either that the shield of British protection will be withdrawn from Moshesh and his tribe, or that the knotty point of the future boundary line between Basutoland and the Orange Free State can be satisfactorily settled, otherwise than by negotiation on the spot. If there be any truth in the generally received opinion that some of the much coveted " conquered territory" is absolutely essential for the maintenance and support of Her Majesty's new subjects—the Basutos, some compromise will have to be effected; and I cannot help thinking that it will be found very difficult indeed to contrive any plan more equitable and beneficial to all parties concerned than that suggested by Sir Philip Wodehouse, of selling farms with British titles, and giving the proceeds of such sale to the bankrupt exchequer of the Free State. Surely, there is not much in the legal, if not under the circumstances rather technical objection, which appears to be founded on " the respect due to international obligations," that the Orange Free State is entitled to *all* the so-called "conquered territory," or rather the territory ceded by Moshesh in 1866, when it is borne in mind that even after this cession on the 22nd of May, 1867, the Free State granted by treaty to Letsea and his minor chiefs, a large slice of that territory for his and their use and occupation. By the Treaty of Imperani also, on the 26th of March, 1866, if I have been correctly informed, a portion of the land annexed by Commandant-General Fick's Proclamation, and afterwards ceded by Moshesh, was allotted to Molappo; and these two treaties certainly seem to amount to an admission on the part of the Free State authorities that some of the

" conquered territory" *properly belonged to the Basutos*, who, having been metamorphosed into British subjects, ought at least to be permitted to convert the land appropriated to them into British territory ; and the grantees or purchasers of the adjoining farms will not, it is thought, be prejudiced by being placed in the same category in this respect with the Basutos, for British titles to land are doubtless of much more value than Orange Free State titles. It may, perhaps, be a nice and intricate point of international law to decide whether Moshesh is right " in holding that the Treaty of Thaba Bosigo was cancelled by the subsequent war," but, at any rate, Sir Philip Wodehouse makes no secret that he " regards the permanent pacification of the country as hopeless without a reasonable modification of it." May it not, therefore, be fairly argued that the Orange Free State will not best consult its interests if it continue obstinately to claim the dominion and entire possession of the " conquered territory," which, according to the authority of some practical men on the spot, " it can neither clear, occupy, nor govern?" So much for the Basuto question, but to me, and, I hope, to many of your readers, the *third* resolution of the Port Elizabeth meeting, which, in the clear paraphrase of the *Eastern Province Telegraph*, " reiterates an oft-repeated statement that the abandonment of the late Orange River Sovereignty was an egregious mistake, and has seriously and most injuriously affected British interests in Southern Africa, and pledges the Port Elizabeth community in favour of the re-union of the Orange Free State with this Colony," and the *fourth* resolution, which expresses the hope that Mr. Wollaston's motion for a Select Committee, which has now been postponed until the 6th of July, " will receive the cordial support of all the members of the Legislature," are most deserving of attentive discussion and approval at the present moment. It may certainly be gathered from your leading article of this morning, that there is much to be said on both sides of the question submitted by the honourable member for Fort Beaufort, but I, for one, give the most decided preference to that branch of your argument which asserts that " the interests of this Colony require that from Cape Point to the Zambezi there should be but one paramount influence, and that must be the influence of Great Britain," and cordially coincide with your practical conclusion contained in the following words :—" If our colonial interests are at all concerned, now is the time to speak out. The plea of non-notice will fail us in the day of trial. England is not bound to consult her Colonies in such cases, but only to keep them informed of what is going on. *In this instance, the papers have been laid before Parliament, and if nothing is said, the Home Government will assume that Parliament has nothing to say.*" From what has already transpired, there is some reason to fear that Mr. Wollaston will meet with opposition, on the ground that the reception of the Basutos is purely an Imperial question, with which the Cape Parliament ought not in any way to meddle ; but it occurs to me to quote an extract from the speech of one of the gentlemen at the Port Elizabeth meeting, as the line of reasoning adopted by him does not appear inapplicable as an answer to the distinction so often made in this Colony between Imperial and colonial questions :—

True it is that hints have been dropped that some exception is likely to be taken to the employment of the Mounted Police force on the occasion in question ; but, he felt persuaded the meeting would agree with him in thinking that it would come with a very bad grace from colonists to raise any objection to the use of the colonial force on what is called ' Imperial service' if under the circumstances they were found better fitted for the particular duty than the regular troops stationed in this Colony. They all claimed the privilege of forming part and parcel of the British nation, and cherished a strong feeling of attachment to the Mother Country, though living in one of her distant possessions ; and ought rather to rejoice at an opportunity being afforded them of helping forward the noble cause she has in hand than to begrudge the limited means at their disposal whenever they could be made available ; neither ought they to forget or lightly esteem the manifold advantages enjoyed, through the liberality of their countrymen at home, by the presence of the Queen's troops, so essential to the progress of civilization in South Africa, as well as to the maintenance of order and good government in the Colony. Let them then encourage the hope that there may be no more grumbling on that score either inside or outside the walls of Parliament.

These truly English sentiments were lustily cheered by the people of Port Elizabeth, and ought to actuate the House of Assembly when they come to the consideration of the Basuto question in its general bearings upon " the progress of civilisation in South Africa."

Saturday, June 20.   COLONIST.

THE BASUTO QUESTION.

SIR,—I take the earliest opportunity of tendering through your columns to " A Subscriber" to the *Standard* my grateful acknowlegment of the flattering terms in which he has referred to me, and of the advice he has so considerately bestowed upon me to desist from attempting to excite further discussion on the Basuto question. " With all deference," however, to him, I cannot admit the force of his reasoning, when he insinuates that the arguments with which I have from time to time endeavoured to uphold, when, in my opinion, unjustly assailed, the conduct of the Queen's Representative in this Colony in giving effect to the instructions of Her Majesty's Government, do not meet with the approval and sanction " of the public generally." At any rate, they remain unanswered, and, therefore, I have no objection to take his hint, and rest on my oars awhile, particularly as there is every prospect of this important subject being argued on all points with much greater effect within the walls of Parliament, on Mr. Wollaston's motion for a Select Committee. Although your rather laconic correspondent is far from complimentary to His Excellency, when he talks about "the meddle and muddle of the Basuto difficulty under his auspices," there is abundant proof that the Eastern, more deeply and directly interested than the Western Province in the restoration of peace on the Border, and in the further extension of British influence northward of the Orange River, cordially supports the reception of the Basuto nation as British subjects, and earnestly applauds "the great energy and discretion" of Sir Philip Wodehouse in the performance of "the difficult task" committed to him by the Home Government. I regret my utter incompetency to grapple with the other abstruse subjects to which my attention has been invited by one who is evidently very anxious that the Cape Community should be instructed in the principles of " commercial morality."

Thursday, 23rd June, 1868.   COLONIST.

Mr. Adderley on the Basuto Question.

Sir,—Although I promised your readers to be silent until the important subject matter of Mr. Wollaston's motion for a Select Committee had passed the ordeal of full discussion in the House of Assembly, the Basuto question seems, in the opinion of many, to have assumed so new a phase by Mr. Adderley's reported statement in the House of Commons, as almost to compel me again to intrude upon your columns. That portion of the Cape Town press, which has persistently deprecated British intervention on behalf of Moshesh and his tribe, as a violent breach of "international obligations," at once exults in the conclusion that Sir Philip Wodehouse has exceeded his instructions, and that his proceedings will not receive the sanction of Her Majesty's Ministers. The *Advertiser and Mail*, while it discreetly and with good taste declines " to rake up all the weary details of the long wrangling contention between" the Free State Government and the High Commissioner, considers, from the tone of the remarks of the Under-Secretary of State for the Colonies, " that the Free State deputation will be able to establish a very strong case indeed for the consideration of Her Majesty's Government." You also, in your editorial column of Tuesday last, appear to think that Mr. Adderley's speech, in reply to the demand of Mr. Cardwell for the production of the despatches from the Governors of the Cape and Natal with respect to the affairs of Basutoland, " is one of the most perplexing of the incidents connected with the Basuto business, and that it will almost compel the intervention of our own Parliament in the way of demanding explanations." I confess I cannot agree either with you or your contemporaries in the construction put upon an official answer in the House of Commons given to a question seeking for information upon a matter still pending. As it seems to me, there is nothing in the statement of Mr. Adderley inconsistent with the Duke of Buckingham's despatch of the 9th December, 1867, which contains the instructions under which Sir Philip Wodehouse has acted. A perusal of that despatch must convince every one " that it was not the intention of the British Government to assume the Protectorate of Basutoland," " under the control of the Governor of the Cape Colony in his capacity as High Commissioner," but, it having been determined that the Queen of England should exercise " Sovereign rights" over the Basuto chief and his people, in concession to their repeated prayers, Her Majesty's advisers decided "that the best and most obvious arrangement would be the annexation of Basutoland to the Colony of Natal." It may perhaps be argued that the strict *letter* of the instructions of "including a settlement of the boundaries between the Free State and Basutoland as an integral part of the arrangement" has not been carried out; but is not this the sole fault of the President and Volksraad, and is not the *spirit* of these instructions the termination of the wretched war between the Boers and the Basutos? "The time and manner of accomplishing this measure, and the terms in which he was to communicate with the Free State on the subject," were entirely left to the " discretion " of Sir Philip Wodehouse, in whose " power to affect an arrangement, which would conduce to the advantage of British interests in South Africa,.to the good of the native tribes concerned, and above all to the preservation of peace," implicit confidence was placed by the Duke of Buckingham.

I fancy I can discern traces of the complete discretion and power vested in Her Majesty's High Commissioner by the Downing Street authorities in the subjoined paragraph from Mr. Adderley's speech :—

As to what events had precipitated measures, we have not yet received any explanation. The reports from the spot which have reached the newspapers are certainly highly coloured and distorted, *but the Boers' invasion and devastation of Basutoland have probably been the cause of hastening and necessitating measures of precaution.*

Notwithstanding, then, all that has been said on the other side, I do not believe that the deputation of the Orange Free State backing up the protest will be received with open arms by His Grace the Duke of Buckingham, or that Mr. Cardwell, his probable successor in the Colonial Office, who had, while in power, " signified his readiness to authorize the establishment of a British agent with Moshesh," will throw his mantle of protection over them, but I am still sanguine that the conduct of Sir Philip Wodehouse will meet with the approval of the Queen's Ministers, whoever they may be, and that the ultimate settlement of the "boundaries between the Free State and Basutoland" will be left to negotiation on the spot. There can be no doubt that you are quite right in the conclusion you draw that, "should the Protectorate be now withdrawn, it is impossible to estimate the damage done," but, in common with all the friends of "the advancement of civilization and Christianity in Southern Africa," you need be under no alarm that Her Majesty will ever recede from the recognition of the Basutos as British subjects, which has been formally made, and you will be forced at length to coincide with me in the conviction with which I have long been most earnestly impressed, that the only practical solution of the Basuto difficulty is the annexation of Basutoland to the Cape, now that Moshesh will have nothing to do with Natal. In the present state of uncertainty as to the truth of the sensational rumours with regard to the revolution or rebellion at Bloemfontein, I purposely abstain from dwelling on this painful topic, further than to remark that, if any credence is to be attached to the explanation given in the latest telegram of the *Argus* from Graham's Town yesterday, of the troubles which are alleged to have arisen from those who have not been released from their natural allegiance to the British Crown declining to go on commando against Her Majesty's *new* subjects—the Basutos, the sooner the serious complications likely to spring from the present relations between the Trans-Orange Republic and Moshesh and his tribe are put an end to by the annexation of the Orange Free State to the British Colonial Empire, the better it will be for all parties concerned. Whatever, then, may be the fate of the motion of the hon. member for Fort Beaufort in the House of Assembly, I, for one, sincerely hope that the Cape Parliament will not separate without some decided expression of opinion in favour of the further extension of British rule northward of the Orange River, which important question certainly demands the investigation, consideration, and report of both Houses of the Legislature, if they have any regard for the "commerce of South Africa," to say nothing of its future prosperity and peace. *Apropos* to this subject, I cannot refrain from, according to my old fashion, transferring to your columns the annexed extract from a late leader of the *Queen's Town Free Press*, commenting on the public meeting at Port Elizabeth, which seems to me so strongly to support my present arguments:—

It is a great gain to South Africa that the Basutos are no longer free, and that Moshesh's days of war and thieving at pleasure are over. This gain would be greatly enhanced were the annexation of the Free State to follow. It is a great mistake that the country was ever given up. Much bloodshed would have been saved. In a commercial point of view both the Colony and the Sovereignty would have been more prosperous. Neither of them would have had the debt they now have. The anti-English feelings, to be expected of the ignorant boers for one or two generations after the overthrow of the Dutch Government, would have been almost extinct, at least unfelt; civilizing influences at work would have been greater, and the circumstances more favourable, and Christianity among the heathen might have been more successful. We see these things now, and feel that it would be wise policy to rectify, if possible, the mistake made fourteen years ago. The most intelligent, both of Dutch and English, in the Free State, feel in the same way, and would hail with joy a re-union with this Colony. The difficulty is how the thing is to be done. The present Government in the Free State will most certainly not entertain a thought on the subject. They are too obstinate to give much heed either to the opinion so prevalent in this Colony, or to the voice of the sensible part of their own people. But the people of the Free State can move in the matter, and must, if anything is to be done. The most of them are British subjects, and as such, they can petition to be received under British protection. Should they do so, they may depend on the warm support of the Colony. In such a petition, as the editor of the *Eastern Province Herald* clearly shows, they may take higher ground than a mere request. They may claim their re-admission into the British Empire as a right, for it would appear that when Sir G. Clerk gave over the sovereignty to a few individuals, it was received by the same with the express understanding that the residents of the country should be freed from their allegiance to the British Crown.

Friday, 3rd July, 1868. COLONIST.

THE TRANSVAAL GOLD FIELDS.

SIR,—The interesting extract from the *Colesberg Advertiser* in your issue of this morning encourages me to reiterate a suggestion before made in your columns, that some action should be taken by the Government of this Colony for the purpose of obtaining precise and authentic information relative to the auriferous quartz said to abound in the Transvaal regions. It may not be long, perhaps, before the excitement which prevails at Hope Town about the news from the South African gold diggings may disturb the even tenor and contentment of the population of the Western metropolis, and lead to the result predicted by the following pretty lines from the ode in the *South African Magazine* of this month:—

>Known is now the land of gold;
>Far and wide the tale is told.
>Forth the banded miners rush;
> Each his tools and rifle sports,
> High in hope and armed to crush
>   Both the savage and the quartz.
>Who the exodus shall stay?
>Who shall bar their onward way?
>Try to yonder stars to climb,
>Stay the rushing wing of time,
>Curb the whirlwind in its wrath,
>Turn the lightning from its path,
>Aye,—but never dream to hold
>Check upon the rush for gold.

The official collection of accurate data upon this question may probably prevent many false hopes being raised only to end in disappointment; but, if there really be rich gold-fields within the dominions of Machuene and Moselekatze, why should not steps be taken, before it is too late, of making favourable terms with them on behalf of British Imperial and colonial interests? The rumoured purchase by Prussia of the Portuguese possessions on the African continent, if consummated, as well as "President Pretorius' annexing proclamation," may throw serious difficulties in the way of the Queen of England granting the prayer of these native chiefs, to become, like Moshesh, British subjects. If the prospect of finding gold be deemed good ground for British intervention beyond the Vaal River, does not the alleged existence of a system of slavery within the territory of the Transvaal Republic justify an appeal to the Imperial Government to extend its influence in that direction? Doubtless the leading article of the *Natal Mercury*, commenting on a communication under the title of "A Voice from the Transvaal Republic," which appeared in the *Standard* of Saturday last, is fresh in the memory of your readers, and I need not therefore fatigue them by referring to the painful details revealed, further than to express an earnest hope that they are not founded on fact. The official correspondence moved for by Mr. Godlonton in the Legislative Council will probably throw more light on this important matter; but it has occurred to me to submit the idea that some member of Parliament might urge the adoption of a respectful address to His Excellency Sir Philip Wodehouse, requesting him to appoint a Commissioner to proceed to the spot with the object of collecting evidence as to the alleged existence of slavery and gold in the Transvaal country, with full power to treat with those chiefs—the original owners of the gold-bearing soil, who would prefer the British either to the Prussian or Transvaal Government. If the report of such Commissioner should establish beyond doubt the substantial reality of slavery and gold in these distant parts, there is not much fear but that the people of England would support Her Majesty's Government in substituting British authority for that of the two Republics in Southern Africa.

Thursday, 9th July, 1868. AFRIKANDER.

The Transvaal Commission.

Sir,—It is a coincidence rather singular that, before I should have seen or heard anything about the Governor's message, "forwarding to the House of Assembly correspondence that has passed with the Chief Macòn, of the tribe of the Bamangwatos, and the Rev. Mr. McKenzie, now residing in their territory," and asking for the "sanction of the necessary expenditure" to enable "the Government to obtain trustworthy information as to the value of the discoveries stated to have been made there, and the general present condition of the country," I should have presumed to suggest, through the medium of your columns, that Parliamentary action should be taken to induce His Excellency to move in this direction. It seems to me to require no argument to convince the representatives of the people in both Houses of Parliament, of the *expediency* of voting the sum required for the appointment of a competent Commission to consider and report upon the prospect of the sanguine anticipations relative to the South African gold-fields being realized ; and I venture to submit that *justice* demands a recommendation, on their part, that the opportunity should be embraced of instituting an inquiry on the spot as to the truth or falsehood of the rumours with respect to the existence of slavery in the Transvaal regions. The *Argus*, in its leader this morning, takes a very practical view of the recent annexation proceedings of the Transvaal Government, when it says :—

A paper proclamation may, however, work serious mischief, and bring about complications in which the British Government may find themselves involved, particularly as Mr. Pretorius has coolly swooped down upon the gold-fields, and appropriated them for the Republic. Our Natal friends, evidently feeling that whatever goes on in these regions to the north of our frontier, which will one day be peopled by Europeans, is of moment to the Colony, have raised the cry of alarm, and invoked the aid of the British Government in checking Transvaal ambition.

Perhaps it may be thought by some that Her Majesty's High Commissioner is rather late in the field for the protection of British interests, which may be found to clash with those of Portugal, Prussia, and the South African Republic, which, like its neighbour, the Orange Free State, is so covetous of land. Is not the date of " President Pretorius' annexing proclamation" subsequent to that of the rejection of the overtures made through Commandant Jan Viljoen to the Chief Macên to hand over his country to the Republic, and if so, may not the former be, in some degree, ascribed to the latter ? Sir Philip Wodehouse, after receiving from the chief of the Bamangwato tribe the invitation " to come and occupy the gold country, in so far as it is at his disposal, and to govern the gold diggers in the name of the Queen of England," wisely "advises him to adhere to his determination to avoid coming under any engagements in any other quarters ;" and the sooner, therefore, legally constituted commissioners are sent to the spot to ascertain whether the gold-fields afford sufficient inducement for Her Majesty's Government to gratify the wish of this native chief, that "his efforts to sustain law and order amongst British subjects in the gold-fields may be superseded by the advent of the power of England," the better it will be for all parties concerned. If the report as to the abundance of gold in South Africa be exaggerated, the sooner it is contradicted, through an official channel, the better it will be for the people of the Cape and Natal ; but, if there really be a prize of gold in these distant parts, why should not steps be taken to secure it, not only for these two British Colonies, but for the Mother Country also ?

Your Cape Town contemporary above referred to quotes certain passages from an article in the *Natal Mercury*, under the title of "A Voice from the Transvaal Republic," for the purpose of proving that, "unfortunately, the Government which now seeks to extend its authority in Central Africa is one of the worst in the world," and I make bold to transfer to your columns the concluding portion of that article as an argument to encourage the Cape Parliament to provide funds for the Commission which Sir Philip Wodehouse so properly appears most anxious to appoint:—

> The origin of the present war is the trade in "black ivory." The way to obtain this is as follows:—Train the old black elephants to kill each other; shoot the females, take their young, and call them ivory. Price of black ivory: one tooth (six years' old), four head of cattle; younger, three head of cattle. Mind, however, that the trade in black ivory has been stopped, with no little ostentation, by Government; so you cannot sell black ivory, but make presents of it, and take a present in return. Some ivory hunters are said to be very clever. I heard of a little band of hunters who placed some female elephants *big with young* in a row and shot them, to try through how many they could put a ball, and afterwards gave some young hunters practical lessons in obstetrical anatomy. I have heard a little anecdote about an affectionate black female elephant. A man took away her young; she loved her young, and crept towards the man who had robbed her, and moistened his veldschoens (or hide shoes) with her own milk. Isn't this funny? A woman took the young elephant and gave it back to its dam, but the man took it away again, and drove the black female elephant away, but—kind-hearted creature he was—did not shoot her. Facts, such as these, come to light day by day, and it is for these reasons that hundreds of Boers and Europeans refuse to fight the Kafirs, but claim that the guilty whites shall be punished first; however, the Government does, or can do, nothing. Our condition is miserable in the extreme. No protection for Kafirs nor against them; no security of property, no trade, no government nor police but a name, no money, no education for the people, no maintaining of law and order but for the well-disposed, and, what is worse, no prospect of better times, except when——?

Few will hesitate to come to the conclusion that this sad picture of inhumanity must be overdrawn, but if such tales of horror and cruelty can find their way into the columns of the Natal press and form the subject of editorial comment, surely the time has arrived when "all persons interested in the progress of African civilization" ought to call out loudly for a commission of inquiry, and for the application of the remedy of the extension of British influence northward on the African continent, if unfortunately there be any foundation for these terrible statements.

Tuesday, July 14. AFRIKANDER.

THE TRANSVAAL COMMISSION.

SIR,—The House of Assembly has done quite right in refusing to listen to the proposal made by the hon. member for Graaff-Reinet, to limit the expenditure of the Commission to the Gold-fields to the sum of £2,000, and has afforded satisfactory evidence of its due appreciation of the desirability and expediency of obtaining official and trustworthy information relative to auriferous quartz and nuggets of gold in the Transvaal regions, by giving to the Governor a *carte blanche*. There is now no excuse for not doing the thing well in the appointment of a Commission in every respect competent to deal with the important subjects to be committed to its consideration and report. As the result of this inquiry, already too long delayed, may be the means of attracting to these shores numbers of the Anglo-Saxon race, as well as other Europeans, and thus exercise a beneficial influence, not only on the prosperity and progress of the Cape of Good Hope, but also "on the advancement of civilization and Christianity in South Africa," it is to be hoped that His Excellency will not for a moment permit any false notions of retrenchment to guide him on this occasion. Your observations in the sub-leader of the *Standard* of this morning, regarding the composition of such Commission, are well worthy of attention, and many will agree with you in thinking that two, if not three, Commissioners, should be appointed. I venture also to suggest that if the services of a gentleman who had some knowledge of the language, habits, and character of the native races could be secured, the labours of the Commissioners, whoever they may be, would be facilitated and be more satisfactory in results. I am glad to find that you adopt the suggestion of the Natal press, which has been repeated in your correspondent's column, that this Commission should not confine its attention exclusively to gold, but "that it might also take the opportunity afforded of inquiring into the alleged existence of slavery in the Transvaal." The idea you throw out that it might also "feel the pulse of that Republic with respect to annexation to this Colony," does not seem to be bad, and might perhaps, with advantage, be made applicable as well to the Orange Free State during the journey of the Commissioners through the dominions subject to the rule of Mr. President Brand. If the policy of this view of the case be sound, I cannot refrain, at the risk of laying myself open to the imputation of an indelicate interference with the prerogative of the Governor, from submitting a suggestion that one of the Commissioners should be a gentleman thoroughly acquainted with the Dutch language, and one in whom the inhabitants of Dutch origin, not only in this Colony, but also in the two South African Republics, would place confidence. The opportunity of promoting the future extension of British influence beyond the Orange and Vaal Rivers by wise conciliation of the Boer element ought certainly not to be lost. If a former member of the Legislative Council, distinguished for his public spirit and independence, and deservedly esteemed by all his countrymen, who has recently turned his thoughts to Free State matters, could be induced to be one of those to accept this important trust, would not Sir Philip Wodehouse be justly adding to his increasing favour with the people of the Cape by availing himself of the services of this gentleman, not deficient in scientific knowledge? The indictment you prefer against the merchants of Cape Town for apathy and indifference about gold, when their brethren at Port Elizabeth and Natal are so much on the *qui vive*, does not appear to be groundless. Why does not the Chamber of Commerce of the Western Metropolis take some action in this matter, and organize a respectable prospecting party to accompany the Commission? Surely, if the best route of reaching the gold-fields—the new Victoria Diggings in South Africa—is *viâ* Hope Town, on the banks of the Orange River, you cannot be far wrong in "believing that this port might be made the most advantageous centre from which to start for Macên's territory." Making a rough calculation, it is thought that Hope Town will be found to be about 600 miles from Cape Town, and rather more than 350 miles from Port Elizabeth; but would not the proximity of Table, as compared with Algoa Bay to England, and the greater facility of providing transport overland at this end of the Colony, give Cape Town some claim to be preferred over Port Elizabeth, by gold-seekers from the Mother Country? The Westerns ought, at least, to make some effort to prevent the tide of emigration from Europe, consequent upon the proof that abundance of gold is a reality in South Africa, being diverted from their port to that of the Easterns or Natalians.

Cape Town, 6th August, 1868.   AFRIKANDER.

The Orange Free State Protest.

Sir,—Having been somewhat disappointed in my expectation that the Governor's message relative to the commission to the Transvaal Gold-fields would have *indirectly* led to a debate in the House of Assembly upon matters affecting "the interests of this Colony in its relations with the Free State, and the progress of civilization in South Africa," I must ask permission to trespass for the last time on your columns with a brief allusion to the Basuto question, in the anxious hope of provoking in the Legislative Council some discussion, before the Parliamentary session closes, on this important subject. The *Argus* of this morning announces the fact that "despatches have been received by the *Dane* from Her Majesty's Government, fully approving of the policy of Sir Philip Wodehouse in reference to the annexation of Basutoland, and concurring in the arrangements proposed by His Excellency." This intelligence cannot fail to be most pleasing to the numerous colonists of the Cape and Natal, who have from the beginning looked with favour upon the British intervention on behalf of Moshesh and his tribe as the best, if not the only, means of restoring peace to South Africa; and it is earnestly suggested that even they, who have hitherto regarded the formal proclamation of Sir Philip Wodehouse, declaring the Basutos British subjects, as a " despotic and tyrannical" infringement of the law of nations, would do well by *now* throwing oil upon the troubled waters, and wisely counselling Mr. President Brand and the Volksraad to give a willing ear to the amicable negotiations of the Queen of England's representative at the Cape. At any rate, the idea suggested by the reported statement of Mr. Adderley in the House of Commons, that it would turn out that Sir Philip Wodehouse had exceeded his instructions from Downing-street, which was at the time made so much of in Cape Town, and which probably also had the effect of confirming the mistaken policy of the Free State authorities to treat Her Majesty's High Commissioner with contempt, is now proved to be groundless; and there is no longer any validity in the argument, which has been urged, that the uncertainty of the fate in England of the celebrated Orange Free State Protest was a good excuse for the studied and continued silence of the Cape Parliament on this interesting topic. Your contemporary further states, " In fact, the whole business is now left in the hands of the High Commissioner;" and, if report speak truly, Sir Philip Wodehouse has full discretion either to annex Basutoland to the Cape or Natal, or temporarily to keep it as a *separate* British possession, " under the control of the Governor of the Cape Colony in his capacity of High Commissioner." It may fairly be presumed that the Imperial Parliament will not, at present at least, repeat the process of compulsory annexation *a la* British Kaffraria, and that the wishes of the Cape and Natal Legislature will be first consulted on this point. If Basutoland then be worth having, has not the time arrived for the Cape Parliament to put in a claim for this valuable prize of territory in opposition to that which has been already preferred on behalf of the rival Colony of Natal by Lieutenant-Governor Keate in the speech with which he opened the Parliamentary session? If Mr. Wollaston had succeeded in obtaining his Select Committee, the report of that Committee might have thrown some light upon the question of the expediency of annexing the rich lands of Moshesh and his tribe to this Colony, or it might have shown that it would be more practicable under existing circumstances, and more to the interest both of the Cape and Natal, that Basutoland and the Orange Free State should together form a *separate* Crown Colony of Great Britain, under the auspices of a Lieutenant-Governor and a Legislative Council. It is now clearly too late in the session to open up the large question of the extension of British rule and protection on the African continent; but would it be quite right in the Legislative Council, which numbers in its ranks many sincere friends of " the cause of civilization and Christianity in South Africa," to conclude its Parliamentary labours, prior to the approaching dissolution, without expressing and recording an approval of the humane policy of Her Majesty's Government in the reception of the Basuto nation as British subjects, as a fitting prelude to the further extension of British influence northward of the Orange River ? This expression of opinion, even by one of the branches of the Cape Legislature, would not only strengthen the hands of Her Majesty's High Commissioner, who has authoritatively and distinctly declared " that the severance of the Free State from the Colony was a misfortune to both communities," but it would also give encouragement to the growing British party within the Orange Free State, where already it is notorious that very many of the boers are only deterred from petitioning for a return of the British Government by the dread of the prevailing Hollander influence over the authorities of this South African Republic. In my last letter I broadly hinted that the people of Port Elizabeth and the Eastern Province generally would greatly regret that the reasonable attempt to excite discussion on "that portion of His Excellency the Governor's speech having reference to Basutoland and the Free State" had been so unsuccessful in the House of Assembly, and I think it may be argued that even in the Free State itself some interest was naturally taken in the result of the motion of the hon. member for Fort Beaufort, which has been shelved, from the subjoined extract from the private letter of a gentleman holding an influential position there :—" What has become of Mr. Wollaston's motion in the House of Assembly ? I had anticipated a lively and interesting debate on the Free State question." As, unfortunately, many of the Eastern members of the Assembly are expected to take their departure by the *Dane* on Monday next, it is useless now to try to get up a debate upon the Basuto question in the Lower House, but this is no reason why the Upper House should not take an early opportunity of correcting this sad omission by discussing at least the bearings of the annexation of Basutoland to the British Colonial Empire upon the future prospects and interests of this Colony as well as of the Orange Free State.

Saturday, 15th August, 1868.   COLONIST.

BRITISH BASUTOLAND AND THE STATE.

SIR,—Although it may fairly form the subject of regret, if not of complaint, both within and without the Colony, that the Cape Parliament should have closed its long protracted session without any discussion upon "that portion of the Governor's speech having reference to Basutoland and the Free State," it certainly will be satisfactory to many to note that not a single voice has been raised within the walls of either House of the Colonial Legislature in condemnation "of the transactions of Her Majesty's High Commissioner with the President of the Orange Free State and the Basuto Chief Moshesh," which have so justly secured the full approval of the Home Government. The laboured protest of Mr. President Brand and the Volksraad has signally failed in changing the benevolent intentions of the Queen of England to make the Basutos British subjects, and their territory part and parcel of the British Colonial Empire. There seems, therefore, good ground to hope that the future boundary line between Basutoland and the dominions of the South African Republic will *now* be easily settled by Sir Philip Wodehouse in amicable conference with the Orange Free State authorities, but there will still remain behind the difficult question of providing in a satisfactory manner for the efficient internal government of the small though populous *new* British possession in South 'Africa. It is true that by this time Moshesh and the other Basuto chiefs have been informed by Mr. Bowker "that Her Majesty's Government, having had under their consideration the report of Sir Philip Wodehouse of the transactions which took place during his late visit to Basutoland, have signified their consent to the tribe being placed at *present* under the control of the Governor as High Commissioner, instead of being annexed either to the Cape or to the Colony of Natal;" but with the experience to be derived from the history of British Kaffraria, it may be taken for granted without argument that this will only be a temporary expedient, and the Duke of Buckingham's despatch of the 9th of December, 1867, appears to warrant this reasonable conclusion. The idea proposed by the old and paramount Chief, that Basutoland should form a kind of Native Reserve, to be annexed neither to the Cape nor to Natal, but to be governed *directly* by the High Commissioner, would, of course, be agreeable to the Basuto nation; but it may be doubted whether it would be attended with equal advantage to their neighbours of the Free State; and may it not be fairly argued that it would be more permanently conducive to the interests and progress of both countries to seize this opportunity of affording the shelter of British rule to the Free Staters as well as to the Basutos? From a leading article of the *Graham's Town Journal*, suggested by the late despatches from England, and written with the proper view of showing that "the settlement of Basutoland involves also the determining of the future relations of the Free State to this Colony," I extract the following truly practical remarks, so pertinent to my present argument:—

But is there no other way of dealing with this question between British Basutoland and the Free State? Mr. Hamelberg is reported to have said, that if Basutoland were to become British, the Free State should also become British. We do not know that Mr. Hamelberg actually did say this, or anything like this; but if he did say so, he never said anything wiser. Unquestionably, this will be the view of the case which will gain adherents in the State, as soon as the first excitement consequent upon the publication of the recent news concerning the fate of the protest and the inevitableness of Basuto annexation, has subsided. There is reason in the State; its common sense has been disturbed of late, but it has not been utterly destroyed; *and it cannot fail to be seen that the continued independence of the State will be but a delusion and a snare.*

If then, as may naturally be expected, the fruitless result of the deputation to England be to damp the ardour of the Hollanders, and to revive the hopes of the British party northward of the Orange River, why should not some decided effort be made by the inhabitants of the Orange Free State to seek for true liberty under the genial influence of the British Crown as a substitute for the "nominal independence" of the existing Republic? At the present moment a practical method of bringing about the happy consummation of a change of dynasty in the land which was once the Sovereignty suggests itself. As each of the three alternatives which have been put forward, the annexation of Basutoland to the Cape, to Natal, or the constituting it a Native Reserve under the sole control of the High Commissioner, is beset with some difficulty, why should not the Free-Staters *themselves* propose the plan "of the annexation of the Free State, and the creation of a large independent British Colony, consisting of that country and Basutoland;" and why should not the colonial communities of the Cape and Natal join in giving their support to a scheme so well adapted to maintain the influence and prestige of the British Government and the British people in South Africa? This idea may perhaps already have presented itself to Her Majesty's High Commissioner—at least it seems worthy of being well discussed *before* much trouble is taken in deciding the intricate question of boundary line, so long the fruitful source of war between the Boers and their sable enemies. If the Free State, *now* that "it must know that Basutoland is British, would only prefer to become British itself," the necessity for "negotiations about boundaries" would altogether cease, and His Excellency Sir Philip Wodehouse be more profitably employed in inaugurating the formation of an important Crown Colony of Great Britain northward of the Orange River—to be annexed hereafter to the Cape of Good Hope, or to be one of the States under the contemplated grand system of Federation, so strongly advocated on all sides. Mr. Godlonton is reported to have referred yesterday, in the Legislative Council, "to the Convention entered into at the time British protection was withdrawn from the Free State," and to have quoted therefrom to show that the Convention had never been carried out by either party, *and that the Free State inhabitants had never been absolved from their allegiance.* It would indeed be difficult to controvert these sound opinions so frequently advocated in your columns and the frontier press, and, if so, may not a reasonable hope be entertained that, if the Orange Free State were to seek for annexation to the British Colonial Empire, the consent of the Home Government would be readily given, "because," as the *Graham's Town Journal* well puts it, "all British South Africa would unite to desire a measure so politic, so healing, and so full of promise;" and does not this hope justify some constitutional agitation within the British Colonies of the Cape and Natal, with the view of inducing and encouraging the people of the Free State to take the initiative in petitioning Queen Victoria to replace them under the wide folds of the flag of Great Britain?

Saturday, 29th August, 1868.   COLONIST.

British Rule for the Free State.

Sir,—If the *Friend of the Free State* felt himself justified, when commenting upon the late debate in the Legislative Council of Natal on the subject of the annexation of Basutoland, to write as follows:—"But any way it must be admitted that the Natal Council has done far better, and displayed more enlightenment than the Cape Parliament has generally done; the latter has, we regret to say, almost invariably proved itself to be hopelessly obstructive of all progress or extension of British territory in South Africa," what will he say now, after hearing that the long Parliamentary session of the Cape Legislature has closed without the utterance of a single syllable in favour of the extension of British rule on the African continent, while the Natal Council has recorded a well-argued recommendation to Her Majesty's Government favourably to receive any proposals which may emanate from the inhabitants of the *two* South African Republics with regard to "their annexation to either the Cape Colony or Natal, or embracing suggestions with respect to any form of allied or separate administration deemed suitable by the majority of the white inhabitants of such States?" The Natal resolutions, which will probably find their way into your columns, will speak for themselves, and cannot fail to give a stimulus to constitutional agitation outside the Cape Parliament, both in this Colony and Natal, with a view of encouraging their neighbours northward of the Orange and Vaal Rivers to seek for the substitution of the regal sway of the British Crown for the Republican form of Government. There is not much new to be said in favour of the Resumption of the Sovereignty, but there can be no harm in repeating arguments upon a political question of such importance to the future progress of South Africa, and, at the risk of again being accused of having "a mania for making extracts," I prefer borrowing the language of the *Natal Mercury*, which most ably argues "that no question bears more directly upon our commercial interests and political condition than the annexation of the Free State," in a leading article from which the subjoined passages are quoted :—

That the Queen's advisers and representatives committed a great mistake when they decided to abandon the Sovereignty, has been and is the common belief of most colonists. No good end has been gained by that policy. It was the beginning of evils. From that time the people who were thus turned unceremoniously adrift have been mixed up in constant warfare with the Basutos. . . . *Had the Free State remained British territory it is more than probable that the Basuto wars which have since prevailed would have been prevented. Moshesh has a wholesome respect for the British lion.*

Again :—

It may be said that neither the Imperial nor the Colonial Governments have taken any part in the wars we refer to. That may be; and yet the evils entailed by the wars are as serious in their effects upon our commercial interests as though we were parties to the strife. There cannot be much less than half-a-million of money due to the Cape and Natal by creditors in the Free State, and yet so long as war lasts, and as the Civil Courts are closed, these claims are practically irrecoverable. In another way the Basuto wars have operated most injuriously. *Nothing can be more disgusting to our natives, and to the tribes around, than the spectacle of another native race constantly at war with the white man.* The natural tendency of such a war is to keep alive instincts and sentiments which had far better, in the interests of peace and civilization, become extinct.

And again :—

Were the Free State and Basutoland both annexed, *and both thrown into one compact and separate Colony*, we believe not only that war would be averted, but that law and order might be re-established and maintained without cost to the Mother Country. *The Basutos and the Free State people together would be able to contribute a revenue large enough for all purposes.* It is absurd on the face of it to deny their capacity to do this. For years the country has kept in the field a large armed and unproductive force, and has done this at incalculable loss to their trade and other interests. At a far less cost to themselves they could afford to maintain a police force of two or three hundred men for the suppression of Basuto thefts. Nor ought the Basutos to bear a small share of this expenditure. Were it not for them, no such force would be required, and we venture to suggest that farms granted or sold within Basutoland should be chargeable either with a rent specially devoted to this defensive service, or, if sold, that the proceeds should be applied to the maintenance of such a police force.

Of course, it remains with the people of the Orange Free State to say whether they will be annexed or not to the British Colonial Empire, but these remarks have been submitted in the hope of exciting discussion at the present juncture, both in this Colony and beyond the Orange River, upon the desirability of restoring, in some shape or other, the Queen's Government to Her Majesty's subjects in South Africa, who were so rudely abandoned in 1854; and it is again maintained with some confidence, that, under all the circumstances of the case, which have been dwelt upon, the plea of permitting the Free State and Basutoland to form together *for the present* a separate British Crown Colony, under a Lieutenant-Governor and a Legislative

Council, will be found to be the most practicable, and the most conducive to the welfare and progress of all parties concerned—the Colonies of the Cape and Natal, the Orange Free State, and the Basuto nation.

Wednesday, 2nd September, 1868.   COLONIST.

THE COMMISSION TO THE GOLD-FIELDS.

SIR,—Few, after the perusal of your sub-leader of this morning, will feel inclined to dispute the soundness of the conclusion at which you arrive, that " when men are preparing on all sides to try their lots in the new gold country," it is only fair to expect the British authorities in the Colony to be on the alert; and that Mr. Black's report furnishes additional force to the general wish for the speedy dispatch of the Commission to the "alleged gold-fields" in South Africa. It is gratifying, however, to find from the Prorogation Speech, that the apparent delay in the appointment of the Commission may solely be ascribed to the difficulty in "the selection of those to be employed" as Commissioners, to consider and report upon this interesting subject in all its bearings. As the Governor well puts it : " To ascertain the existence and quantity of gold forms but a portion only of the duty they will have to perform. Irrespective of the existence of gold, the colonial trade with those regions is of much importance, and I hope that our relations with the tribes that inhabit them, and those through which access to them must be obtained, may be much improved through the efforts of the contemplated Commission."

If the right men only are found for this important mission, their labours cannot fail to bear good fruit, not alone in proving or disproving the reality of the gold discoveries, but " in paving the way for beneficial changes in due season on the northern bank of the Orange River." This idea, which has been suggested at Natal, of making the mission to the new Victoria Gold-fields " bear a partially political character," certainly deserves consideration, and the annexed quotation from the *Mercury* may not altogether be deemed out of place :—

Nothing can be of greater importance in the present phase of South African affairs than that the influence and prestige of the British Government and the British people should be maintained. Never yet has there been so general a desire on the part of the natives to assume the obligations of British subjects. Never yet has there been so wide-spread a reliance upon the *bona fides* of our Government on the part of the aborigines. Mr. Shepstone's great diplomatic abilities would enable him to make this assurance in the native mind doubly sure, and to establish relationships which would virtually amount to the extension of British supremacy over all the territories that intervene between Natal and the Zambezi.

Some of your readers may, perhaps, recollect that so far back as January last, their attention was called to a suggestion of the *Graham's Town Journal* that the British Colonies of the Cape and Natal should take action in concert with the view of obtaining authentic intelligence as to the alleged Gold-fields in the territory of Moselikatse, and of making favourable terms with the native chief. Although there may be a fair rivalry between Cape Town, Port Elizabeth, and Durban, as to which is the best port for European emigrants to make as the starting point in South Africa for the Victoria Gold-diggings, both the Cape and Natal are alike interested in establishing the reality of gold, and in the further advancement of Great Britain's influence over the native chiefs and their tribes in the interior of this continent, and why should they not therefore have a joint commission? Both British Colonies ought to be equally interested in the question of the supposed existence of a system of slavery in the Transvaal regions, so opposed to the progress of civilization amongst the native tribes, and so injurious to the influence of the white race, although the Natal Legislature has *alone* spoken out on the subject. Having read the Natal resolutions, which appear in your columns of this morning, I cannot help thinking that a splendid opportunity is afforded to Sir Philip Wodehouse to refute the calumny thereby conveyed that "the office of High Commissioner, as exercised at present in relation to the Colony of Natal, is inimical to the maintenance of the prestige and influence of Her Majesty's Government amongst the native tribes of South East A'rica," by assigning to the Commission, as part of its duty, on its return from the Gold-fields, to endeavour to institute " a *bonâ fide* inquiry" as to the scandal which now attaches, perhaps unjustly, to the Transvaal Republic. Surely, it can never be contended that Great Britain, who has gained such laurels by her active exertions in the abolition of slavery, ought tacitly to consent to an infringement of the positive terms of a treaty, merely because "it would be beyond the power of the Transvaal Republic, admitting it to have the inclination, to put down a trade which the Boers must find very tempting and profitable." No one who has read what has been so aptly described as "the admirable and genial address from the Governor, which will long be remembered as a fitting word of farewell to the Parliament, with whom he has worked with varying success," can for a moment doubt the deep interest taken by Sir Philip Wodehouse in the future welfare and progress of South Africa; and it is diffidently submitted that the well-considered report of a competent Commission may in some degree be instrumental in enabling him, or his successor at the Cape of Good Hope, to carry out his good purpose of "creating beyond the river a large and well-organized Government, bound to this Colony only by a common allegiance, by the ties of kinship, by congenial laws, by just covenants, and by a common desire to extend the blessings of Christianity, peace, and civilization to all within their reach." I venture, therefore, with all respect, to take the liberty of so far trespassing upon the exercise of the prerogative of the Governor as again to suggest " that one of the Commissioners should be a gentleman thoroughly acquainted with the Dutch language, and a person in whom the inhabitants of Dutch origin, not only in the Colony, but also in the two South African Republics, would place confidence"; and thus a good opportunity would be afforded of conciliating the Boer element both in the Orange Free State and the Transvaal, where already, if report speak truly, there is a growing opinion in favour of the Queen of England's Government. As His Excellency also properly lays great stress upon the expediency of availing of the occasion to improve our relations with the native tribes, would it not be as well to secure the services in aid of the Commission of some gentleman who can speak the native language?

Saturday, 5th September, 1868. AFRIKANDER.

BRITISH SUBJECTS IN THE FREE STATE.

SIR,—Your leading article of Saturday last upon the late trial of Mr. Bowden, at Philippolis, in the Orange Free State, concludes with the remark that " you feel quite satisfied that, in the hands of the Governor, international rights will be strictly observed, and the honour of the British Crown be preserved intact." If it be true, as alleged, that an appeal has been made to Sir Philip Wodehouse, a favourable consideration of the case of the unfortunate convict may fairly be anticipated, for there cannot be much doubt as to the opinion of His Excellency on this point after the short but telling despatch of the 31st of July to Mr. President Brand, in which the " recently commenced prosecution for high treason against a British-born subject, who protested against being called upon to march against his fellow-subjects," is prominently put forward, in conjunction with the contemptuous treatment of Her Majesty's High Commissioner, the protest to England, and the continued " destruction of the crops and huts of the Basutos," as condemnatory evidence of " the policy adopted and persevered in" by the Government of the Free State. If Her Majesty's High Commissioner had legal jurisdiction, he probably would reverse the judgment of the Orange Free State Court of Law, but the fear is, that, although the Volksraad will *now* amicably negotiate with Sir Philip Wodehouse as to the settlement of the boundary line of Basutoland, they will be slow to admit his power to nullify and set at defiance the commando law of the independent South African Republic. Whilst the deep-rooted and earnest loyalty and devotion to the British Crown of the *thirteen* Englishmen, who boldly united in declaring that they would not forfeit their natural allegiance to the Queen of Great Britain, from which they had never been legally released, and that they would not wage war against their *new* fellow-subjects—the Basutos—merits the warmest admiration ; there is, doubtless, much in the argument you have advanced, that an English citizen of the Orange Free State is bound to obey the law of the land in which he permanently resides, and to take his share of the military duty of defending the frontier of that State, when called upon in his proper turn to do so. Unless, then, Mr. Bowden is to be incarcerated in a vile dungeon for the term of twelve months, as a punishment for not performing "a service required at his hands, which his duty to his Sovereign prevented him rendering," and thus to furnish good ground to Great Britain for a *second* Abyssinian Expedition, that is to say, if she be desirous of preserving her consistency in defending the liberty of Englishmen in foreign countries, is not the practical solution of the "embarrassing" question, which seems to perplex you—the formal declaration of the Free Staters as well as the Basutos to be British subjects ?

The numerous friends on both sides of the Orange River, of the further extension of British rule in Southern Africa, will rejoice to hear that the *Norseman* brings the cheering intelligence that action has been taken in England to prevent the delegates from the Orange Free State having it entirely their own way at the Colonial Office, to which department of the British Government they have been quietly, but not without courtesy and kindness, handed over by Lord Stanley, Her Majesty's Secretary of State for Foreign Affairs. The well-drawn memorial, giving an accurate history of the origin and abandonment of the Sovereignty, which has been prepared for presentation to the Duke of Buckingham, and signed by the principal Cape merchants resident in London, will, no doubt, appear in your columns, and best speak for itself ; but I cannot refrain quoting, as singularly illustrative of my present argument, *two* of the principal reasons put forward by the memorialists in support "of the re-asserting British authority over the Orange Free State." They are as follows :—

a. The anomalous position of residents in the Free State, who, as subjects of the Queen, and separated only by geographical lines from the Colonies of the Cape of Good Hope and Natal, are allowed to exercise independent authority, and are regarded and treated as foreigners.

b. The inevitable complications which must result from the altered position of the Basuto nation in relation to Great Britain and the Orange Free State.

The *Graham's Town Journal*, with reference to the well-timed resolutions of the Legislative Council of Natal, "affirming the desirableness of Free State and Transvaal annexation to British South Africa," most aptly remarks :—

We can only say that we wish our Parliament had had the spirit to record and transmit to the Colonial Office a similar expression of opinion. The

Natal resolution prays Her Majesty's Government to favourably consider any proposal which the authorities of either State may make towards union. *This is exactly the kind of encouragement which the annexationists in the Republic require, and it is exactly the kind of action which the Colonies could take without offence to those in the Republics who are opposed to annexation.* Had a resolution like this been sent home from the Cape and Natal Parliaments, at the time when the Free State protest and deputation left for Downing-street, it would have been timely and serviceable. In this respect Natal has, strangely, been a little slow; while, not at all strangely, the Cape has been altogether stagnant.

The Prorogation Speech, however, I confess, makes me almost indifferent about the silence of the Cape Parliament on the Basuto question, and no one can consistently quarrel with the well-expressed opinions of Sir Philip Wodehouse on this important and interesting subject. He tersely says:—

There remains still for final adjustment one question of importance in its effect on the native tribes—that of the reception as British subjects of the tribe of the Basutos; which I sincerely hope may be so accomplished as not only to secure their welfare, *but to pave the way for other beneficial changes in due season on the northern bank of the Orange River.*

If there could exist any substantial doubt as to the nature of the changes in contemplation, it would be removed by the following passage from the Governor's last speech:—

What is to be hoped for, in my opinion, is the creation, beyond the River, of a large and well-organized Government, bound to this Colony only by a common allegiance, by the ties of kinship, by congenial laws, by just covenants, and by a common desire to extend the blessings of Christianity, peace, and civilization to all within their reach.

Many will most cordially sympathize with His Excellency in these statesmanlike views, and the only impediment in the way of the resumption of British authority at no distant day northward of the Orange River, so much desired by the Cape and Natal colonists, really seems to be the want of expression in "some unmistakeable form," on the part of the people of the Free State, of their consent and concurrence with the substitution of the regal sway of the Queen of England for that of the South African Republic. The Aliwal North correspondent of the *Great Eastern* writes as follows of the Orange Free State:—

The country is divided against itself—composed of many elements, and these elements are in a state of solution. The Hollanders mistrusted, the English crying out for annexation, and the Boers longing for peace and prosperity. The condition of many of the farmers is very sad and grievous; many are ruined, and the people generally know not whither to turn. Many of the Boers are so disheartened and dispirited that I am well assured that a word, yea, the least hint, from the High Commissioner would cause them to go hand-in-hand with the English in their prayer for annexation.

This may, perhaps, be an exaggerated picture of the misery beyond the Orange River, but surely a case is made out to justify *the people of the Cape Colony* in agitating in favour of the resumption of the Sovereignty, not with the intent of dictating to their neighbours of the Orange Free State, but with the anxious and earnest hope of convincing them that it will be to

o

their interest *speedily* to give some practical proof that they agree with Sir Philip Wodehouse " in regarding the measures which severed from their allegiance the European communities in those regions to have been founded in error; and that it will be a blessing for all if, with their general and hearty concurrence, they can be restored in a general sense to their former position."

Saturday, 12th September, 1868.   COLONIST.

THE FREE STATE.

SIR,—In the *Standard's* leading article of this morning, written for transmission to England by the *Roman*, you say, "the Free State and Basuto question remains *in statu quo*," and, curiously enough, your contemporary the *Argus* makes use of the same expression. I presumptuously venture to differ from you both, and to submit that this interesting and important question may fairly be said to have derived a new aspect and more cheering phase from the resolutions recorded by the Natal Legislative Council recommending the annexation to the British Colonial Empire of the two South African Republics—the Orange Free State and the Transvaal—as well as from the decided opinion expressed by Sir Philip Wodehouse in favour of "other beneficial changes in due season on the northern bank of the Orange River" having the effect of largely increasing the number of British subjects in South Africa. To me it seems that the annexed popular paraphrase by the *Port Elizabeth Telegraph* of that portion of the "conciliatory" prorogation speech having reference to this subject is calculated to convey to our friends in England a clearer insight into the true position of the Basuto-Free State difficulty:—

Referring to Transgariepean affairs, His Excellency gave it as his matured opinion that the abandonment, by the express action of the Imperial Government, of the Orange Free State territory (formerly the Orange River Sovereignty), was a mistake, and seems to have come to the conclusion that the readiest way of meeting the emergency that has arisen in connection with the chronic warfare, so long kept up by its inhabitants and the neighbouring Basuto tribe, would be to unite their respective territories, and erect them into a British Colony, under a Government somewhat analogous to that of the Colony of Natal. This, however, can only be effected by and with the consent of the majority of the Free State people—an influential minority of whom are understood to be favourable to such solution of their present difficulty with their sable neighbours, now Her Majesty's Basuto subjects. On the return to Bloemfontein of the Free State delegates (believed to be now on their way back from England) it is hoped that the Free State Government will be ready to negotiate with Her Majesty's High Commissioner for a solution of its difficulty with the Basutos on the basis of mutual concessions, and a willingness to also come under British rule in the manner suggested in the Governor's prorogation speech.

It is, perhaps, no more than might under the circumstances

be expected that the Orange Free State Government should, in the words of the President's reply to the Governor's despatch of the 17th of August, "await the result of their mission," rather than at once, in compliance with His Excellency's reasonable request, submit " some proposals which might form the basis of further negotiations and the ultimate adjustment of all pending questions ;" but it would, indeed, be "madness" on the part of " the Bloemfontein Administration" obstinately to persist in declining " to treat with Sir Philip Wodehouse" after the return of the delegates from England. As the *Graham's Town Journal* well puts it :—" Unless the deputation should gain from Downing-street what the protest has failed to secure, the High Commissioner must promptly, President or no President, carry out his already declared intention of placing the Basutos and Basutoland under British Government. He has no other course. If Mr. Brand declines to be a contracting party to the arrangement, he will only be playing the fool at his own cost, and to the injury of the country he is bound to rule, not with the passions of a child or the sullen fury of a lunatic, but with the prudent wisdom of a full-grown and sane man. It ought to be seen by Mr. Brand and his advisers that their friends in the Colony, who approved of his conduct when there was some hope of a favourable reply to the protest and deputation, may very well withdraw their support when it is found that resistance is hopeless." The *Friend of the Free State* wisely counsels the people of that State, "as one man, to demand that negotiations should at once be entered into with Sir Philip Wodehouse ;" and, perhaps, these negotiations might, with great advantage to all parties concerned, be now no longer confined to the settlement of the boundaries of Basutoland, but might also embrace the preliminary steps in the formation of a *new* British Crown Colony northward of the Orange River in lieu of the existing South African Republic. The comprehensive and well-argued memorial from the Cape merchants resident in London to the Duke of Buckingham may not only have the desired effect of inducing the Home Government to reverse the fatal policy of the abandonment of the Sovereignty, but it may also be the means of convincing the Africander Boers that it is to their interest to make common cause with the British party in the Orange Free State, and to take the initiative in asking from the Queen of England, through the instrumentality of Her Majesty's accredited agent at the Cape of Good Hope, for the re-assertion of British authority over their country. The annexation resolutions which passed the the Natal Legislature have appeared in your columns, and speak for themselves; but I cannot help thinking that the *original* resolution, "That, in the opinion of this House, the consolidation of the Free State and Basutoland as a separate British Colony would put an end to the demoralizing war which has been so long carried on between the Free State and the Basutos, and would place on a sound footing the extensive trade between the Republic and the neighbouring British Colonies, but which, owing to the closing of the Civil Courts and the general insecurity of the country, has suffered serious and disastrous injury during the duration of the war," which Mr. Robinson moved, was more practical, and less difficult to be put into immediate operation, particularly as it seems to accord with the ideas of Sir Philip Wodehouse, as expressed in the Prorogation Speech. There may be, however, consistently difference of opinion as to the *form* in which British rule is to be extended over the Free State, without in the least degree affecting the soundness of the argument that the Free Staters and the colonists of the Cape and Natal should live under the protection of a common national flag—that of Great Britain. It is worthy of remark that the *amended* resolutions, which speak of "the comparative dependence of the Orange Free State on the Cape Colony and Natal," as justifying the belief that that State would "be desirous of returning again under the dominion of the British Government, to which indeed it but recently belonged," were framed by Mr. J. N. Boshoff, the former President of the South African Republic, and will not fail, it is hoped, in producing a salutary effect upon the people of the Free State, and prevent them from blindly continuing under the baneful influence of the Hollander party. Report says that, although the majority of the Afrikander Boers are in favour of Brish rule, they are "too timid to sign petitions" to the Queen of England in favour of it, as they have been taught to believe that "it would be high treason to apply to a Foreign Power." If the Burghers of the Orange Free State be "wearied of their nominal independence and fruitless freedom," they incur no danger in openly avowing their wishes. The inhabitants of the land which was once the Sovereignty, have not been "formally absolved from their allegiance to the British Crown, and to this day, therefore, they are legally British subjects." It is to be hoped, then, that I have succeeded in showing that the Basuto question is not precisely *in statu quo*, and that the cry, " Hurrah for Sir Philip !" which has been raised at Fort Beaufort, and echoed in your editorial columns, may welcome Her Majesty's High Commissioner " on the northern bank of the Orange River," when he goes in a short time to endeavour to settle the relations of the Colonies of the Cape and Natal with the Free State and Basutoland on a peaceful and satisfactory basis, and that his efforts may redound in the "extending of the blessings of Christianity, peace, and civilization" beyond the limits of Her Majesty's present dominions in South Africa.

Saturday, 19th September, 1868.   COLONIST.

A "SUFFERER" AND "COLONIST."

SIR,—If the complaint of your correspondent be really *bonâ fide*, I should indeed regret that my long "disquisitions" regarding the Free State and Basutoland should have caused such pain. I cannot, however, admit "that the question is not sufficiently pressing to be worked up just now," although it may be wanting in interest to many of your Cape Town readers. It strikes me as rather singular, that immediately under your editorial note, evidently sympathizing with poor "Sufferer," you should have inserted the well-timed letter of "British Subject," which proves beyond doubt that the anomalous position of Englishmen, compelled by the law of the Orange Free State to wage war with their *new* fellow-subjects—the Basutos, is worthy of fair discussion, at least by those who have the true interests of this Colony, as well as of the Free State, at heart. Surely, when the Cape merchants in London, usually so apathetic and indifferent about Cape politics, think it absolutely necessary to address the Duke of Buckingham on this subject, and when even His Grace, if we may judge from the paragraph, "British Extension," which appears in the same issue of your journal, "is prepared to extend to the Zambesi the red line which marks down on our maps the boundaries of the British Empire, home and colonial," well meant attempts to concentrate public attention in Cape Town upon "the blessed Basuto" question ought not to "bore" the constituents of the *Standard*. As "Scotus" has been referred to, I can assure the gentleman who honours me with "his friendly warning" that while I admire greatly the talents, outspokenness, and terse writing of this valuable contributor to the *Argus*, I never felt in the least annoyed by his reiterated rebuke of my "quoting propensities." The truth is, I am always glad to quote what appear to me to be the well-expressed opinions of others, if they fortify my argument, and I have from time to time made copious "extracts" from the *Graham's Town Journal*, because it always was, as I thought, particularly happy in its consistent support of the recent peaceful policy of Her Majesty's Government towards South Africa, and the conduct of Sir Philip Wodehouse in carrying it out. Although it may be dangerous to incur the further hostile criticism of "Scotus," I must venture the remark that the best part of even his forcible condemnation of the rigid action of the Custom House authorities, was, in my opinion, his quotation from Adam Smith.

Saturday, 26th September, 1868.   COLONIST.

Letters to the Editors of the Cape Argus.

THE FREE STATE.

SIRS,—Whatever may be said in general of the address to the Governor, a copy of which appeared in your Thursday's issue, there is one point of it which we think the community ought not to overlook. We refer to the suggestion that the Governor should exert his influence in order to have a union effected between the Free State and Her Majesty's dominions in South Africa. It appears from all accounts, though it may be quite possible that nothing better could be accomplished, that affairs between this Government and the Orange Free State territory are meanwhile in very anomalous, unsafe, and unsatisfactory condition. Suppose for instance (a thing very likely to happen), that depredations to a large extent were to be made by the Basutos on the property of the people in the Free State. What would the consequences be? The Free State cannot apply to our Government; for it does not admit its right to interfere, nor will it condescend to hold any official communication with our Governor. The course most likely to be adopted, and which they appear to contemplate by continuing their commandoes in the field, is to make reprisals, and thus immediately we find ourselves at war with them. It may be said it is more their interest than ours to avoid such an issue. This may be perfectly true, but it is small consolation to us, if we have to suffer, that greater suffering is caused to them. In the present posture of things, they would not be wholly inexcusable in punishing aggression; and as for self-interest, whilst the well-disposed and more respectable sort of people in the Republic may be more anxious to avoid a collision with us than we with them, it is well known that there is a number of wild spirits there who wish for it; and once blood is up, it is not so easy to allay it again. We believe no one for a moment proposes to annex the Orange territory by forcible means, or without the consent of the inhabitants, expressed through their representatives and Government. And the gain to the peaceably disposed part of the community would be much greater on their side than it would be to us. At the same time, there are very important interests which we ought to have at heart. The cause of humanity is one of these. No really good man can be indifferent to bloodshed, and burnings, starvation, and hangings carried on and suffered without any appearance of coming to an end, on our own borders. But the finer sensibilities of humanity cannot be wounded without damage to lower and more material interests. A small, independent community of white people on our frontier, with whom we have no right to interfere, and who by their fewness cannot impress the natives with respect, and by their losses are sooner or later prompted to repel injury in the spirit of revenge, cannot long be expected to maintain peaceful relations with them ; and when war breaks out between the two parties we cannot enjoy the assurance and advantages of peace. There is also another most material point, which appeals to the most selfish regard which it is possible for any of us to have, to our own personal interests, not as a community only but as individuals also. The impoverishment of others affects the interests of everybody, whether rich or poor, in a variety of ways. There is less to be done, less to be sold, a greater scarcity of money, with corresponding damage to the general credit ; and whilst our power to sustain the public burdens is lessened, we have severally to bear them to an increased amount. We are induced to employ such transparent truisms, addressed to the lowest degree of capacity and order of character, from the acknowledged apathy in this country, as compared with most others—we say it with regret—to claims of a higher kind, and from our deficiency, as a people, in public spirit. Now, we understand that here in Cape Town, and more particularly at Algoa Bay, an amount of money, reckoned by hundreds of thousands, is at stake, and which may very possibly be altogether lost unless things are speedily made to flow in their former peaceful channel in the Free State, credit there restored, and the courts of justice again thrown open. Had we not more than exhausted the space to which such a letter as this must be confined, we would have gone on to show of what vast importance it must be to the members of the Free State to become incorporated with us, or at least to become subjects of the British Crown. On this head, as well as on some others, such as the mode in which the union may be brought about, we shall in one word refer to the sensible letters in the *Standard* by " Colonist," with whose views on the subject we may say that we very generally agree.

May 20, 1868.   PAX.

SLAVERY IN THE TRANSVAAL REPUBLIC.

SIR,—The Natal Legislative Council, in their natural abhorrence of " the system of slavery, under the guise of child-apprenticeship," which is said to disgrace the country of the Transvaal Republic, has spoken out decisively with the laudable intention of inducing Great Britain to apply some practical remedy to an evil fraught with danger to the peace, civilization, and progress of South Africa. They have been, however, perhaps too sanguine in anticipating that " the representatives of Her Majesty's authority at Natal were they freed from the control of the High Commissioner, would be able successfully to interfere in the matter without entailing any troublesome or costly complications on the Home Government." The Natal resolutions, which have appeared in your columns, were evidently meant to convey the opinion that Sir Philip Wodehouse had treated with apathy and indifference the appeals which had been made to him on this subject by Lieutenant-Governors Scott and Maclean; but it is thought that His Excellency, if fairly judged, will not be found deserving of such an unworthy imputation. Your readers will forgive me for reminding them that as far back as December, 1855, Mr. Surtees, then Arbitrator in the Mixed British and Portuguese Commission at the Cape, concluded a well-written despatch to the Earl at Clarendon, as follows: " In 1852 a treaty was concluded between Sir George Cathcart and the Transvaal Boers, when their independence being recognised, one of the articles stipulated that slavery should not exist in the Transvaal territory; but the treaty omitted to provide any mode by which the stipulation was to be enforced. Since the conclusion of that treaty, as before, it has been constantly rumoured throughout this Colony, that the children of the Bushmen and other natives were kept in slavery by the boers, sometimes being obtained by barter, but often by force. The proclamation of Pretorius has now established the truth. I am bound to state to your Lordship my conviction that this evil, so long unchecked, and at length openly acknowleged, as it is of no light character, is one that calls for a speedy remedy." Mr. Surtees also enclosed a memorandum of Mr. Shepstone, of Natal, and other documentary evidence, clearly tending, as he maintained, " to establish a known and openly practised system of kidnapping natives and holding them in unremunerated servitude." This matter was referred by the Foreign Office to Her Majesty's Secretary of State for the Colonies, Mr. Labouchere, who in February, 1856, called upon Sir George Grey " for a full report of the circumstances alleged in the communication from Mr. Surtees, as far as it might be in his power to make one, in order to enable Her Majesty's Government to judge what steps might be advisable." The lucid report of Sir George Grey, contained in his despatch of the 22nd of May, 1856, too long for insertion here, may now be consulted with advantage on this point; but I am tempted to make the annexed extract therefrom in the hope of justifying the conclusion, at first sight perhaps unsound, at which Sir Philip Wodehouse arrived, when applied to by Lieut-Governor Maclean, " that he was really quite at a loss to discover in what manner he could interfere with any prospect of success":—

(2.) The subject has engaged much of my attention, and I should have reported regarding it at an earlier period, if I had seen my way clearly to the course which I thought Her Majesty's Government ought to pursue in reference to it. *But this is a difficult thing to decide.* It is easy to say that measures should be taken to put a stop to such practices; but what are the measures which will do this, is the question at issue? whilst the danger to be avoided is, taking measures which will only aggravate and prolong the evils complained of, instead of putting an end to them.

(3.) Upon our north-eastern frontier we have two Republics, established as such, and duly acknowledged as such by Great Britain, and this, in the instance of one of them, *in spite of the earnest entreaties and remonstrances of a large number of the most wealthy and respectable of its inhabitants.*

(4.) These Republics number amongst their populations many persons who were for years the proprietors of slaves in a slave country, and whose affections were in a great degree alienated from the British Government by the manner in which slavery was put a stop to the Cape Colony.

(5.) The European inhabitants of the two Republics are also, comparatively speaking, few in number, and are surrounded by dense masses of natives. Amongst them are many persons who, having lived for years on the outskirts of civilization, unwillingly submit to any laws or restraints.

Does not this line of reasoning corroborate the opinion apparently entertained by Sir Philip Wodehouse, that it would be in vain to attempt to put down slavery in the Transvaal regions, by merely making formal representations to the Transvaal Government in condemnation of it? Is not, indeed, the only practical remedy for "the atrocities from which the native races of South Africa are suffering," the extension "of the salutary and beneficent influence" of the British Government beyond the limits of its present jurisdiction on the African continent? With respect to the "alleged capture and sale of children and other persons by Europeans residing without the limits of this Colony," the Queen's representative at the Cape may be right in saying that "a *bonâ fide* inquiry would be almost impracticable, and, moreover, it would be beyond the power of the Transvaal Republic, admitting it to have the inclination, to put down a trade which the boers must find very tempting and profitable;" but it is confidently submitted that this is no valid argument in support of Great Britain, so renowned for the successful advocacy of the cause of the slave in all parts of the world, continuing to take no step in exacting the fulfilment of the positive stipulation in the agreement with the Assistant Commissioners in 1852, "that no slavery is or shall be permitted or practised in the country to the north of the Vaal River by the emigrant farmers." The despatch of Sir George Grey above referred to aptly concludes by advising Her Majesty's Government "to authorize the High Commissioner *either to abrogate* or to modify, from time to time, the treaties now existing with the Republics in our vicinity if they, on their part, do not exert themselves to adhere to their engagements to prevent slavery, *or if they use the powers given to them by those treaties in a manner or for purposes which could never have been contemplated by Great Britain at the time they were concluded;*" and it is suggested that the time has arrived when a due regard to the interests of all parties concerned demands the *abrogation* of these treaties, which guarantee the independence of the

Orange Free State and the Transvaal Republic, and prevent all alliances of the British Government "with the coloured nations north of the Vaal River." Even then, if the Commissioners about to be appointed by the Governor of the Cape of Good Hope to visit the new gold-fields in South Africa, already honoured with the name of Her Most Gracious Majesty, should fail to establish the reality of gold in sufficient abundance to remunerate the digger, their labours will not be lost if they be in any degree instrumental in proving to the satisfaction of the British people that justice alone requires the substitution of British rule for that of the two South African Republics.

Cape Town, 26th September.　　　　　　　　　　　　CIVIS.

THE COMMISSION TO THE GOLD-FIELDS.

SIRS,—Your correspondent "Inquirer" only represents the general feeling when he complains of the apparent inaction of the Cape Government in procuring trustworthy information regarding the alleged gold-fields in the Transvaal country. The difficulty of finding, as you say, in the Colony a competent "professional gold surveyor" may be deemed by many satisfactory to account for the delay in the appointment of the Commission, but your practical suggestion of "letting the diplomatic commissioner start in advance" seems to merit the favourable consideration of the Governor. The anxious curiosity about "the richness and extent of the auriferous regions" is certainly not confined to Cape Town ; for the *Graham's Town Journal*, in referring to the Port Elizabeth and Queen's Town diggers already far advanced in their journey to the South African gold mines, amusingly asks, "When will the Commission—the Government party—leave Cape Town ?" and "strongly recommends His Excellency to appoint himself," or "if Sir Philip cannot go, to send the new Board of Examiners." A gentleman also of long standing in the Orange Free State, most competent from local experience as a traveller to form an opinion, writes thus :—"I do not think anything of the difficulties and dangers to be encountered in reaching the Goldfields, but I can easily foresee that great difficulties and dangers will arise after the fields have been reached, unless the Government takes early measures to prevent them. I do not know Sir Philip, and therefore cannot say whether he be equal to the emergency; but were Sir George Grey here, he would act sharp in the interests of England and her people, and have the British Government represented without delay in the gold region." If the Natal press be at all correct in its sanguine predictions "that the new gold workings, carried on by free European men, will have the wholesome and happy effect of stopping the vile traffic in young native children now carried on by the Boers of the Transvaal, under the false pretext of apprenticeship," would not Sir Philip Wodehouse be exercising a wise discretion in giving Her Britannic Majesty's Commissioner of the Mixed British and Portuguese Commission at the Cape the opportunity of making himself useful in collecting authentic information as to the quantity and quality of the auriferous quartz in the territory of Macên, who is so desirous of becoming a British subject ? If Mr. Layard be only half as anxious as his predecessor, Mr. Surtees, to preserve the consistency of Great Britain with respect to the emancipation of slaves and the checking of the slave trade on the East Coast of Africa, he would work with zeal and energy to establish the reality of gold in South Africa, and, perhaps, if he were successful, the Imperial Government might be induced to contribute to the costs of the Commission, which would be an agreeable surprise to the Cape Parliament, notwithstanding its recent liberality in having given the Governor a *carte blanche* in the matter. I know that the evidence which as yet has been produced makes many persons look with suspicion on the pictures which have been drawn of the resources of the new Victoria Gold-fields; but, as even in the present uncertainty of the real state of things, many are not prevented from "trying their luck" at the South African Diggings, the sooner some official report can be published on the subject, the better for all parties concerned.

Cape Town, 1st October, 1868.   ANGLO-AFRICAN.

THE FREE STATE BURGHERS AND THE BASUTOS.

SIRS,—It is somewhat remarkable that Mr. President Brand's reply to the requisitions sent him to stand again for the Presidentship, in which he makes an appeal to the "*faithful burghers, trusting in Providence, to work together in unity and love for the prosperity of the State,*" should appear in your columns this morning in juxtaposition to a communication from a correspondent of the *Graham's Town Journal*, which discloses a demoralizing system of robbery and bloodshed alleged to be "tolerated at least, if not sanctioned, by the Free State Government." Your editorial comments upon the new complexion thus given to "the Basuto raids" seem practical and just; and it is but natural that you should express the hope "that, when the boundary line is fixed, and Basutoland occupied by the British Government, these scandals will cease." Many, however, who, in common with you, duly appreciate the good intentions of the Queen's Ministers to restore peace to South Africa, will, I think, concur with me in doubting whether you be not rather too sanguine in anticipating that the mere settlement of the geographical line which is in future to divide Her Majesty's new territory—Basutoland—from that of the Republic—the Orange Free State—will be completely efficient in putting an end to the wretched and chronic warfare between the Boers and the Basutos. When in 1842 Her Majesty's Secretary of State for the Colonies was called upon to provide a remedy for the then existing state of hostilities between "the emigrant Dutch farmers from the Cape of Good Hope and the Zoolahs and other tribes," he decided " upon the recognition of the territory of Port Natal as a British Colony," whose subsequent peaceful career with its large native population is the most convincing proof that he was right. The lucid despatch, bearing date 13th December, 1842, of the Earl of Derby, then Lord Stanley, is well worthy of being referred to at the present moment, and might, perhaps, afford some useful hints even to the High Commissioner in his coming negotiations with the Free State authorities; and, as throwing light upon the point under discussion, I must crave leave to make a quotation from that despatch.

I fear, moreover, that in the present state of the population, many of their acts, whether towards each other, towards the native tribes within their limits, or towards those who surround them, might be such as the British Government could neither approve nor permit; that disunion and jealousies among themselves would require the intervention of some supreme authority, and that Her Majesty could not safely entrust the emigrant farmers with the unchecked management of the Kafirs within their territory, nor repose entire confidence in the moderation and temper with which they might repel the aggressions or avenge the occasional depredations of the border tribes.

A Bloemfontein correspondent of the *Friend of the Free State* reports that Mr. Adderley, the Under Secretary of State for the Colonies, had "told the deputation that the abandonment of the Sovereignty was a great mistake;" and, perhaps, after all, the Rev. Mr. Vandewall, on his return from England, which is very shortly expected, may have it in his power to satisfy the people of the Orange Free State that if they only ask for the re-assertion of British authority over that State, their prayer will be granted. At any rate, it is submitted that the line of reasoning adopted by the Earl of Derby, who, doubtless, still possesses great influence over Her Majesty's present advisers, when he declined in 1842, " to admit the independence of the emigrants at Natal, and to disclaim all responsibility respecting them," would justify an appeal to the Home Government from British subjects on the northern bank of the Orange River, in favour of the reversal of the fatal policy of abandonment on various good grounds, besides the fact that Sir George Clerk's Convention had never been ratified and confirmed by Act of Parliament. It remains to be seen whether the many conditions upon which Mr. Brand " accepts the candidateship as President" will be fulfilled. If the *Friend* be at all a fair exponent of public opinion in the Orange Free State, it seems doubtful whether " *the result of the election will show that it is almost the unanimous wish of the burghers to see again at their head*" one who so strenuously opposed the peaceful British intervention to stay the bloody hands of war, and took so decided and active a part in inducing the Volksraad to treat Her Majesty's High Commissioner with contempt when he was prepared to negotiate, and "to give the fullest consideration to the just claims of the Free State." But perhaps you are right in thinking that "your enlightened and plucky contemporary of the Free State, the anxious advocate of the resumption of the British Sovereignty over the territory beyond the Orange River," is too "hard upon Mr. Brand," in ascribing to "his maladministration of the Government" the misfortunes of the State. The republican system of government is ill-suited and weak, and the welfare of the Burghers and Basutos, as well as that of the British Colonies of the Cape and Natal, requires a total change of dynasty northward of the Orange River. All South Africa must become British. It is idle to attempt to make separate nationalities out of the same races—for what are we at the Cape, Natal, the Free State, and the Transvaal, but Englishmen and Boers? Whether, then, Mr. Brand be triumphantly returned or not on the 12th of November, it is hoped that his presidential career will not be long, because the opinion which has been expressed, "That the Free State can never be really independent, happy, or glorious until the British flag once more waves on the Fort of Bloemfontein," is earnestly believed to be founded on truth and justice, and to be entitled to favourable consideration by the constituents of the President and Volksraad, *before* Sir Philip Wodehouse enters upon the puzzling question of amicably deciding the future limits of Basutoland on equitable terms, satisfactory to all parties concerned.

Saturday, 10th October, 1868.   CIVIS.

The Two South African Republics.

Sirs,—Although the Cape Parliament seemed to dread even to discuss during the last long session the tedious Basuto question, it is consolatory to know that, about the same time that the Natal Legislature resolved to recommend to the favourable consideration of Her Majesty's Government the annexation of the two Republics situated on the borders of this Colony and Natal, the Cape merchants in London were usefully engaged in bringing to the notice of His Grace the Duke of Buckingham their faithful *resumé* of the history of the Sovereignty, which may be regarded as a " counter-blast" to the representations of the delegates from the Orange Free State. In a former letter I ventured to transfer to your columns a telling extract from the despatch of Sir George Grey of the 22nd May, 1856, reporting upon the then alleged existence of slavery in the Transvaal country; and I now presume to trespass upon the patience of your readers by annexing a further quotation from that statesmanlike document, which appears to me to be particularly appropriate to the present crisis in Southern Africa.

On another point connected with this subject I have formed opinions which I ought to express. The treaties at present existing between ourselves and the Transvaal Republic and the Orange Free State amount, in fact, to this : That we must enter into no treaties with native tribes ; that we must allow no native tribes to obtain arms and ammunition ; that we must allow the two Republics to obtain such arms and ammunition as they require. I think that power ought to be given to me in some measure to modify these treaties, if a necessity for my so doing arises. *In my mind, these treaties amount on our part to a declaration that we abandon the coloured races to the mercy of the two Republics.* If, from a determination to embark in no further operations in South Africa, we had resolved to remain strictly neutral, I could understand it. But in this case we do much more than remain neutral ; and if, as is now asserted by many well-informed persons, a general combination of the coloured tribes is being attempted to be formed against us, I fear that these treaties have naturally had some influence upon the chiefs who have joined the confederacy. *It would be well, I think, to consider how far such stipulations consist with the honour and greatness of Great Britain, or, at least, whether there are not many circumstances under which such stipulations ought not to be maintained.*

By the Transvaal Convention of 1852, "Her Majesty's Assistant Commissioners disclaim all alliances whatever and with whomsoever of the coloured nations to the north of the Vaal River ;" and the second clause of Sir George Russell Clerk's Convention of 1854, the fruitful source of bloodshed beyond the Orange River, is as follows :—" The British Government has no alliance whatever with any native chiefs or tribes to the northward of the Orange River, with the exception of the Griqua Chief, Captain Adam Kok ; and Her Majesty's Government has no wish or intention to enter hereafter into any treaties which may be injurious or prejudicial to the interests of the Orange River Government." We know that the Free State Volksraad, under the auspices of Mr. President Brand, has protested against the recent reception of the Basuto nation as British subjects as a breach of the contract on the part of Great Britain ; and if the *new* Victoria Gold-fields on the African continent should fortunately turn out so rich in auriferous quartz as to justify the British people in urging upon Her Most Gracious Majesty to grant the prayer of the Bamangwato chief, Macên, to be placed on the same footing with Moshesh, the Transvaal Government, with Mr. Pretorius at their head, may perhaps raise a similar objection. Although there may not be much legal force in this objection, the spirit of these two ill-judged Conventions certainly seems to be " the abandonment by Great Britain of the coloured races to the mercy of the two Republics ;" and, therefore, the sooner they are totally abrogated, the better. It will be recollected that Sir George Grey, in the despatch above referred to, suggested "that the High Commissioner should be authorized either to abrogate or to modify, from time to time, the treaties existing with the Republics in our vicinity ;" and it is much to be hoped that the Queen's present representative at the Cape, when he repeats his promised visit to the banks of the Orange River, will be clothed by the Home Government with the necessary "power" recommended by his far-seeing and justly popular predecessor. When Sir Philip Wodehouse was last at Aliwal North, his reported speeches on the reception of the ten gentlemen from Bloemfontein, and the delay in his acknowledgment of the letter from the chairman of the Port Elizabeth Chamber of Commerce, which conveyed the hint " *that it would be a source of immense relief to this Colony if, in the course of the negotiations with Mr. President Brand, it should so happen that His Excellency were to see the way to bring the Orange Free State again under British rule, by annexation, federation, or otherwise,*" led to the conclusion that he was rather too delicately scrupulous about being accused of tampering with the independence of the Orange Free State Republic. But it is respectfully submitted that it would not be a very extravagant hypothesis now to assume that His Excellency, after having on his return to Cape Town clearly coincided with the opinion expressed " that the severance of the Free State from this Colony was a misfortune to both communities," and *after* having also declared in the Prorogation Speech " that he regarded the measures which severed from their allegiance the European communities in those regions to have been founded in error ; and that it would be a blessing for all if, with their general and hearty concurrence, they could be restored in a general sense to their former position," will, in the coming conference to settle the boundaries of Basutoland, be found to be less anxious " to avoid giving the Free State Government a pretext for asserting that he was plotting its overthrow," as well perhaps as that of the Transvaal Republic.

Cape Town, 26th October, 1868. CIVIS.

BRITISH SUBJECTS IN THE FREE STATE.

SIRS,—While the *Advertiser and Mail* laudably reiterates the opinion that " it is in the highest degree desirable that British rule should be resumed over the interior Republics," it scornfully derides the idea that the case of Mr. Bowden, of Philippolis, who has been punished by the Orange Free State authorities for " drawing up a strong protesting document" against Englishmen being compelled to go on commando against the Basutos, calls for the intervention of Her Majesty's High Commissioner. Many, however, who cannot help thinking that the real point at issue is involved in the question so forcibly put by the " plucky" editor of the *Friend of the Free State*, " What British-born subject, unabsolved from his allegiance, would, after reading the Proclamation of the 12th of March, 1868, ' of which all Her Majesty's subjects in South Africa are required to take notice,' have the hardihood, or feel at liberty to wage war with the Basutos ;" will hesitate to bow implicitly to the decision of your contemporary, that any appeal by Mr. Bowden or his friends to Sir Philip Wodehouse would be "utterly unreasonable and absurd." To me, at least, it seems that the point will well bear discussion, and without admitting or denying the soundness of the conclusion, that a citizen of the Orange Free State, so long as it remains an independent Republic, is bound to fight against Moshesh and his tribe, I desire rather to submit, through the medium of your columns, that, if the argument of the learned professor based upon the analogy of "the case of an English-born subject domiciled in the United States of America during the late war" be sound, the anomalous position of British subjects "on the northern bank of the Orange River" would justify Great Britain in *at once* planting her flag at the fort of Bloemfontein, as well as at Thaba Bosigo. Without attempting to argue the question, which perhaps would be tedious to your readers, I prefer to quote the two annexed extracts, speaking for themselves, from the despatches of the late Duke of Newcastle to Sir George Clerk, bearing date 14th November, 1853, and 14th January, 1854 :—

> The precise form and substance of the instrument by which Her Majesty's authority is to be terminated is yet under discussion, but you may rely on it that sufficient care will be taken in framing it not to render it operative until all necessary preliminaries are accomplished. With regard to the question which appears to have been raised, whether the inhabitants of the Sovereignty would be fully released from their allegiance to Her Majesty, I have to state that they undoubtedly will be so from that allegiance which results at present from their being domiciled in a portion of her dominions. *Whether or not such of them as were born elsewhere, subjects of the Crown and emigrated as such to the Sovereignty, will be freed from that native tie of allegiance, is a question which I am not immediately prepared to answer, and which perhaps the parties interested have themselves not fully considered,* inasmuch as the severance of that tie, while it would scarcely produce them any real addition to their independence, would make them strangers and aliens in the event of their returning to their former country, and deprive them of the power of inheriting lands and other privileges of British subjects within British dominion.

And again :—

> It will be competent to Her Majesty's Government to have recourse to Parliament afterwards, should occasion arise, in order to obtain additional authority, to obviate any difficulties which may arise from the abandonment; but they are not at present aware of any probability that this will be necessary. *With respect to the question of the allegiance of the inhabitants who may have been born in British dominions either within or without the Sovereignty, there is, I believe, little doubt that no measure resting on the Queen's prerogative only for its authority could release them from the tie of such native allegiance. An Act of Parliament would be required for such a purpose. But for the reasons already adverted to in my despatch of the 14th November last, I do not consider it necessary to apply to Parliament on this ground.* It is probable that the inhabitants of the future commonwealth would generally prefer to retain the rights of British subjects rather than become wholly aliens, and subject to the ordinary capacity of aliens within Her Majesty's dominions.

The principle of law referred to in the above extracts by the Duke of Newcastle is thus laid down by Blackstone :—" Natural allegiance is such as is due from all men born within the Sovereign's dominions immediately upon their birth; it cannot be forfeited, cancelled, or altered by any change of time, place, or circumstance, *nor by anything but the united concurrence of the Legislature."* Does it not therefore follow that Her Majesty's "Orange River Territory Proclamation" of the 30th January, 1854, together with the celebrated Convention of Sir George Clerk, were insufficient in law to make the British subjects who inhabited the land which was once the Sovereignty " a free and independent people?" Is not the subjoined allegation in the memorial from the Cape merchants in London to His Grace the Duke of Buckingham a true version of the story ?

When, in the year 1854, the fatal measure of withdrawing British rule was decided upon, and the territory was abandoned to the inhabitants, *they were not formally absolved from their allegiance to the British Crown, and to this day therefore they are legally British subjects,* a fact which has either been lost sight of by the Home and Colonial Governments, or otherwise disregarded for obvious reasons.

The *Advertiser and Mail* says : " Mr. Bowden was determined to make a martyr of himself, and perhaps many British subjects on both sides of the Orange River will see cause to regret that ill-health has prevented him from pining in a dungeon at Bloemfontein, and thereby exciting the commiseration and securing the interposition in his behalf of the Queen of England's representative at the Cape of Good Hope." It seems almost a pity that the *læsa majestas* of " the Independent Republic " was appeased by so small a sum as £25 sterling, particularly if a larger fine or a longer term of imprisonment would have had the effect of ensuring a due " vindication of the rights of British subjects" within the Orange Free State.

Cape Town, 16th November, 1868.   CIVIS.

Leading Articles of the Friend of the Free State.

Bloemfontein, July 24, 1868.

To believe, as we believe, that it would have been better for the Free State to compromise matters with His Excellency, and to agree to join him in a petition to the Home Government for the re-annexation of the Free State to the Colony—to believe this,—will not help the matter under discussion, which is, what should be done now that the Free State has pursued a diametrically opposite course? We only see two sources of hope for the Free State now; and that is, first, that events may so shape themselves that, instead of the present Government, there may be one in office prepared to treat for re-annexation ; or, second, contrary to all hopes, that the delegates of the Free State, now on their way home, should have " secret instructions," authorising them to compromise matters and to consent to waive all claims, provided re-annexation were agreed to. There is very little apparent hope to be entertained in either case, and in the meantime matters will probably remain as they are, and one of the finest sections of South Africa be left a prey to the most miserable of Governments.—*Eastern Province Herald.*

We take over the above paragraph from the *Eastern Province Herald*, last week received here. We do so because we think it just possible, though we must say it is more than we can expect, that, as suggested by our Port Elizabeth contemporary, our delegates now, if all be right, arrived in London, may have received " secret instructions, authorising them to compromise matters, and to consent to waive all claims, provided re-annexation were agreed to." We repeat, we do not anticipate that this is the course to be adopted by our delegates; but still, as drowning men are said to catch at straws, so we would catch at this idea, and would fain hope that some such clause may form part of the " secret instructions" delivered by the Raad to Messrs. Van de Wall and De Villiers, at its final interview with those gentlemen, which, it will be remembered, took place with " closed doors." And now that the *Herald* has refreshed our memory, we call to mind that Mr. Advocate Hamelberg was understood to have declared that, provided he had seen his way clear to undertake the mission to England, he would not have done so, without first receiving full authority, in the event of the protest proving ineffectual, to demand of the Home Government the conditions on which this State might or would be re-annexed to the British Empire. This report may or may not be true; but such was currently reported and believed at the time. The delegates (Van de Wall and De Villiers) are, we know, personally neither of them opposed to re-annexation; but would, on the contrary, up to a very recent date, have greatly rejoiced if " a consummation so devoutly to be wished" could by any means have been accomplished. These gentlemen are, however, doubtless bound to act as nearly as possible in accordance with the spirit of their instructions, whatever these may be. At any rate, for the present, we will hope that our legislators had the good sense to give their delegates a *carte blanche* to act as they thought best for the good of the State, after every argument had been tried and had proved unavailing, to induce the British Government to withdraw its protectorate from over the Basutos. The delegates sent home by this country in 1853, the Rev. Andrew Murray and Dr. Fraser, were despatched on a widely different mission, viz., solemnly to protest against the abandonment or withdrawal of the British Government from this State. They arrived in England too late. Though they admittedly represented and were delegated by the only duly elected and real representatives of the people, Sir George Clerk seized the opportunity of their absence to treat with certain spurious representatives who came to Bloemfontein, armed with what was popularly termed at the time a *lastbrief* or warrant, the collective signatures to which, from all parts of the country, amounted, we are credibly informed, to no more than 227. The result was that these individuals, representing 227 men and boys, had come to terms with Sir G. Clerk, and had agreed to take over the Government almost before the Rev. A. Murray and Dr. Fraser had sailed from the Cape. We do not say that history will in this case repeat itself, but it is not by any means improbable. We should not be surprised, even next week, to hear that the *Cambrian* had brought a despatch to His Excellency Sir P. Wodehouse, containing full and final instructions on the subject ; and if so we may rest assured that the present deputation, like that of 1858-54, will have arrived too late. Should the Home Government, on receipt of the Proclamation and the first despatches of Sir Philip, have come to a final decision on the Basuto question, no deputation nor any amount of protests will affect that decision. Mr. C. B. Adderley, it is true, talks in such a way in the English House of Commons, when replying to the queries of his political opponents, as to raise the hopes of the Government party here ; but still there is no material divergence between his remarks and the text of the despatch of the Duke of Buckingham, under which the Basutos were proclaimed British subjects. Mr. Adderley has, of course, to be very guarded on such occasions when he is called upon, after due notice, to act as the mouthpiece of Government in enunciating the views of Her Majesty's Ministers on any great colonial question. He, like the Hon. Richard Southey in the Cape, must not tell too much, or by so doing he would be playing into the hands of the opposite party. The sole object of his reply was evidently to show that the new arrangements were to be carried out without expense to the Imperial treasury. It is a matter of gratulation to all well-wishers of this country, that by the last mail-steamer we learn that the present (Disraeli) Ministry will remain in office till the end of the session, and therefore till this Basuto and Free State imbroglio shall be settled. Nothing could be more disadvantageous to this State, under its present circumstances, than a change of Ministry in England. But whatever may be the result of the protest, we have no apprehensions for the future. Re-annexation, sooner or later, must come : it is merely a question of time. From whence came (and are coming still) the population of the Orange Free State ?—The *British* colonies. For one foreigner who may find his way here during the next ten years, there will be a hundred British colonial-born subjects. What will this country be twenty-five years hence, provided the present system be permitted to continue so long ? What is the spirit of antagonism to Great Britain here to grow to—Hollanders playing pitch and toss with British interests and English subjects, to the latter's ruin ? What an anomaly for British subjects, unabsolved of their allegiance, to be repairing to the *Foreign* Office for the redress of their grievances ; and actually threatening to appeal to Foreign powers! Such a state of things cannot long continue. Besides, the British Government might now resume its sovereignty here without additional expense. It might be stipulated beforehand that we were to bear the whole of the charges of our Government. Since 1854 the annual revenue of the country has risen, in times of peace, to about £55,000 annually; and for this a decent and respectable Government might very well be carried on. Our annual exports too have increased in spite of war and bad government, till they have been estimated as follows: —Wool, £280,000; ostrich feathers, £15,000; hides and skins, £10,000; cattle and horses, £10,000;—together, £265,000. Most of the diamonds too discovered up to the present time, have been found on this side of the Vaal River, in the Free State districts of Boshof and Jacobsdal. Then the Free State is the highway to the newly-discovered South African Goldfields, and forms the connecting link between the two British Colonies of the Cape and Natal. Both these Colonies, moreover, are strongly in favour of the re-annexation of the Free State, and have always been closely connected with it by trade and family ties. In conclusion, then, we trust that the ultimate result of the deputation to England will be the re-annexation of this State to the British Empire, either as a separate Colony or as a province of the Cape or Natal. Nothing less will help us. If longer left to ourselves, we shall, both as a State and people, inevitably be reduced to beggary and ruin.

RE-ANNEXATION.

Bloemfontein, July 31, 1868.

An esteemed correspondent at Harrismith writes us by the last post, under date the 24th inst. :—"A strong feeling prevails here that this division (Harrismith district) ought to be annexed to Natal;" while a second correspondent, residing at Abrikooskop, writing on same day, remarks that "The Boers here, to get out of their present difficulties, would not object to become British subjects." These we look upon as healthy signs of the times, and go far to show which way public opinion is tending. It is but natural that Harrismith should feel a desire to be annexed to the British Colony of Natal, situated as it is on the immediate border of that Colony, and thus enjoying constant and continual intercourse with its inhabitants. The people of Harrismith cannot but feel the superiority of the form of Government under which their neighbours are living, which, though perhaps not all that the pushing and intelligent Natalians would wish it to be, is still far preferable to our own. For instance, in Natal the people are seldom if ever called out to serve on commandoes against the native tribes, and consequently are never mulct in fines for breaches of the commando law; even-handed justice is dealt out alike to all, by three competent judges learned in the law; British coin is in circulation, in place of bluebacks and good-fors as here; and, moreover, the large native population have such trust and confidence in British justice, that all wars with them have been avoided from the time that the English Government took possession, now some twenty-three years since; while here we have had nothing but wars for the past four years, to say nothing of the three little wars in the days of Presidents Hoffman and Boshof. Harrismith has, moreover, all along complained that it derives no appreciable benefit from its union with the Free State or Bloemfontein Government, beyond being graciously permitted to pay taxes, quit-rents, non-occupation tax, transfer dues; likewise to send its burghers on our commandoes, and in return to receive no protection or fostering care in any shape whatever. No bridges or ponts are erected at the river drifts, as in Natal, no roads constructed, but everything left to a state of nature. Such, whether well or ill-founded, are some of the complaints against our paternal Government. Should Basutoland be annexed to Natal, there is but little doubt that Harrismith would shortly thereafter make application to be permitted to enjoy the same privilege. We cannot but believe that it would prove an unspeakable blessing to the whole community were the Free State, as far as the Modder River, united to Natal, and the other half to the Cape Colony. The pretended freedom of the Free State has already proved, and is proving, a very serious obstacle to progress and to the advance of civilization in South Africa. Does any one doubt this, we would remind them of the following painful facts:—The proposed electric telegraph has been turned aside, and the idea of its passing through the State abandoned; the bridge over the Orange River thwarted; foreign banks expelled; the influx of capital checked; railways not to be thought of; Christian missionaries driven out of Basutoland; educated and enlightened men and capitalists prevented by our wars and obnoxious laws from settling here. These are some of the special disadvantages of our mis-called freedom; but Republics have moreover proved a curse in all ages, and in all parts of the world. Instance the greatest of modern Republics, the so-called United States of North America, its recent civil war, and present attempts to coerce and rule the losing or weaker party with a rod of iron, the one President (Davis) kept for years in chains and suspense, awaiting his trial for high treason, and the other, the President of the victorious states, impeached by Congress, and standing his trial before the Senate; the consequent commotion and instability which has all to be paid for, and must come out of the pockets of the people. Look at the Republics of South America, the whole of which are wealthy and powerful compared to ours; these are even now at war; and never, for any length of time, are at peace with their neighbours or themselves. They seldom retain the same president for many years or months together. In these Republics even life is not secure. Internal broils and commotions are of constant occurrence, in the midst of which a president or general, or some man of mark, is sure to be assassinated. Compare this for a moment with the blessings of a monarchy, with representative institutions and equal laws, in which no periodical upheavings, shakings, or divisions ever take place. What is the freedom which is not to be found under a monarchical form of goverment? What is it that our boer population desire? If not peace, plenty, equal rights, and low taxation, we really wish they would explain. What are our true interests? Certainly not the supporting of the machinations of crafty and designing men. Why should this fine and productive country ever remain the prey of such? In the year 1858, when our commandoes had been beaten back and had retreated from before Thaba Bosigo, Mr. Boshof, and even the Hollanders (only a few were then here) were in favour of, and pleaded for, annexation or federation; but in 1863, on the petitions for federation being read in the Volksraad, J. Serfontein, instigated by Hollanders, opposed the movement, and proposed a counter resolution, which had been carefully prepared and placed in his hands. The 1550 memorialists at that time pleaded for annexation to avoid war with the Basutos; but the Hollanders, fearing the loss of their independence, and firmly believing that we, unaided, could smash up that tribe, would not listen to reason, and persuaded the boer members to look at the question in the same light. Our Dutch farmers, like many greater and wiser people, were easily persuaded that they were a mighty nation, and that they could or ought to put down the *zwart natie* with comparative ease. The result was, our burghers, for an undisciplined force, fought upon the whole well—to a certain extent subdued the Basutos—and we really believe that this State would have long since enjoyed permanent peace, had it not been for the surpassing folly of our Volksraad and Goverment; firstly, in depriving the Basutos of too much land; and, secondly, in leaving the country unoccupied for a whole year after the signing of the treaty ceding the same. Nothing could have been more unwise, nay criminally and wilfully foolish, than at that time to shut our eyes to the fact that the ceded territory would inevitably be again re-occupied by its former owners, the Basutos. But this was all of a piece with our other blundering and dishonesty. To encourage the burghers to fight, a fair division of the spoil—corn, live stock, and *land*, had been promised by high authority, if not by the Raad, and the latter, if not previously, afterwards promised a fair division of the proceeds of the sale of the same. What is the result? The land has been sold to the highest bidder, and the division of the proceeds are *nil!* The money which had at first been separately lodged in the Bank, has since been drawn out by order of the Volksraad, mixed up with the general revenue of the country, and appropriated towards defraying the debt caused by the wilful waste and foolish extravagance of our Government, for by what other language can it be designated, when we consider that it has gone to keep a force in the field, doing nothing from April last, from which time we might have entered into a satisfactory and permanent arrangement with Sir Philip Wodehouse; in supporting a weak and silly protest; and in sending a deputation to England, which is merely another scheme to enslave us to the so-called independence. If England would but recognize her manifest mission in this land, she would and ought, as in India, to reach forth her hand ahead, and place Government agents with the different native tribes of the interior, with a view to their gradual absorption and incorporation in the "Empire on which the sun never sets." She cannot stand still. Not to advance is to retrograde. How can England pretend to fulfil her high mission and large Christian professions, if she allow the aborigines to be handed over to the tender mercies of the advancing and lawless bands of her white subjects, who are even now pouring into the interior? Nay, she must and will advance into this opening continent, in spite of herself and of all opposition. She keeps the reins, the seaports, and can undoubtedly rule the whole continent, up to the Portuguese settlements, *without troops*. Her name and support, and *our* arms are sufficient. The name of England everywhere works wonders with niggers.

STATISTICS OF THE ORANGE FREE STATE.

(COMPILED FROM THE "FRIEND.")

Value of annual imports into the Orange Free State from England, the Cape Colony, and Natal	£300,000
Value of annual exports, viz.:—	
Wool, 23,000 bales, value each, £10 .... £230,000	
Ostrich feathers, &c. 15,000	
Hides 10,000	
Cattle and Horses 10,000	
	265,000
Value of exports in 1854, year of the British abandonment	25,000
Colonial trade through the Free State to the Transvaal	25,000
Trade with the Transvaal Republic, about £20,000 imports, and a like amount of exports yearly.	
Amount of debts owing to the Standard Bank and other colonial banks and loan companies	100,000
Amount owing to Port Elizabeth and other colonial merchants	550,000
Amount of land and other property in the Free State held by colonists and other British subjects	150,000
Amount of Government paper bluebacks in circulation	125,000

Amount of debts of the Free State Government, viz. :
Balance Governmentnotes (bluebacks) £39,000
Due local banks 51,000
Sundry debts 15,000
———— £105,000
The amount of Government paper (bluebacks) originally issued was £130,000, but £5,000 have lately been redeemed, and of the £125,000 now in circulation £86,000 have been lent out to the Boers and others on the security of property, &c., which loans yield an annual revenue of £5,160 to the Government. The £86,000 here mentioned as an ·asset, and the Government debt under the head of paper circulation (bluebacks), is therefore left at £39,000, as before stated.
Annual expense of carrying on the Government in the time of peace 55,000
Number of sheep in the Orange Free State 2,500,000
Total white population of the country....................... 37,000

NOTE.—No census having been taken since 1855, either of the population, number of sheep, &c., the figures are, of course, but an approximate calculation.

REVENUE AND EXPENDITURE OF THE ORANGE FREE STATE FOR THE YEAR ENDING THE 1ST APRIL, 1868.

I. REVENUE.

Quitrents	£7,710	11 11
Sales of Public Lands	131	8 0
Transfer Dues	10,077	8 9
Licenses...	4,359	3 4
Fees of Office	1,422	8 1
Fines	1,335	13 8
Postage Receipts	2,456	18 9
Stamps	2,947	13 9
Auction Dues	715	10 8
Inspection of Lands	31	14 6
Sale of Ammunition	4,762	15 0
Commando Receipts	1,707	7 3
Tolls and Pontage Dues	847	8 9
Succession Duty	565	16 6
Native Hut Tax	529	19 11
Pound Sales	212	1 2
Miscellaneous	705	14 10
Fees (Orphan Chamber)................................	357	7 5
Import Duty on Munitions of War	718	12 3
Sale of Postage Stamps	480	6 2
Funds for Ruined Burghers	2,428	0 3
Cape Government Postal Allowance....................	600	0 0
Cape Colonial Postage................................	150	0 0

Total Revenue for the year ending 1st April, 1868 .... £45,254 0 11
Balance in hand 1st April, 1867 .... £1,562 16 0
Borrowed Capital 68,400 0 0
                                                    ————— 69,962 16 0
                                                              ——————
Total of Year's Receipts....................£115,216 16 11

II. EXPENDITURE.

Civil and Judicial ·...................................	£10,365	8 11
Police..	2,323	10 7
Church and Schools...................................	3,602	11 6
Ammunition ....:..................	12,330	19 0
Stationery	1,007	1 2

217

Administration of Justice	£2,234	17	0
Gaols and Police	2,084	3	8
Hospitals	973	6	1
Ministers (Consulent)	32	0	0
House-rent	353	8	6
Wagon-hire	204	8	9
Conveyance of Mails	3,185	6	10
Public Works and Buildings	566	16	9
Presents to Native Chiefs	97	8	10
Roads, Streets, and Bridges	17	1	6
Allowances to Members of Raad	2,301	5	6
Land Commissions	374	10	0
Commando Expenses	31,869	11	4
Border Police	6	0	0
Artillery Corps (Treasurer-General)	4,250	0	0
Carrying Expenses	218	13	6
Heemraden and others	93	10	6
Unforeseen Expenditure	4,110	13	5
Printing	933	5	10
College	270	0	0
Interest on Loan	2,592	16	0
Import Duty	19	14	2
Artillery (Paymaster)	4,952	3	11
Remittances to Landdrosts............ £32,523 13 10			
Less received from Treasurer-General 31,511 15 3			
	1,011	18	7
Stolen out of the Chest	464	8	5
Balance—Miscellaneous items not specified	22,369	16	8

Total Expenditure £115,216 16 11

SPEECH OF THE HON. JOHN ROBINSON, ESQ., IN THE NATAL LEGISLATIVE COUNCIL, AUGUST, 1868.

Mr. ROBINSON moved :—" That, in the opinion of this House, the consolidation of the Free State and Basutoland as a separate British Colony, would put an end to the demoralising war which has so long been carried on between the Free State and the Basutos, and would place on a sound footing the extensive trade which exists between the Republic and the neighbouring British Colonies, but which, owing to the closing of the civil courts, and the general insecurity of the country, has suffered serious and disastrous injury during the duration of the war." It was hardly necessary for him to go to any length into a historical review of the events in the neighbouring territories, which had led to the war referred to in the resolution, before moving the resolution itself, as, in his opinion, the best way of putting an end to them. The Free State had been proclaimed to be British territory in 1848 ; in 1851 it had been declared by letters patent to be a distinct and separate colony ; in 1853 a Commission had been sent out, which resulted in the country being formerly abandoned in 1854, and by letters patent declared to be independent. He believed it was

Q

generally held by all the inhabitants of South Africa that this step was both cruel and unwise; it was one of those very few acts on which the enlightened Government of the Mother Country must, he thought, look back with regret, and he traced all the evils which had since beset the Free State back to the adoption of that policy. It had always appeared to him that the people of the Free State had a great claim to indulgent treatment at the hands of all European people. A people of pastoral habits, and in no way fitted for the task, they had yet been suddenly called upon to assume all the responsibilities of self-government. Whatever mistakes, therefore, might have been committed, there was every reason for judging of the policy of the Free State Government in the most indulgent manner. He (Mr. Robinson) was not one of those who disclaimed all sympathy with men of his own colour, and avowed the tenderest feelings for those of another race. He believed that all the Europeans in South Africa must feel that the burgher residents of the Free State had been placed in a very peculiar position by the English Government, and could not have behaved better than they had done under the very trying circumstances in which they had found themselves. Since their abandonment by the British Government they had been constantly at war with the Basutos, which nation even the statesmen of England had found it very difficult to deal with, and it might be that, on this very account, the country had been abandoned. Experience, too, ever since that time, had shown how great a mistake England had made in carrying out the policy which it had done; for, although on the Free State had rested the sole responsibility of dealing with the Basutos, yet the other countries adjacent, which were really British territory, had been most disastrously affected by these protracted wars. Hon. members were aware that large sums of money were owed by the Free State to Natal merchants, amounting probably to not less than a quarter of a million sterling, and for the payment of this large sum no security existed whilst this war was still going on. It was hardly necessary for him to say that the late war had been very demoralising in its effects. It had been demoralising because it kept up a constant state of antagonism between the black and the white races, and led them to regard each other as hereditary enemies; it had been demoralising because it prevented all enterprise and caused the cessation of all trade on a solid basis; it had been demoralising because it was productive of an entirely abnormal and unnatural state of things. At the same time, though he was of opinion that it was highly desirable that the Free State should be annexed to the English crown, yet he thought it was also desirable that the Free State and Basutoland should form a distinct territory under a separate government. The Free State was differently situated from Natal or the Cape, and her requirement was chiefly that of a strong Government, which should afford equal protection to all classes of the population, but she was not in a position to exercise advantageously the rights of Responsible Government. It had been suggested to him that this resolution would, to some extent, be conflicting with that recently passed by the House relative to the annexation of Basutoland. He candidly stated that, of the two alternatives, the annexation of Basutoland to Natal, or the constituting that country and the Free State into a separate government, the latter was, in his opinion, by far the better way of getting out of the scrape. But as this could not meet the approval of those hon. members who had voted for the annexation of Basutoland on the previous occasion, he proposed somewhat to modify the resolution so that it would stand as follows:—" That in the opinion of this House it is highly desirable that the Orange Free State should once more be brought under British rule, inasmuch as this House has reason to believe that a strong feeling in favour of such a policy exists among the residents of that Republic, and as the re-annexation of that territory by the Crown would put an end to the demoralising wars which have, from time to time, been carried on between the Free State and the Basutos, and would place on a sound footing the extensive trade which exists between the Republic and the neighbouring British Colonies, but which, owing to the closing of the civil courts and the general insecurity of the country, has suffered serious and disastrous injury during the war." No hon. members would be disposed to deny that it was the wish of the great majority of the people of the Free State to come again under British rule. The time, he thought, had now arrived when the Home Government could, with great advantage, retrieve the false step it took in 1854, when these unfortunate people had been, to adopt a phrase made use of the other evening, "left out in the cold." The whole question would now come under consideration in connection with the annexation of Basutoland, and he thought if it were brought before the Home Government they might be led to consider the expediency of re-annexing the whole of the Free State as well as Basutoland. . . . . . .

FEDERATION MEMORIAL PRESENTED TO SIR PHILIP WODEHOUSE, AT ALIWAL NORTH, APRIL, 1868.

Unto His Excellency Sir PHILIP EDMOND WODEHOUSE, *K.C.B., Governor of the Colony of the Cape of Good Hope, High Commissioner, &c., &c.*

The Memorial and Petition of the undersigned Proprietors, Traders, and other Citizens, of the Orange Free State, Humbly Representeth,—That, in February, 1854, in spite of the almost universal opinion and reiterated remonstrances of the people, the Sovereignty of Her Majesty the Queen over the territory now called the Orange Free State was summarily withdrawn, and its future Government transferred to comparatively a few individuals, whom Sir George Russell Clerk, K.C.B., Her Majesty's Special Commissioner, had, with considerable trouble, prevailed upon and induced to take over and assume the future management thereof. That in such haste was Sir George Clerk to withdraw British Supremacy, that several questions of vital importance to the future tranquillity and prosperity of the country, in its new character of a self-sustaining Republic, and more especially questions of territorial rights and boundaries with neighbouring tribes and states, were left in an undefined and unsettled condition—a variety of promises made, and inducements held out, by the said Sir George Clerk, in the name of the British Government, having, however, never been fulfilled or realized. That, to the crude, ill-considered, and precipitate mode of shaking off the future responsibility of Her Majesty's Government, thus adopted by Sir George Clerk, and the isolated position the Free State has since occupied, are, and will be undoubtedly due, the harassing wars which have well nigh ruined the country, as well as the complications and troubles likely to arise out of boundary disputes and differences now pending with native tribes and the South African Republic. That, taking every circumstance into consideration, your petitioners are humbly of opinion, that the future peace and prosperity, not only of the Orange Free State, but of civilized South Africa generally, would best be promoted and secured by the introduction of such a system of federal union as (whilst securing to each separate State or division, under the paramount rule of the Queen, and subject to equitable conditions, local self-government, with the privilege of administering its own revenue for its own personal development and improvement), would at the same time confer and impose on the union itself the right as well as obligation of exercising control over the general affairs of the confederation, and more especially of upholding individual States against the aggressions or encroachments of countries and peoples not embraced in the union.

May it therefore please your Excellency to take this Memorial and Petition into your immediate and favourable consideration, and to adopt all steps and measures necessary and calculated to accomplish, in the end, the object and desire of the Memorialists. And in case you may not consider yourself at liberty to act at once in the matter, may it further please your Excellency, with all convenient speed, to transmit this Memorial and Petition for the gracious consideration of Her Majesty the Queen. And your Petitioners, as in duty bound, shall ever pray.

(Signed) G. A. FICHARDT, J. T. JOLLIE.
G. H. DEXTER, THOMAS WHITE, &c., &c.

www.ingramcontent.com/pod-product-compliance
Lightning Source LLC
Chambersburg PA
CBHW021822230426
43669CB00008B/841